THE BATTLE OF MONMOUTH

London: Humphrey Milford
Oxford University Press

THE
Battle of Monmouth

BY THE LATE

WILLIAM S. STRYKER

ADJUTANT-GENERAL OF NEW JERSEY
PRESIDENT OF THE NEW JERSEY SOCIETY OF THE CINCINNATI
PRESIDENT OF THE NEW JERSEY HISTORICAL SOCIETY, ETC.

Edited by

WILLIAM STARR MYERS, Ph.D.,

PROFESSOR OF POLITICS, PRINCETON UNIVERSITY

PRINCETON
PRINCETON UNIVERSITY PRESS
1927

PRINTED AT THE PRINCETON UNIVERSITY PRESS
PRINCETON NEW JERSEY, U. S. A.

Printing Statement:

Due to the very old age and scarcity of this book,
many of the pages may be hard to read due to the
blurring of the original text, possible missing pages,
missing text and other issues beyond our control.

Because this is such an important and rare work, we
believe it is best to reproduce this book regardless of
its original condition.

Thank you for your understanding.

Tennent Church, Still Standing on the Battlefield

FROM AN OLD PICTURE

WITH THE GRACIOUS PERMISSION OF

MRS. STRYKER

THIS BOOK IS DEDICATED TO

The Officers and Members of the
Monmouth County Historical Association

WHOSE EFFORTS ARE SUCCESSFULLY

DIRECTED TOWARD THE PRESERVATION

OF THE MEMORIES OF THE GREAT EVENTS

THAT HAVE MADE THEIR COUNTY FAMOUS

AUTHOR'S PREFACE

*T*HE kind reception accorded to my work on "The Battles of Trenton and Princeton" has induced me to follow it with a history of that other great battle of the Revolutionary War on New Jersey soil. Under the direction of the late Professor George H. Cook, State Geologist of New Jersey, in the year 1885, a special survey of five square miles of the battle-field of Monmouth was made for me and this survey was afterward used in the series of fine geological maps of our State issued by this distinguished scientist. I then had a most accurate relief map made from this survey and with this map I began a study of the varied features of the fight. The topography of this tract of land has altered very little since Revolutionary times, and the high ground, the water courses, the ravines and marshes are virtually the same as they were a century ago. Taking up, in the first place, the "General Court-Martial of Major-General Charles Lee," all the movements of Lee, of Dickinson, of Lafayette and of Washington were carefully determined and marked on the topographical map, in the light of all the sworn testimony of officers who took part in the battle. Continuing this plan, every contemporaneous document and diary and all the traditions current in the neighborhood were examined, the marching of the different detachments of troops traced on the map and the accuracy of each statement verified by the facts furnished in the trial of General Lee. Representing the State as one of the members of the Monmouth Monument Commission, in the erection of the beautiful memorial shaft at Freehold, I became almost as interested in the Battle of Monmouth as in the fight on the streets of Trenton. With some confidence, therefore, I send forth this companion volume for the perusal of all lovers of history.

W. S. S.

TRENTON, NEW JERSEY
JUNE 28, 1899

INTRODUCTORY NOTE

M ORE than twenty-seven years ago the late General William Scudder Stryker prepared a full and exhaustive account of the Battle of Monmouth Court House, but his untimely death, a short time after its completion, prevented its publication. Mrs. Stryker, with great generosity, has recently placed this manuscript in my hands for publication by the Princeton University Press, leaving the method of preparation entirely to my discretion, with the one reservation that General Stryker should get the credit he so richly deserved for the extensive research and painstaking work he successfully accomplished. In substantiation of this, the following pages speak for themselves.

Other conditions of publication have made necessary the partial abridgement of the narrative and also the omission of some hundreds of pages of documents most of which are now easily accessible in the various libraries throughout the country. I have made the endeavor to include everything of especial value and also, in making minor corrections, to preserve the original form and style of presentation as far as possible. A choice has been made among the large number of illustrations of persons and places which General Stryker had intended should be included in the book.

In bringing the narrative up to date and adding certain matters of contemporary interest, I have been greatly assisted by Mr. Samuel Craig Cowart, of Freehold, New Jersey, himself an enthusiastic student of the history of the battle, who kindly spent several hours with me in examining the battle-field on a recent August day which, most appropriately, was intensely hot and sultry.

WILLIAM STARR MYERS

PRINCETON, NEW JERSEY
AUGUST 18, 1926

CHAPTER I

AS a prelude to the history of a great battle in the war for the independence of America fought on the soil of old Monmouth County, it is necessary to note some of the events which immediately preceded it and to give some outline sketches of life in the hostile armies during the one hundred days prior to that memorable hot Sunday in June. The great feature of camp life in the American Army in 1777 and 1778, the first thought which comes to the mind when the name of Valley Forge is spoken, is the wonderfully patient endurance of keen physical suffering by the soldiers of the young republic in those huts on the bleak hillside of the Schuylkill River. At the same period Philadelphia must forever be associated with a winter of the gayest revelry, of wild dissipation of every kind, of flagrant vice, of a demoralization of discipline in the British Army caused by the idle and dissolute character of their commanding general. The toils, the trials, the bitter hardships and exposure in the cold and cheerless encampment of the one stands out in sharpest contrast to the ease and warmth, the luxury and pleasure of the troops in the other army in the Quaker City.

The closing months of the year 1777 were crowded with events important to America in the struggle for national freedom. On September 11 the army of Britain came to close quarters with General Sullivan's column of Continentals on the left bank of the Brandywine, and after giving and receiving some severe punishment, the patriot army was obliged to retreat. In the morning of September 26 Lord Cornwallis, at the head of the British Line and of the German contingent, marched into the capital city of Philadelphia, scattered the Federal Congress and assigned his army to quarters in the homes of the people. On October 4 the Continental troops of General Sullivan and General Wayne rushed furiously on the embattled ranks of the British Foot and their Light Infantry detachments and drove them through the streets of Germantown, and sturdy old Maxwell with his Jersey Blues sent volleys of leaden hail at the vigorous defenders of the Chew House. But the result of that battle was another disaster to the American arms and the patriot blood spilled in those streets makes a sad page in history. Then followed the operations on the Delaware River at Red Bank, at Fort Mifflin and Fort Mercer, until these positions, important because they controlled the water route from the ocean to the great city, finally yielded to determined assault and the heavy guns of the British fleet at close range. On the fourth day of December the British troops moved out of the city for the purpose of drawing the American Army from the camp at White Marsh. During the three following days they tried to provoke a battle, but failed to do more than receive into their own breasts the bullets fired by Morgan's riflemen; then they withdrew for the season into the festive city of Philadelphia. But amid all the disasters of the latter part of the year 1777 there came from the upper waters of the Hudson River the glad news of General Stark's victory with his Green Mountain boys over a combined force of English, of Germans and of Indians, and of the surrender of General Burgoyne and his entire army on the field of Saratoga.

Notwithstanding this victory which Providence had vouchsafed to the northern army, the "end of our warfare—independence, liberty and peace," as Washington announced, seemed still not likely to be realized in the immediate future. The chieftain then thought it necessary to say that he did not dread the force of Britain exerted alone, that the soldiers of America were full of fortitude and patience under the fatigues they were called upon to endure and that France had already shown a kindly disposition to grant them every aid they asked.

But the winter was upon them, with all its bitter cold,

its dreadful trials, its impending sufferings, and something must be done to furnish quarters for the little army and keep them together for another campaign. Where should the place be which would "most effectually prevent distress and give the most extensive security?"[1] Some officers, at a council of war held November 30, urged Wilmington, Delaware, a place too far south, however, for any effective stroke at an enemy crossing the Jerseys; others said, form the winter camp at Reading and Lancaster, Pennsylvania, and in the country lying between those villages; still other officers favored Trenton, New Jersey, a place which might constantly have been menaced by a strong naval force on the Delaware River. According to Washington's custom, the opinions of the general officers of the army were required and given with great detail in writing, and after much careful study he issued his own decision in orders. With great wisdom, as all military students now agree, he selected a place in Pennsylvania near enough to Philadelphia to be a daily menace to the British Army, far enough away for the American troops to feel themselves secure from any unexpected attack by the light horse of the enemy, and with a fair advantage in rapid pursuit of the British Army if they should march at any time toward the north or start out on a southern campaign.

On the sixteenth day of December, 1777, the advance of the American Army reached Valley Forge on the west bank of the Schuylkill River, about twenty-two miles by wagon road from the city of Philadelphia. On December 19 the army under General Washington had arrived there and by his orders, issued the previous day, commenced the erection of huts for their winter encampment and dug intrenchments for its defence. On the rugged hillside in this "wilderness," as De Kalb described it, the log huts, fourteen by sixteen feet in size, were built in the midst of thick woods by the confluence of the frozen waters of

[1] From the Orderly Book, December 17, 1777, Sparks' *Writings of Washington*, Vol. V, Appendix, p. 523.

Valley Creek and the Schuylkill River. With great patience and severe toil the soldiers yoked themselves to wagons, because horses were scarce, and in this way brought the timber on the ground. Thus in a few days the forest was changed into a hutted camp. The encampment was not completed until January 15, 1778. Potts' Forge was situated at this point in the Great Valley and a few cottages thereabout made up a very primitive village on the Old Gulf Road. The headquarters of the Commander-in-Chief were at Isaac Potts' two-story stone house near the mouth of Valley Creek.

The action of General Washington in thus placing his troops in winter cantonment was not without protest from some of the people of the colonies. Even the Legislature of Pennsylvania took action on the subject and a communication was sent to Washington remonstrating against his conduct in the matter. In this document such expressions are used as that by the proposed encampment a "great part of this State, particularly that on the east side, together with the State of New Jersey, must be left in the Power of the Enemy, subject to their ravages"—"that many of our People are so disaffected already that nothing but the neighborhood of the Army keeps them subject to Government."[2] This drew from General Washington a prompt and pertinent letter addressed to the President of Congress, December 23, 1777, couched in such stirring language as this: "I can assure those gentlemen, that it is a much easier and less distressing thing to draw remonstrances in a comfortable room by a good fireside, than to occupy a cold, bleak hill, and sleep under frost and snow, without clothes or blankets. However, although they seem to have little feeling for the naked and distressed soldiers, I feel superabundantly for them, and, from my soul, I pity those miseries, which it is neither in my power to relieve or prevent."[3]

[2] *Pennsylvania Archives*, First series, Vol. VI, p. 104.
[3] Ford's *Writings of George Washington*, Vol. VI, p. 261.

General Washington's Headquarters, Valley Forge, Pennsylvania

FROM PHOTOGRAPH TAKEN FEBRUARY 1, 1899

And the snow fell, the storms of wind and sleet increased, the bitter cold became still more intense, until the soldiers of the poor army had really to struggle for bare existence. The feeling of patriotism, however, was still alive in these rude huts, but the spirit of every champion of liberty was sorely tried in the struggle to keep from perishing, without the very necessities of life. Even while they were building their huts, one-half the army, it is said, had no proper shoes and stockings and their bleeding feet crimsoned the snowdrifts. Their clothing was by no means suitable for wintry weather—so thin and tattered had it become. Very few of the men had blankets to wrap around them at night, many had no breeches and were compelled to huddle around the fires and so pass away the long uncomfortable hours of night in uneasy sleep. One writer describes some of the men as with "a dirty blanket around them attached by a leathern belt around the waist." Another visitor in camp speaks of "twenty-six men in a New York regiment without a shirt." And still another says, "A few of the men wear long linen hunting shirts reaching to the knee, but of the rest no two are dressed alike, not half have shirts, a third are barefoot, many are in rags." On one occasion—referring to six commissioned officers and two hundred and fifty-five men of his command as unable to do any duty—General Wayne said, "of those returned sick present is for want of clothing, being too naked to appear on the parade; our officers in particular are in a most wretched condition." General Washington said to a friend, "Through the want of shoes and stockings and the hard frozen ground you might have tracked the army from White Marsh to Valley Forge by the blood of their feet." And just before Christmas he wrote, "few men having more than one shirt, many only the moiety of one and some none at all. . . . We have by a field-return this day made no less than two thousand eight hundred and ninety-eight men now in camp unfit for duty, because they are barefoot and otherwise naked."[4]

In addition to the great want of clothing, arms and equipments in the American Army, there came also a terrible scarcity of food. The utter failure of the commissary department to supply the necessary rations was fully discussed at general headquarters and various stern and quick methods were suggested to avert the impending famine. Some of these plans were tried but not always found effective. The suffering from hunger increased as the weary days of the dull winter dragged along until the cheerless hour arrived when the officer in charge of the supplies was forced to say that he had not a single head of cattle for the butcher's ax and that not twenty-five barrels of flour could be had in all the camp.

Cold, naked and hungry, without pay, without provisions, without rum, sleeping on the bare earth in their huts, the army kept together in a pitiable existence. In their dire adversity sickness came in their midst and the death rate increased week after week. With great reluctance General Washington then began a system of compulsory requisition. It is only necessary to read his letters at this time to see how distressing these plans were to his mind, but as a temporary expedient they had to be put in force. General Washington issued orders to all the farmers within ten miles of Valley Forge, requiring them to thrash out one-half of their grain by the first day of February and the other half by the first day of March, under penalty of having "all that shall remain in sheaves seized by the Commissaries & Quartermasters of the army and paid for as straw."[5] Many loyalist farmers refused to obey, defending their grain with their rifles and burning what they could not defend. To these Tories it seemed far better to sell to the British Army in Philadelphia and receive pay in gold than to give their grain to the men at Valley

[4] Ford, Vol. VI, p. 260.
[5] Proclamation December 20, 1777, Ford, Vol. VI, p. 248.

Forge and be paid in certificates for which Congress had as yet failed to provide any mode of redemption. Wonderful indeed was the love of country displayed in these trying hours, when the brave men and zealous patriots gathered around Washington's quarters, looking to him as the only resource in their dire extremity. Surely no sketch of these times has exaggerated their condition. And what must have been the sorrow of the great chieftain as he witnessed their calamity and felt that he was not fully supported by the power of the government—as every day the currency became more and more depreciated and he himself could do but little to mitigate their distresses? Certainly nowhere in the annals of the world can it be shown that a party of half-naked and hungry men bore their trials with greater fortitude and truer resignation in the name and on behalf of liberty.

CHAPTER II

IT is well to make a brief note of events that occurred
during the early part of the year 1778, among the people and with the militia in the southern part of New Jersey
so soon to aid in harrassing the march of the British Army
across their own farm lands. On March 21 a detachment
of the British Army, while on a foraging expedition, made
an attack on the troops of Cumberland and Salem Counties at a place now known in history as Hancock's Bridge,
and again, two days later, at Quinton's Bridge. The Jerseymen were severely repulsed. The next day Colonel
Charles Mawhood, the same officer who had led the British
foot at Princeton's battle, wrote the American officer in
command that, "induced by motives of humanity," he
asked them "to lay down their arms and depart each man
to his own home." If they did not do so, he threatened to
put arms in the hands of their Tory neighbors, to burn
their houses, and reduce their wives and children to beg-
gary. He added to his letter a list of the "first objects to
feel the vengeance of the British nation"—the names of
the principal men and most active patriots in that section
of the State.[1] Colonel Elijah Hand, of the First Battalion
of Cumberland Militia, replied to these strange "motives
of humanity," accusing the British not only of "denying
quarters, but butchering our men who surrendered themselves prisoners in the skirmish at Quinton's bridge" and
"bayonetting at Hancock's bridge, in the most cruel manner, in cold blood, men who were taken by surprise,"
adding the remark, "to wantonly destroy will injure your
cause more than ours: it will increase your enemies and our
army."[2] These little affairs were of no great importance,

[1] Johnson's *Historical Account of Salem in West Jersey*, p. 159.
[2] Barber and Howe's *Historical Collections of the State of New Jersey*,
p. 421.

but they exhibited the temper and spirit of the Jersey
troops at this critical time in the Revolutionary struggle.
The object of these expeditions of the British was probably more to gather corn and steal cattle than to inflict
any special punishment or to gain any glory to their arms.
The farmers of the State, embodied in her militia, sought
only to resist a spoliation of their garnered grain and a
raid upon their fattened herds.

While the mind of General Washington was filled with
grave concern regarding the deplorable condition of his
army, he began to realize that a strong intrigue was forming to supplant him in the chief command of the military
force of the republic. Enemies about him in the camp,
men actuated by sinister motives in Congress, began to
talk of battles fought which only ended in disaster, of
movements of troops executed which only proved useless
and ill-judged. The laurels gained over Burgoyne at the
capitulation of Saratoga, although we now know that General Schuyler more properly deserved them, made General
Gates aspire to be placed in the supreme command of the
army. Joined with Gates were several other officers who
were jealous of Washington's prominent position before
the American people and of the glory that was sure to rest
upon him and his reputation in after years should he succeed in wresting this young nation from the thraldom of a
kingly power. In an indirect way a little coterie of men
sought to interfere with the proper workings of the several
departments of the army, and they prepared important
documents in Washington's name, which he had never
seen and never signed. As a willing abettor of the victor of
Saratoga's battle, there was a foreign officer, General
Thomas Conway, an Irishman by birth, but of late a
colonel in the army of France, a "worthless soldier" as
General Greene called him, who stirred up this intrigue
most vehemently, hoping in some way to gain promotion
in the success of Gates, who had just been made President
of the Board of War. An attempt was made to induce

Lafayette to join in this conspiracy and the Board tried to flatter the young French officer with a separate command, organized without consultation with Washington, for the purpose of invading Canada. But Lafayette refused the honor and the service unless he could report direct to the chieftain whom he had learned to love. Many prominent men were more or less connected with this secret plot, ever afterward known as the "Conway Cabal," and Congress did nothing to crush it but rather encouraged it by commissioning Conway a Major-General and Inspector-General of the army over his seniors in commission. The movements of this malignant faction at length became public and reached the ear of one of General Washington's truest friends, Major-General Lord Stirling, and the dire machinations were stopped by the public sentiment that was quickly aroused. The desire to affect the standing of Washington with his army utterly failed and the insidious plot only cemented more closely the bond between him and his trusted followers. The gallant Philadelphia soldier, General Cadwalader, checked General Conway's career with the bullet of a duellist on July 4, 1778, and caused him, in view of his expected death, to beg pardon for his wrong-doing. He had already tendered his resignation to Congress, April 28, and on recovering from his wound returned to France. It seems sad indeed that in addition to the daily sight of sick, ragged and hungry men whom General Washington longed so much to assist, his mind should be harrassed with the knowledge that some of his general officers desired to injure forever his fame. But through all these intrigues he preserved his dignified bearing, which, while it annoyed his enemies, encouraged his friends, who rallied closer around him; and nothing could shake the confidence of the people nor supplant him in the affections of the rank and file of the army.[3]

[3] For particulars concerning the cabal, see Sparks' *Writings of George Washington*, Vol. V, Appendix, p. 483 *et seq.*

In June, 1777, seven letters were published in London under the title of "Letters from General Washington to several of his Friends in the year 1776. In which are set forth a fairer and fuller view of American Politics, than ever yet transpired, or the Public could be made acquainted with through any other Channel." These letters were spurious, and when brought to the attention of the Commander-in-Chief he immediately denounced the forgery; but just at this trying period of the war they caused the General great anxiety, as may be seen by an extract from his letter to Richard Henry Lee, of date May 25, 1778.—"If anything of greater moment had occurred, than declaring that every word contained in the pamphlet, which you were obliging enough to send me, was spurious, I should not have suffered your favor of the 6th instant to remain so long unacknowledged. These letters are written with a great deal of art. The intermixture of so many family circumstances (which, by the by, want foundation in truth) gives an air of plausibility which renders the villany greater; as the whole is a contrivance to answer the most diabolical purposes.—Who the author of them is, I know not."[4] The letters referred to, purporting to be written by General Washington, one to Mrs. Washington, one to John Parke Custis and five to Lund Washington, and captured with a servant at Fort Lee in 1776, were reprinted in New York City in 1778, under the auspices of the loyalists, for the purpose of wider circulation in America and to show that the real feelings of Washington were widely different from his pronounced opinions, and in this way do the patriot cause infinite damage. During the rest of his life General Washington had to combat this attack from time to time and as late as the year 1796 the letters were republished. On March 3, 1797, General Washington, then about to retire from the Presidency, wrote a strong letter to Colonel Timothy Pickering, Secretary of State of the United States, which

[4] Ford's *Writings of George Washington*, Vol. VII, p. 22.

he desired to be deposited in the Department of State, in which he denied with great emphasis that his servants, any part of his baggage or any of his attendants, with these letters in their possession, had ever been captured during the whole course of the war. He ended this statement with the "solemn declaration that the letters herein described are a base forgery and that I never saw or heard of them until they appeared in print."[5] In the midst of all the hardships, dangers and cabals of Valley Forge, General Washington had to bear this cruel attack with equanimity and to appear to his soldiers calm, unmoved and self-reliant under every change of fortune or base charge of his enemies.[6]

On April 20, 1778, General Washington addressed a letter to all the general officers on duty at Valley Forge, in which he expressed this opinion: "There seem to be but three general plans of operation, which may be premeditated for the next campaign; one, the attempting to recover Philadelphia and destroy the enemy's army there; another, the endeavouring to transfer the war to the northward by an enterprise against New York; and a third, the remaining quiet in a secure, fortified camp, disciplining and arranging the army till the enemy begin their operations and then to govern ourselves accordingly.— Which of these three plans shall we adopt?"[7] The replies to these letters were all promptly sent in to headquarters and were very different in the views expressed. Generals Maxwell, Wayne and Paterson favored an early demonstration on Philadelphia, according to the first of Washington's suggestions. Generals Varnum, Knox, Poor and Muhlenberg desired to endorse the second plan and push across the State of New Jersey, to threaten and attack

---

[5] Ford, Vol. XIII, p. 378.

[6] In Ford, Vol. IV, p. 132, these letters are ascribed to "John Randolph, the last royal attorney general of Virginia and long the ablest lawyer in the colony. He went to England in 1775." The letters are to be found in the same volume, pp. 132, 160, 177, 219, 254, 264 and 288.

[7] Sparks, Vol. V, p. 319.

New York City. General Lord Stirling would try both plans, and Generals von Steuben, Lafayette and Duportail, the foreign officers, were decided in their opinion of the inexpediency of an attack on the British at this time. They thought every effort should first be made to complete, if possible, the arming, equipping and disciplining of the force, so that success might be made more certain. General Greene differed somewhat from all these opinions, for he would have a special column of four thousand selected men to push rapidly to New York, to be joined there by the militia from New England, and have the commander-in-chief go in person with this division and General Lee remain in command of the rest of the army in the camp at Valley Forge.

After a full study of the views advocated by all these officers, General Washington decided to remain at present where he was intrenched and await events.

On May 11 and 12, 1778, the officers of the Continental Army took the new oath of allegiance as required by a resolution of Congress dated February 3, 1778.[8] The resolution is in these words:

"Resolved, That every officer who holds or shall hereafter hold a commission or office from Congress shall take and subscribe the following oath or affirmation: I —— do acknowledge the United States of America to be free, independent and sovereign States, and declare that the people thereof owe no allegiance or obedience to George the third, King of Great Britain; and I do renounce, refuse and abjure any allegiance or obedience to him; and I do swear (or affirm) that I will to the utmost of my power support, maintain and defend the said United States against the said King George the third, and his heirs, and successors, and his and their abettors, assistants and adherents, and will serve the said United States in the office of —— which I now hold, with fidelity, according to the

---

[8] *Pennsylvania Magazine*, Vol. I, p. 174, and Lossing's *Field Book of the Revolution*, Vol. II, p. 146.

best of my skill and understanding. So help me God."[9]

The officers of the army, according to an order of General Washington issued the previous day, met at the General's headquarters at eleven o'clock in the morning of May 12 and took the required oath.

There were a few officers not on duty at Valley Forge at the time, or on duty but not in the camp, who did not take the oath of allegiance that day. Among these was Major-General Lee, who had not yet returned from York, Pennsylvania. On June 9 these officers also renewed their oaths to Congress. At this time a very singular thing happened, especially pertinent to the events soon to follow. As the officers came before General Washington to subscribe to this renewed profession of fealty to the cause of national independence for which they had taken up arms and risked their lives to maintain, it was noticed that General Lee withdrew his hand from the Bible. General Washington asked him why he did this singular act. He replied, "As to King George, I am ready enough to absolve myself from all allegiance to him, but I have some scruples about the Prince of Wales." The officers all laughed at this very odd remark, but it clearly displayed his opinion of the ultimate failure of the cause. It was a faint expression of the treason in his heart which had already developed itself while he was a prisoner of war. As soon as silence had been restored after this unusual episode, General Lee took the oath of allegiance with no doubt a wicked mental reservation that he would act as he thought his own personal interests required.

Before we turn away from the dreary picture of life at Valley Forge, let us speak of one auspicious event which for a moment diffused joy among the suffering soldiers in the huts on the Schuylkill River.

The news of the surrender of Burgoyne, which reached Paris December 4, 1777, seems to have given great pleasure to the court at Versailles. On December 12 a meeting

[9] *Journal of Congress*, Vol. IV, p. 66.

took place between the American Commissioners and the Count de Vergennes, then Minister of Foreign Affairs of France. At this meeting the preliminaries of a treaty of alliance and commercial intercourse were discussed. On February 6, 1778, Louis XVI of France, prompted by a desire to humble the power of England, determined to acknowledge the independence of America and a treaty was signed in which it was stated that it was the desire of France "to maintain effectually the liberty, sovereignty and independence, absolute and unlimited of the United States as well in matters of government as commerce." To accomplish this important act, Doctor Benjamin Franklin, Silas Deane and Arthur Lee had been laboring with all the diplomacy they could command and they were efficiently aided by Pierre Augustine Caron de Beaumarchais, the intimate friend of Count de Vergennes. Silas Deane wrote of him as one "to whom the United States are on every account greatly indebted; more so than to any other person on this side of the water."[10] The news of the signing of this treaty was not known in London even during the celebrated debate in Parliament on the American question February 17; but when it was announced in that city it was regarded as a declaration of war and Lord Stormont, the English Ambassador, was instructed to leave the French court immediately. In anticipation of this event, a French squadron was in readiness which started from Toulon about the middle of April under the command of the Count Charles Henry Theodat d'Estaing, and sailed toward the United States. The flag-ship of the squadron carried Monsieur Conrad Alexandre Gérard, first minister of France to the United States, and Silas Deane, one of the American commissioners. On March 20 Benjamin Franklin and his associates had been received at court as the representatives of an independent nation.

On April 13, Simeon Deane, a brother of the diplomat

[10] Wharton's *Revolutionary Diplomatic Correspondence of the United States*, Vol. II, p. 201.

Silas Deane, arrived in Falmouth harbor, now the city of Portland, Maine, in the fast-sailing French frigate "La Sensible," Captain Marigny, and brought the news of the recognition by France of American independence and the promise of a military contingent and an efficient fleet to assist in securing the rights of the American people.

It was not until May 2 that the news of the signing of the treaty reached York, Pennsylvania, where the Continental Congress was in session, and it infused new life in the breasts of the patriot statesmen assembled there. When it was announced at Valley Forge the previous day it aroused wild excitement among the soldiers in that camp. Throughout the whole country this action of the French king diffused great joy among the American people.

On May 4 Congress resolved unanimously to ratify the treaty of amity, commerce and alliance between the most Christian King of France and Navarre and the United States of America, and they desired the commissioners representing the States in that country to present the grateful acknowledgments of Congress to him and to assure him that "it is sincerely wished that the friendship so happily commenced between France and these United States may be perpetual."[11] General Washington issued his quaint and characteristic order, May 6, for a due celebration of this auspicious event to be made the day following. By his direction divine worship was conducted by the chaplains of the army at nine o'clock in the morning; at ten o'clock he reviewed the troops under arms, and one o'clock that day a Continental salute of thirteen guns was fired, followed by a running fire of musketry through the whole front line of the army and a return fire on the second line. A loud huzza was given—"Long live the King of France!" The huzza was repeated with the shout "Long live the friendly European Powers!" and a third time the artillery fired and the *feu de joi* of infantry rattled along

[11] *Journals of Congress* from January 1, 1778, to January 1, 1779, Vol. IV, p. 257.

the lines as the troops cheered to the sentiment, "Prosperity to the United States of America." In the afternoon General Washington gave a collation to the officers of the army, at which Lady Washington and Lady Stirling assisted, and toasts and cheers followed each other until the party broke up at five o'clock with loud shouts of "Long live General Washington!"

On May 8 an address was ordered by Congress to be prepared and copies of it scattered among the people of the country announcing the joyful news of a powerful ally willing and ready to aid the young struggling nation, and urging upon them strenuous, unremitting exertions to further the cause in which they were engaged.

So an alliance was formed with a strong Continental power fully able to send an army and a navy, with material of war to aid in securing the independence of the United States. War was then declared with England by the King of France and an agreement made with the Continental Congress that neither nation should cease its warfare until the freedom of America was secured.

CHAPTER III

TURNING now from the encampment on the hillside of Valley Creek, we look for a moment at the gay life of the young British officers in the former rebel capital of Philadelphia. One of their own number, Charles Stedman, has said in his history that they "killed dull hours at the dance, the faro-table and the theatre." Utterly regardless of the duty they owed their king, to crush out armed rebellion among his colonists, these young soldiers, led by their commanding general, busied themselves to find new ways of pleasure. They made gay feasts, they invited the Tory families to merry dances. Every week the ball-room at the City Tavern was crowded with fair women and their soldier gallants in the minuet and noisy with the hilarity of the Virginia reel. Every few days a crowd of choice spirits would gather at the cock-pit on Moore's Alley. Some of the royal officers could be found every night at the Bunch of Grapes and the Indian Queen in wild gambling parties, or engaged in great convivial merriment at the brilliantly lighted rooms of the London Coffee House. From January to May the officers had weekly entertainments in the wooden building of the Old South theater, and Captain John André, of the Twenty-sixth regiment of foot, and Captain Oliver De Lancey, of the Seventeenth regiment of light dragoons, led off on the boards in "No one's enemy but his own," "The Mock Doctor" and "The Deuce is in him." Then when the beauty and wit of the city, who had applauded their efforts to amuse, had retired, the gay actors sought wine, revelry and a night's carouse in the club room of the City Tavern. In this way, with pleasant days and festive nights, they killed the dull routine duties of a soldier's life.

During the spring the British made one effort to show that they had been sent to America to subdue a rebellion.

In the early hours of May 7 two large galleys, with several flat-boats, containing about six hundred men of the Second battalion, British light infantry, Major John Maitland commanding, went to Bordentown, New Jersey, near the head of tide-water on the Delaware River. On this raid the enemy burned or sunk in Barnes', Watson's and Crosswicks' creeks two large frigates, one made for thirty-two and the other for twenty-eight guns, nine large ships, three privateers for sixteen guns each, twenty-three brigantines and several sloops and schooners. They burned the store-house that contained the commissary supplies and made themselves free in the handsome residence of Francis Hopkinson, a signer of the Declaration of Independence. This house they fired, but Captain Johann Ewald of the Hessian Yagers, allowed the citizens to extinguish the flames. The British also destroyed the residence in Bordentown of Colonel Joseph Borden, formerly of the First regiment, Burlington County New Jersey Militia, and of Colonel Joseph Kirkbride, of the First battalion, Bucks County Pennsylvania Militia, on the Pennsylvania side of the river. Although his entire property was destroyed, Colonel Kirkbride was able to write this patriotic sentence in a letter to Thomas Wharton, President of the Supreme Executive Council of the Commonwealth of Pennsylvania,—"Notwithstanding, I can say with Sincerity I had rather loose ten such Estates than to be suspected to be unfriendly to my Country."[1] The next day the British went up to Biles Island intending to raid on Trenton, but hearing that a force under Major-General Philemon Dickinson, commanding officer of the New Jersey Militia, had arrived there and was ready to oppose them, they abandoned their object. Eight men were killed and four cannon captured on this expedition. The British fleet returned on Sunday, May 10, with all

---

[1] *Pennsylvania Archives*, First Series, Vol. VI, p. 503.

their booty and were received with great hilarity in Philadelphia.[2]

On February 17 Lord Frederick North, Prime Minister of England, made his great speech in the British House of Commons, in which, in the most eloquent manner, he advocated the passage of two bills for the purpose of conciliating the American people. One bill was "For removing all Doubts and Apprehensions concerning Taxation by the Parliament of Great Britain in any of the Colonies and Plantations of North America" and one of the distinct features thereof was that the duty on tea was to be removed and the government pledged not to impose a tax of any kind whatever on His Majesty's colonies except such duties as were necessary to be levied to regulate commerce, and even the moneys derived therefrom were to be used only for the benefit of the colonies. The other bill appointed five commissioners with extraordinary powers, among which were, to grant pardons, to suspend any Act of Parliament passed in reference to America since February 10, 1763, to appoint Governors of the colonies, to proclaim, if they saw proper, a cessation of hostilities on sea and land, for any period and under such conditions as they might deem best, and, in fine, "to agree upon the means of quieting the disorders now subsisting in certain of the Colonies of America."

The speech of Lord North, the action of the House of Commons March 3, and the royal assent proclaimed from the throne March 11, 1778, may be summed up in this way: The British authorities, alarmed at first by the surrender of Burgoyne and then by the French alliance, were at last willing to agree to any form of conciliation, except absolute independence, and to accomplish this they were ready to repeal any law, relinquish any heretofore asserted right and acquiesce in any plan which would end the quarrel and still preserve the territory to the crown.

[2] For a minute description of this affair, see Woodward's *History of Burlington County, New Jersey*, p. 464 *et seq*.

These conciliatory bills were sent across the ocean, reached New York City on April 14 and were proclaimed by the royal Governor, William Tryon of New York, on the following day. The Governor, filled with the usual zeal of an ardent Tory and thinking that now a settlement of every difficulty and an end of the war would soon be made and that he would commend himself to the King for his activity, with unblushing coolness wrote a letter, dated April 17, to General Washington at Valley Forge, and sent him a package of the "Bills," urging him, a most "extraordinary and impertinent request," to assist in distributing them among his troops and among the people of America. In the American camp it was at first supposed to be a forgery and it was but the work of a moment for the General to decide what was best to do with this bundle and he packed it off by an express rider to Congress at York, Pennsylvania.

It is quite plain, however, that General Washington had some fears as to the effect these documents, called by the patriots "deceptionary bills," might produce upon the people of the several states at this time. He knew well that many were anxious for peace, and to know that this end could be reached by the acceptance of the very terms first demanded by the colonies, would perhaps tempt the weak-hearted, who were weary of fighting. If this spirit should gain much ground, cause disaffection among the people, distraction in public councils and interference in the approaching campaign, longer and more grievous would be the struggle for freedom, and the result more uncertain. Therefore, in his letter transmitting the package, he begged Congress to make every effort to counteract their malignant influence.

From a letter of General Washington, dated April 21, to John Banister, a delegate to the Continental Congress, we find this strong remark, "The enemy are beginning to play a game more dangerous than their efforts by arms (though these will not be remitted in the smallest degree) which threatens a fatal blow to the independence of America and of course to her liberties. They are endeavoring to ensnare the people by specious allurements of peace. . . . Nothing can be more evident than that a peace on the principles of dependence however limited, after what has happened, would be to the last degree dishonourable and ruinous. . . . Nothing short of independence, it appears to me, can possibly do. A peace on other terms would, if I may be allowed the expression, be a peace of war. The injuries we have received from the British nation were so unprovoked and have been so great and so many, that they can never be forgotten."[3]

When the patriot Governor of New York, George Clinton, heard of the propositions looking toward peace, he said, "Lord North is two years too late with his political maneuvres."

Governor Trumbull, of Connecticut, wrote, "There was a day when even this step might have been accepted with joy and gratitude, but that day, sir, is passed irrevocably."

Robert Morris said, "No offers ought to have a hearing of one moment unless preceded by acknowledgment of our independence."

According to the official return now on file in the Public Record Office in London, the British force in Philadelphia March 26, 1778, was,—British, 13,078; Germans, 5,202; Provincials, 1,250, making a total of 19,530 men.

General Washington estimated the force in Philadelphia to be about 10,000 men and this he thought might be increased to 14,000 by relieving the troops then on duty in New York City. Following this opinion of General Washington, we find Marshall in his history computing the British effective force in Philadelphia as 10,000; Gordon, as from 9,000 to 10,000 rank and file, and Irving, as from 9,000 to 10,000 men. Von Elking, in his valuable work, says they had scarcely 13,000; but Captain John Montresor, the Chief Engineer on the staff of General

[3] Sparks' *Writings of George Washington*, Vol. V, p. 323.

Howe, says than on June 6 the British Army in Philadelphia consisted of 20,000 effectives, 17,600 of whom were
fighting men.[4] Justice Thomas Jones, of the Supreme
Court of the Province of New York, with a proneness to
exaggerate, says in his history of New York, "Sir Henry
crossed the Delaware with his whole army, nearly 30,000
men."

On August 15, 1778, a return of the British Army was
made, and from this it appears that the troops in and about
New York numbered 19,586, an increase since the return
of March 26 of 9,130 men; on Long Island they numbered 8,117, which is an increase by that amount; in
Rhode Island, 5,789 men, an increase of 2,019. Leaving
out the two German regiments that went to New York in
the ships, perhaps 1,000 men, we arrive at the conclusion
that Clinton had more than 18,000 men ready to march
and give battle outside of Philadelphia.

It appears strange indeed that with a large fleet[5] to
cover with its guns the city of Philadelphia, Sir William
Howe, with his magnificent army, did not make a vigorous
demonstration in force on the impoverished camp at Valley
Forge, only a day's march distant, and scatter with one
blow the ragged and starving soldiers who, as an army,
represented the military power of the republic. In the
warm houses of Philadelphia General Howe thought of
the intense cold, the heavy snows, and the toil and trouble
of a winter attack. He knew that his foe were starving,
freezing and dying by the side of the icy river, but the
habit of easy procrastination and inactivity took possession of his soul and the opportunity slipped away. The
Americans could not have remained in the fortified can-

---

[4] *Pennsylvania Archives*, Vol. II, p. 290.
[5] The British fleet on the Delaware River consisted of the *Phoenix*,
a 40-gun ship, the *Eagle*, a 24-gun ship, the frigates *Andromeda, Lizard*
and *Thomas*, the packets *Cadiz* and *Harriet*, the galleys *Cornwallis* and
Hussar, the sloops *Porcupine, Fanny, Brune, Camilla, Somerset, Liverpool,
Roebuck, Daphne, Nautilus, Isis, Alert, Maidstone, Pearl, Richmond, Trident, Vigilant, Active*, and thirty other small sailing vessels, in all one
hundred and twenty vessels, anchored off Philadelphia in June, 1778.

tonment for many days if they had been surrounded, for they would soon have died of starvation. They could not have sallied out without the loss of large numbers of the half-naked soldiery and they could not have retreated with safety to any place where they could with more certainty have made a good defence. As week after week passed by and no attempt was made to break up their winter retreat, the foreign officers, Generals von Steuben and Lafayette, Duportail and De Kalb, expressed themselves as astonished that Howe failed to make a demonstration. General Duportail had frequently told his brother officers that Howe could have exterminated the American force at any time after the fight at Brandywine. But Howe excused himself on the ground that it was "imprudent until the season should afford a prospect of reaping the advantages that ought to have resulted from success in that measure but having good information in the spring that the enemy had strengthened the camp by additional works and being certain of moving him from thence when the campaign should open, he dropped thought of an attack." He said also, "that he must receive large reinforcements from England if he attempted what was clearly expected of him." The Tory history before referred to says on this subject, "To put an end to the rebellion the only object should have been the destruction of the army under Washington, . . . and to the surprise of everybody Howe never attempted to beat up the rebel quarters."[6] Colonel Henry Lee puts the case in the most pointed language,— "Knowing, as sir William ought to have known, the sufferings and wants of every kind to which Washington was exposed at Valley Forge, as well as that his army was under inoculation for the small-pox, while he himself was so abundantly supplied with every article requisite to give warmth and comfort to his troops, it is wonderful how he could omit venturing a winter campaign, to him promis-

<hr>

[6] Jones' *History of New York*, Vol. I, pp. 236-7.

ing every advantage, and to his antagonist, menacing every ill."[7]

On April 19 General Howe wrote to the British minister, "The enemy's position continues to be at Valley Forge and Wilmington. Their force has been diminished during the course of the winter by desertion and by detachments to the back settlements where the Indians make constant inroads; but the want of green forage does not yet permit me to take the field, and their situation is too strong to hazard an attack with a prospect of success."[8]

And so the winter wore away in inaction and in revelry in the gay city during which the gallant officers forgot war and war's alarms. But one morning they knew that this wild life must come to a sudden end as the news rapidly spread around the city that General Howe was ordered to report in England and that his command would soon be assumed by Sir Henry Clinton.

Great was the grief among the young officers of his army and the lively, fun-loving belles of the city when they learned that Sir William Howe had been superseded. What should they do to testify to the beloved commander the feelings with which they regarded him? After many consultations a great scheme was decided upon by twenty-two of the commissioned officers "to exhibit a something before unknown to the New World, perhaps to the Old."[9] On May 18 the famous Mischianza was fully carried out, with the wildest folly and extravagance, on the streets, on the river, in private grounds, in the public halls of Philadelphia. General Howe accepted with great pleasure this fulsome adulation, knowing full well, however, that it was a severe and open criticism of the action of his king.

While the merry dancers were engaged in their midnight frolic, Major-General the Marquis de Lafayette was leading a chosen body of troops toward Philadelphia

[7] *Lee's Memoirs of the War in the Southern Department*, p. 32.
[8] *Parliamentary Register*, Vol. XI, p. 465.
[9] Jones' *History of New York*, Vol. I, p. 241.

for the purpose of restraining the British forage parties and obtaining some intelligence of their intended movements. It was not many hours before the news reached General Howe's quarters that Lafayette's "tattered retinue had abandoned their mud-holes" and with twenty-five hundred men and eight cannon had crossed over the Schuylkill River and were moving between that stream and the Delaware River. At half-past ten on the night of May 19 a party of fifty-three hundred men under General James Grant, consisting of the Second battalion, British light infantry, the Queen's rangers, the Sixteenth and Seventeenth regiments of light dragoons and the First and Second brigades of British foot, were despatched to capture the American detachment. After promising the ladies of Philadelphia to bring Lafayette back to dine with them, General Howe started out the next morning with fifty-seven hundred more troops, accompanied by Clinton and Knyphausen and his own brother, Lord Howe. But Lafayette was not so easily entrapped, for he eluded their movements in an orderly style; the men, responding quickly to the tactics in which they had been disciplined, made "a handsome retreat" in great order over the Schuylkill at Matson's Ford, and General Howe returned to Philadelphia after a fruitless march to Barren Hill. The whole affair was generally considered a fine display of tactical knowledge by Lafayette and it certainly was an event of keen disappointment to the British.

CHAPTER IV

SIR Henry Clinton reached Philadelphia May 8 but did not immediately assume command of the British Army in that city. On May 11 General Sir William Howe issued an order to his troops announcing the change of commander.

On March 21 instructions had been sent Sir Henry Clinton from London with reference to his future movements. These orders reached him May 23. After giving directions to send certain troops to the British West Indies and to Florida, the order reads, "When these detachments shall have been made or while they are making, Philadelphia is to be evacuated; all the troops to be embarked, with everything belonging to the army, and to proceed thence to New York, where they will wait the issue of the negotiation, which the commissioners have been authorized to propose to the Congress."[1]

In the secret despatches of March 8, sent by Lord George Germaine, Colonial Secretary, the following passage occurs: "It is recommended not to pursue an offensive warfare against the interior, but leave men enough to defend the posts and embark a detachment on board the King's ships and attack the harbours along the coast between New York and Halifax. . . . If this service cannot be executed, without detaching so many men from Philadelphia as to leave that place insecure, then such a post may be taken on the Delaware River and fortified, as may be defended by a small number of men, the shipping thereby protected and the navigation of the river obstructed. Philadelphia may then be evacuated, leaving only a garrison at the above post and taking the remaining troops to New York, except such as are wanted for the expedition against the northern seaports. Not that the

[1] Sparks' *Writings of George Washington*, Vol. V, Appendix, p. 550.

retaining of Philadelphia is not thought a very important object and it is to be abandoned only on the condition that the northern service cannot be effected without it."[2]

It is quite certain that Clinton would have preferred to have taken his whole army in vessels by way of the Delaware River and Bay and up the New Jersey coast to New York City. The heavy baggage, cannon and shells had been placed on the transports on May 14; but Clinton soon found that with all the sail he had they would not be able to carry one-half the soldiers and citizens, whom it was necessary to take with them, and the vast materiel of war, the horses, wagons and incumbrances of various kinds. He therefore wrote Lord Germaine that he "found it impracticable to embark the forces in order to proceed to New York by water, as there are not transports enough to receive the whole at once and therefore a great part of the cavalry, all our provision train and the persons whose attachment to the government has rendered them objects of vengeance to the enemy must have been left behind. . . . These reasons have induced me to resolve on marching through Jersey."[3]

General Clinton found it necessary to vacate the city of Philadelphia as soon as he possibly could do so. In the early part of June he learned that a French fleet had sailed from Toulon for the Capes of the Delaware and that if he wished to escape with his army by water or even to allow some of his baggage and heavy munitions of war to be transported in that way to New York and the New England coast he must act instantly, before it became too late. He saw clearly that he must place his army as soon as possible in a city on the seaboard, which could not so easily be blockaded by a hostile fleet. Every hour's delay made safety more uncertain. He dared not cherish the idea, as his predecessor did, that he could at any time attack Washington in his quarters at Valley Forge, but must get

[2] Sparks, Appendix, Vol. V, p. 549.
[3] *ibid.*, Vol. V, p. 396, footnote.

away quickly from a city known to contain partisans of the rebel cause, who were not slow in giving the patriot chieftain information of all the movements in the shipping on the river.

The various orders issued by General Howe during the closing days of his administration and the instructions given by General Clinton when he assumed command preparatory to the movement of his army from Philadelphia are interesting at this point in the narrative.

After a review of the British troops the following congratulatory order was issued by General Howe on May 4: "The Commander-in-Chief desires that Lieutenant-General Knyphausen and the Hessian Troops under His Excellency's command will please to accept of his acknowledgments and thanks for the magnificent appearance they exhibited this day of which he shall not fail to make the most faithful report to His Majesty."

On May 3 Captain John Montresor, General Howe's chief engineer, began to erect defences on Cooper's Creek in New Jersey, under the protection of the galley-ship Cornwallis and the Fifty-fifth and Sixty-third regiments of the British foot. It took three days to finish these redoubts and then the Pennsylvania and Maryland regiments of loyalists joined the troops just mentioned in garrisoning the forts. On May 8 Brigadier-General Alexander Leslie was sent over the Delaware River with an escort of Captain Richard Hovendon's Provincial company of light dragoons, to take command of the British force on Cooper's Creek. On May 14 some of the heavy impedimenta of the army was ordered to be prepared for shipment, the officers were directed in this way "to lighten their baggage for the field as much as possible," and on May 20 the general officers of the army were ordered to see that all the tents, baggage and stores not necessary in field service were placed on the transport ships.

This was the condition of affairs when Sir Henry Clinton received his orders, May 23, took command of the army and abandoned the plan of taking them by water to New York. At nine o'clock in the morning of May 25 orders were issued, dated the previous day, for all the men, women and children unfit to march to be instantly placed on the transports "under the command of a careful non-commissioned officer and to report the number, that provisions may be ordered," and that these boats fall down the river at one o'clock that day. On May 26 an order was issued for the marching troops to carry twenty days' provisions in wagons and four days' food in their packs. On May 28 the Seventh and Twenty-sixth regiments of foot were ordered to report to General Leslie in the redoubts on Cooper's Creek and the Fifteenth regiment to report to Brigadier-General Courtlandt Skinner, commander of the brigade of New Jersey volunteers (loyalists) stationed at the fort at Billingsport, New Jersey. On May 29 a "review of arms, accoutrements, ammunition and necessaries took place at three o'clock in the afternoon." According to order, the men brought to this review their camp kettles, canteens, tomahawks and every article they were to carry on the march.[4] At this time General Leslie became alarmed to find that the New Jersey militia was hovering around his post and he ordered "roll to be called often, no one allowed to quit camp, no soldier to go beyond the sentries as the regiments may be subject to sudden alarms and the

[4] The staff of Lieutenant-General Sir Henry Clinton on May 30, 1778, consisted of James Paterson, Sixty-third regiment, colonel and adjutant-general, relieved to go to England June 19, 1778, by Lieutenant-Colonel Lord Francis Rawdon, who was made adjutant-general; Stephen Kemble, major and deputy adjutant-general; George Hutchinson, Twenty-third regiment, captain and deputy adjutant-general; James Cramond, Forty-second regiment, lieutenant and assistant adjutant-general; Lord Francis Rawdon, volunteers Ireland, lieutenant-colonel and aide-de-camp promoted; Duncan Drummond, regiment artillery, major and aide-de-camp; William Sutherland, Fifty-fifth regiment, captain and aide-de-camp; Lord William S. Cathcart, Seventeenth dragoons, captain and aide-de-camp; William Crosbie, Thirty-eighth regiment, captain and aide-de-camp; —— Wilmousky, Prince Carl regiment, captain and aide-de-camp; Frederick Ernst von Munchausen, regiment Louisburg, captain and aide-de-camp; John Smith, Thirty-seventh regiment, captain and military secretary; Andrew Bell, deputy muster-master of provincial forces.

men's accoutrements must be hung up conveniently so that
they may be able to turn out instantly and form in front
of their huts."

All night of June 8 the baggage wagons of the British
Army were being transported over the Delaware River and
placed under the care of General Leslie. This fact, how-
ever, soon became known to the Americans, for Brigadier-
General Joseph Reed, hearing of it, wrote to his wife
June 9,—"Many persons are very sanguine that the enemy
must evacuate Philadelphia after having sent their baggage off." At two o'clock in the morning of June 9, the
Hessian battalions of Anspach and Bayreuth were placed
on board the transports. These battalions were sold by the
Margrave Charles Alexander to the British king. In
March, 1777, they had mutinied at Ochsenfurth on the
Main, the little village from which they afterward embarked for America. The Margrave was then brought to
them by express, and with a keen view of the £18,000
soon to be his and of the pleasure this would bring him, he
soon quelled with threats this incipient riot. These battalions were now put in vessels at Philadelphia instead of
crossing New Jersey. The diary of Quartermaster Johann
Heusser, of the von Lossberg regiment, says it was "because they were unable to march," but the British reports show that Clinton did not trust them. He feared
they would all desert. These organizations, however, remained in the service and were captured at the battle of
Yorktown."[5]

On June 9 the Forty-sixth British regiment joined General Leslie at Cooper's Creek. On the evening of June 11
"the sick of the army absolutely unable to march" were
ordered to be "at the lower ferry at five A.M. precisely
to-morrow morning in order to their being sent on board
the hospital ships." On June 12 the last of the wagons, all

[5] Lowell's *The Hessians and the other German Auxiliaries of Great
Britain in the Revolutionary War*, p. 47. Johnston's *The Yorktown Campaign*, p. 119.

the light artillery, and on June 14 and 15 all the horses of the army, draft as well as officers' horses, were ferried over into New Jersey. On the latter day, "with deep expressions of discontent at the movement," a brigade of Hessian troops, accompanied by the Thirty-third regiment of British foot, went over the river in flat-boats. On June 16 the Sixteenth and Seventeenth regiments of light dragoons, with Generals Knyphausen and Grant, passed over the Delaware River. The Hessian regiments of grenadiers also went with them by a misinterpretation of orders, as it was intended that they should form a rear guard.

During all these movements General Washington made no attempt to prevent the British from securing a foothold in New Jersey, so as to begin a march across that State. He preferred, rather, as a German writer says, "to build a bridge of gold for a flying enemy."[6]

As has been mentioned, General Howe had received despatches April 9, directing him to return to England. Notwithstanding his military abilities and his soldierly presence and bearing, being tall, with fine figure, pleasing countenance and dignified appearance, he was constitutionally inert and procrastinating, always reluctant to engage in anything but his own personal pleasures. Withal, he was not a favorite of Lord Germaine, the Colonial Secretary, and although he claimed a relationship with the king, George III did not care to protect him from the hatred of his executive officer. In the early morning of May 24, General Howe turned over the command of the army to Lieutenant-General Sir Henry Clinton, and at half-past one in the afternoon he went on board the frigate *Andromeda*, Commodore Brine, with Captain Frederick George Mulcaster, Forty-third regiment of foot, his military secretary. The sorrow of the young officers in Philadelphia was very great as they bade adieu to their **boon**

[6] For details of these movements of the British Army, see journal of Captain John Montresor, *Pennsylvania Magazine of History*, Vol. VI, p. 189 *et seq.*

companion, as well as military chief, who had set them an example of wild license and of heavy gambling, instead of at least assuming a spirit of adventure in an attempt to surround and destroy the ill-clad and poorly fed army of America a few miles distant. General Knyphausen, representing the older soldiers, attempted to say some words of compliment and farewell, but his feelings overcame him and he had to stop his remarks.

After leaving the wharf, the British frigate made but little headway down the river against a fresh southerly wind and it was not until May 26 that she cleared the Capes of the Delaware. The vessel reached England July 2, 1778. Horace Walpole remarked, when he heard of the arrival of General Howe, that he was "much richer in money than in laurels."

Sir Henry Clinton was now in full command of the troops in and about Philadelphia. He was an officer rather under size in stature, portly, with a prominent nose, somewhat reserved in his manner and not given to much intimacy with his other general officers. Consequently, he never became very popular with them and perhaps appeared more cool and distant than he really was, coming so close after and in such strong contrast to the affable and friendly manners of Howe. The German soldiers liked him because he spoke their language. He had studied and practised the art of war and as aide-de-camp to Ferdinand, Duke of Brunswick, had seen much service in the Seven Years' War. He was slow and very cautious for a general officer but forty years of age, yet he was personally a very brave man and in his eagerness for victory, never hesitated to assume any personal risk or danger.

In speaking of General Clinton, it is well not to omit mention of General Cornwallis, who was without doubt the best equipped soldier the British government had in the United States. He was an officer of great influence in war circles on account of his family connections and rank. Although much like Clinton in figure, he had a pleasing face and expression and was greatly admired and loved by the men of his command. His lordship, who had left Philadelphia for England December 19, 1777, returned to Philadelphia in the same vessel with the Commissioners for peace, at eleven o'clock on the morning of June 6, 1778.

On Saturday night, June 6, in the midst of a fierce rain storm, the three commissioners referred to in Lord North's conciliatory bills, to "treat, consult and agree upon the Means of quieting the Disorders now subsisting in certain of the Colonies, Plantations and Provinces of North America," having sailed from England April 22, arrived at Philadelphia in the English vessel *Trident*. General Clinton announced their arrival in General Orders that evening and ordered the army to pay them every respect. When General Lafayette heard of their arrival, he said he feared these men more than ten thousand troops. In this, however, he was mistaken. In the early morning of June 7 a salute was fired in their honor and the commissioners entered the city, the heavy rain of the night making a cheerless reception. These officials were, Frederick Howard, Earl of Carlisle, George Johnstone, once Governor of West Florida, and Sir William Eden, afterward Lord Auckland, a member of Parliament and Under-Secretary of State. To this commission it was proposed to add Lord Howe and General Howe, and General Clinton took the place of the latter officer. Doctor Adam Ferguson, Professor of Moral Philosophy in the University of Edinburgh, came with the commission as their secretary. On June 9, through Sir Henry Clinton, they requested General Washington's permission and safe-conduct for Doctor Ferguson, whom they desired to send to New York with a letter and a copy of their instructions to Congress. This request was refused. These documents, however, were sent to the Continental Congress the next day, were received June 13, and by that act the commission gave Congress its official and rightful recognition. It may be noted that the letter of the commission was sealed with "the image of a fond mother caressing her children."

In these communications to Congress they guaranteed freedom of legislation and internal government, representation in parliament, exemption from the presence of a military force, except with their own permission, in fact, the gratification of every wish that the Americans had ever expressed, save only that of independence. In after years the King said that many of these offers were made without authority. It may with truth be stated, however, that at the time they were made all these concessions seemed more a sign of weakness than of any real desire to benefit the colonists. The letter from the commissioners was read in Congress at York, Pennsylvania, but elicited no favorable response. A slight reflection on the conduct of the King of France caused an interruption, the further reading was stopped and the business laid over.

The committee in Congress, to which these letters and documents were referred, said it was quite evident that these concessions were intended to create diversions and defections in the ranks of those who had so zealously espoused the cause and that in their opinion "these United States cannot with propriety hold any conference or treaty with any commissioners on the part of Great Britain, unless they shall, as a preliminary thereto either withdraw their fleets and armies, or else in positive and express terms acknowledge the independence of the said States."[7]

The commissioners found at the very beginning of their labors that Congress had previously acted on the purpose of their mission, that the Americans were feeling new spirit at the news of the strong alliance with France and that an order from Lord Germaine had preceded them to quit Philadelphia at an early day. From the very first hour they could not but feel that their mission was doomed to failure. They complained bitterly to the home government

[7] *Journals of Congress*, January 1, 1778, to January 1, 1779, Vol. IV, p. 347 to 354.

in thus embarrassing them at the outset by giving up to the Americans the former capital of their country, and said that this retreat dispelled every hope of success they had cherished.

These unexpected measures of the ministry of England excited astonishment and indignation in the British Army. The officers thought it a personal indignity that the commissioners were willing to concede so much. These conciliatory bills seemed to them a kind of substitute for the reinforcement of 20,000 men which they had been led to expect. The loyalists thought, and so intimated to the commissioners, that all their public and private hopes and the expected gratification of their personal resentments were cut off at a blow.

In this way, and because of these attempted negotiations, the march of Sir Henry Clinton's army and the abandonment of Philadelphia were delayed from day to day. The army was kept in check for the sake of diplomacy. General Gates remarked, June 17, "Thank Heaven for the precious time the enemy have so foolishly lost."[8]

During the time the commissioners were urging their plans upon Congress and the American people, a curious attempt was made by them, through a Mrs. Ferguson, to bribe General Joseph Reed, President of Pennsylvania, with the offer of ten thousand pounds sterling. He indignantly spurned the effort with the caustic reply that he was not worth purchasing, but such as he was, the King of Great Britain was not rich enough to do it.

On August 11, 1778, notice was taken in Congress of the plans of the commissioners by the adoption of the following resolution:

"Resolved, That Congress will not in any degree negotiate with the present commissioners in America for restoring peace." This was in the form of a declaration and was ordered to be published to the world.

[8] For Washington's opinion of the conciliatory bills, see letter to John Banister, Delegate in Congress from Virginia,—Sparks, Vol. V, p. 321.

The action on the part of those loyalists who had determined to leave Philadelphia with the troops was equivalent to the sacrifice of their property, except so much thereof as they were allowed to carry on ship-board. To quit the city was to exile themselves, bid farewell to former friends and associates and to begin life anew in some untried locality. To those loyalists who preferred to remain, it meant ostracism by the patriots, who would soon return, and, as it afterward proved, imprisonment and death to some of them. Von Elking says, and certainly with much truth, that they "contemplated the arrival of the colonists with terror and stupefaction."

On June 2, even before his army had possession of Philadelphia, General Washington advised the greatest moderation, forbearance and charity toward those who would remain. He warned Congress that for want of the offer of protection, "hundreds, nay thousands of people and among them many valuable artisans, with large quantities of goods, will be forced from Philadelphia who otherwise would willingly remain. From report, their reluctance and distress upon this occasion are scarcely to be paralleled." And the loyalists said, as they gathered up their movable property, "If Philadelphia is left to the rebels, independence is acknowledged and America lost." The poor Tories were indeed in a terrible plight, for their faint hearts were filled with dread of patriot revenge. The loyalist ladies who, with their beauty and presence had made the winter gay for the young soldiery of Britain, saw that the end of their jollity had come and that they must keep in close retirement, if indeed they remained at all in the city soon to be in control of the American arms.

CHAPTER V

AGAIN looking for a moment at the camp at Valley Forge, we find that early in May the warm sunshine followed the chilling blasts of winter, and spring infused joy and good spirits into the ranks of the worn soldiers of the republic. Yet it must be remembered that it was during that long season of intense cold and suffering, borne with sublime heroism, that the American Army first learned the discipline of the true soldier. Baron von Steuben, who had been taught the art of war under the great Frederick and who joined Washington's army February 23, had begun in March to recreate an army, and every day and all day he labored to make a force of skilled soldiers. He thought that under tattered clothing he saw good material for a fighting column, and he tried to develop it. With strange German oaths he drilled the awkward squad, himself acting as sergeant, and when his own vocabulary of sharp profanity became exhausted he called on his aide, Captain Benjamin Walker, to assist him in words adequate to the occasion. The men saw that he was sincere and they admired him. In after days they thanked him from their patriotic souls when they saw that they were brought to victory by the methods which he had so carefully taught them. On March 28, as we find by Washington's orderly book, von Steuben had begun to exercise the duties of Inspector-General of the army, in the place of General Conway, although it was not until May 5 that he was commissioned to that office, with the rank of Major-General, by the Continental Congress. On May 30, Colonel Jacob Morgan of the Pennsylvania militia wrote, "regiments of the army perform manoeuvres with great exactness and dispatch and are well disciplined."

The Quartermaster's department was now working more smoothly under the management of the noble-hearted

General Greene. He was ably seconded by Colonel John Cox and Colonel Charles Pettit, Assistant Quartermaster-Generals, and by Colonel Clement Biddle and Colonel Jeremiah Wadsworth in the department of the Commissary.[1]

With a better supply of food and clothing the men forgot their past sufferings, turned with cheerfulness to the school of the soldier, and were drilled into a force fit to cope with any of the troops of Britain.

About the last of April some six hundred men joined the army from the New England States and Lieutenant-Colonel Eleazer Oswald wrote from the Artillery Park at Valley Forge, May 15, to Colonel John Lamb, the commanding officer of the Second regiment Continental artillery, "Our army is now very formidable, but not such as enables Gen'l Washington to attack the enemy in Philadelphia. . . . Reinforcements have lately arrived—a few more will give us superiority of our enemy."

On June 10 the soldiers left their winter huts and pitched tents for the few days they expected to remain on that soil.

General William Maxwell's Continental brigade was ordered May 7 to march to New Jersey and be prepared to harass the enemy in case they proceeded to New York by land through that State. The whole army, as General

---

[1] The Staff of General Washington consisted of Alexander Scammell, colonel and adjutant-general; Nathaniel Greene, major-general and quartermaster-general; Frederick William Augustus von Steuben, major-general and inspector-general; Louis Lebèque Duportail, brigadier-general and chief of engineers; Henry Knox, brigadier-general and chief of artillery; John Lawrence, colonel and judge advocate-general; Jeremiah Wadsworth, colonel and commissary-general of purchases; Charles Stewart, colonel and commissary-general of issues; Clement Biddle, colonel and commissary-general of forage; Alexander Hamilton, lieutenant-colonel and aide-de-camp; Richard K. Meade, lieutenant-colonel and aide-de-camp; John Laurens, lieutenant-colonel and aide-de-camp; John Fitzgerald, lieutenant-colonel and aide-de-camp; Tench Tilghman, lieutenant-colonel and aide-de-camp; Robert H. Harrison, lieutenant-colonel and military secretary; James McHenry, assistant secretary; Joseph Reed, brigadier-general and volunteer aide-de-camp; John Cadwalader, brigadier-general and volunteer aide-de-camp.

Washington says, was placed under marching orders the same day.

The Continental Congress ordered a council of war to be held at Valley Forge. This was done on May 8. At this meeting there were present Major-Generals Gates, Greene, Stirling, Mifflin, Lafayette, De Kalb, von Steuben and Armstrong, and Brigadier-Generals Knox and Duportail. The council was called at General Washington's quarters to determine the plan for the general operations of the army during the approaching campaign, and especially to decide whether it was best to attempt any important movement at that time. It was then determined "that the line of conduct most consistent with sound policy and best suited to promote the interests and safety of the United States, was to remain on the defensive and await events, and not attempt any offensive operation against the enemy, till circumstances should afford a fairer opportunity for striking a successful blow." The storming of Philadelphia had been suggested but this was deemed very imprudent and impracticable with the present force, and for the same reason siege could not be laid against that city. When General Lee arrived in camp twelve days after the council he agreed to the policy of avoiding all offensive demonstrations and so gave his signature to the written action of the meeting of general officers. The very discussion of the subject, however, proves that at the opening of spring the American officers began to feel that they were nearly ready to commence some bold operations on the enemy.

The common topic in the huts of the American Army at this time was, the probable destination of Clinton's Army. As early as May 18 Washington wrote Lafayette that the "enemy were preparing to evacuate Philadelphia." Some thought it possible even then that the British would march into interior Pennsylvania, make a demonstration on the American cantonment and disperse the Congress at York. Some supposed they would move southward and others thought they intended operations on the Hudson River. General Gates expressed the last opinion and added that he thought they intended to carry desolation through New England.

On May 27 the following notice appeared in the *New Jersey Gazette*: "The militia of this State are desired to be particularly attentive to signals, as a movement of the enemy is soon expected."

Christopher Marshall wrote in his diary May 28, "It was thought the army intended to make a push across the Jerseys for Amboy."

On May 29 General Washington wrote to Governor Clinton, as follows: "That the enemy mean to evacuate Philadelphia is almost reduced to a certainty. It is as much so, as an event can be, that is contingent. Their baggage and stores are nearly if not all embarked; and, from our intelligence, there is reason to conclude that many days will not elapse before they abandon it."[2]

Sir Henry Clinton could not conceal the fact that he was about to make some great strategic movement, but the place of his operations he tried to keep secret. General Washington, however, was thoroughly apprised by his true friends in Philadelphia of every intended movement of Clinton's forces. He knew when the attempt to take them by water to New York was abandoned and when it was determined to march the troops across the State of New Jersey. On June 2 he wrote Major General Philemon Dickinson, commanding the New Jersey Militia,—"appearances and a thousand circumstances induce a belief, that they intend to pass through the Jerseys to New York."[3]

About this time Deputy Quartermaster-General Moore Furman wrote a letter from Trenton, New Jersey, to William Lowrey, a quartermaster at Flemington,—a document still preserved by his descendants in Trenton—

[2] Sparks' *Writings of George Washington*, Vol. V, p. 387.
[3] *ibid.*, p. 395.

informing him that the British would soon cross the State of New Jersey and that the American Army would go in pursuit of them. It is evident that General Washington had informed his trusted friend at Trenton so that supplies for his army might be collected immediately.

The total strength of the American Army under the immediate control of General Washington was about 16,000 men.

On June 24, 1778, General Washington wrote that he had "on the ground 10,648 rank and file, besides the advanced brigade under General Maxwell of about 1200, and 1200 Militia in New Jersey." To this force must be added the commissioned officers, non-commissioned officers and musicians of the army. The historian Marshall computed the American Army at between 10,000 and 11,000 effectives. General de Peyster, in a very careful computation, estimates the American Army as at least one-fourth larger than the British force in Philadelphia.

It is quite apparent that the number as stated above is very close to the full strength of the army, counting every soldier under General Washington's control. The official field return of the army on June 22, 1778, herein fully displayed, gives a total of 13,503 officers and men.[4] Add to this the number of men who appear on the return of July 4 as "present fit for duty" in General Maxwell's brigade, namely 1297, and from 800 to 1000 New Jersey militia, and the grand total of all organizations and all arms of the service under Washington's direct command must have been about 16,000 men. Probably from this gross amount we should deduct about 2000 or 2500 as men on leave of absence, on detailed duty, and in hospitals and we then have Washington's effective force, between 13,000 and 14,000 men. These are about the figures estimated by General de Peyster in his critical articles on the Battle of Monmouth, and by Winthrop Sargent in his life of André.

[4] See Appendices I and II.

On April 23 a distinguished officer of the Continental Army, Major-General Charles Lee, arrived at Valley Forge after more than fifteen months' captivity within the British lines. He left Philadelphia on his parole of honor April 5 and was declared exchanged April 21 for Major-General Richard Prescott of the British Army. He received from the officers and men in the American Army an ovation too great for his past services, and very inappropriate in the light of his conduct during the subsequent three months.[5] As he appears so prominent in the pages of this work it seems proper that some mention should be made of the previous history of the senior Major-General of the American Army.[6] In November 1776, General Lee commanded a column of troops at White Plains, New York, which were ordered to reinforce the army under General Washington on the west bank of the Delaware River. On the morning of December 13 he was surrounded and taken prisoner by a detachment of the Sixteenth regiment, Queen's light dragoons, near Baskingridge, Somerset County, New Jersey, four miles outside of his own lines. During his long confinement, he seems to have revived his esteem for his former comrades, his love of the glory of the British arms and to have expressed again and again his contempt for the apparent weakness of the force con-

[5] The Honorable Elias Boudinot, LL.D., in after years the President of the Continental Congress and signer of the treaty of peace with Great Britain gives this description of the entrance of General Lee into the lines of the patriot army: "All the principal Officers of the Army were drawn up in two lines, advanced of the Camp about 2 miles towards the Enemy. Then the troops with the inferior Officers formed a line quite to head Quarters. All the Music of the Army attended. The General with a great number of principal Officers and their Suites, rode about four miles on the road towards Philadelphia and waited till Gen'l Lee appeared. Gen. Washington dismounted & rec'd Gen. Lee as if he had been his brother. He passed thro' the Lines of Officers & the Army, who all paid him the highest military Honours to Head Quarters, where Mrs. Washington was and here he was entertained with an Elegant Dinner and the Music Playing the whole Time. A Room was assigned him back of Mrs. Washington's Sitting Room and all his Baggage was stowed in it. . . . Gen'l Washington gave him the command of the Right Wing of the Army, but before he took charge of it, he requested leave to go to Congress at York Town, which was readily granted."—*The Boudinot Journal*, p. 78.

[6] See Appendix III.

tending in liberty's name. But worse than all is the discovery made by the learned historiographer, the late Doctor George H. Moore, that on March 29, 1777, he submitted a "plan" to the commanding officers of the army and navy of the Crown as to the best mode of conquering America. Among other things he said, "If the Province of Maryland or the greater part of it is reduc'd or submits, and the People of Virginia are prevented or intimidated from marching aid to the Pensylvania Army the whole machine is dissolv'd and a period put to the War," and he advised that "four thousand men be immediately embark'd in transports, one half of which shou'd proceed up the Potomac and take post at Alexandria, the other half up Chesepeak Bay and possess themselves of Annapolis. . . . These Posts may with ease support each other, as it is but two easy days march from one to the other, and if occasion requires by a single days march. They may join and conjunctly carry on their operations wherever it shall be thought eligible to direct 'em, whether to take possession of Baltimore or post themselves on some spot on the Westward bank of the Susquehanna, which is a point of the utmost importance."[7]

These few lines give us some idea of the plans which this bold, unscrupulous man, while a prisoner of war, had the impudence to offer for the consideration of the representatives of England's power in America. These words give an outline of his treasonable scheme to subvert and destroy the future liberties of a people struggling in a holy cause, to "unhinge and dissolve the whole system of defense" and thus end the war. It is clear that by thus betraying the cause in which he was engaged his idea was that when the whole plan of self-government had been acknowledged a failure, it would be his fortune not only to have secured his own personal safety and protection but also, perhaps, his old commission, with pay attached. For he expected that the humanity of his Majesty's Commis-

[7] Moore's *Treason of General Lee*, p. 87.

sioners would "incline 'em" in that supreme moment of victory to "have consideration for Individuals who have acted from Principle."[8] If they would only act as he suggested, he ventured to assert with the penalty of his life that the war would end in less than two months.

It appears that for some time General Washington had been making very active exertions to have General Lee exchanged, because, as he said, he had never been "more wanted by him than at the present moment." But the interview which Colonel Elias Boudinot, Commissary General of Prisoners, had with Lee, wherein Lee said to him, "It is in vain for Congress to withstand british Troops in the Field," and indeed the whole conversation, proves him not to have been a true and zealous patriot.[9]

General Lee was exchanged April 21, as has been said, received with great honor in the American camp April 23, left immediately for the Continental Congress then in session at York, Pennsylvania, and on the twentieth day of May again reported for duty at Valley Forge. Ten days thereafter he was ordered to command the First Division of the army.[10]

This is the man who was destined to take so prominent a part in two war councils of the patriot army in the ensuing campaign and who was to play such a questionable rôle on the field of Monmouth. General Lee, with overweening vanity, thought that at the suggestion of General Howe and Lord Howe, General Clinton would certainly follow the plan suggested by a soldier of such merit and experience as himself, and march his army toward the lower parts of the Susquehanna River. From some of the dispositions of General Howe there is no doubt that at one

[8] *ibid.*, p. 85.
[9] Boudinot's *Life and Services of Elias Boudinot*, Vol. I, p. 140 *et seq.*
[10] The staff of General Lee consisted of Lieutenant-Colonel John Brooks of the Eighth Massachusetts regiment, adjutant-general; Colonel the Marquis Francis de Malmedy, Major John Francis Mercer, formerly Captain of the Third Virginia regiment, Major George L. Turberville, formerly Captain of the Fifteenth Virginia regiment, and Captain Evan Edwards, of Hartley's Continental regiment, aides-de-camp.

time he intended to do so. Fully impressed with this opinion, having "particular reasons" to think they would do so, and anxious, if such a movement were made, to be able to say that he himself had predicted it, General Lee wrote a letter to General Washington June 15, in which he gave his professional opinion of the situation, what he thought the British would do and the way the Americans should act in the predicted contingency.

General Washington replied to General Lee's artful communication the same day. It was a very courteous letter, but it is clear that the Commander-in-Chief was not shaken in his belief that the design of the British officers was to march across New Jersey.[11]

[11] *Lee Papers*, New York Historical Society Collections, 1872, pp. 399, 402.

CHAPTER VI

ON June 16 Sir Henry Clinton determined to start immediately on his march through New Jersey by way of Brunswick to the city of New York. That very evening he sent General Stirn with a small command across the Delaware River into New Jersey. The visit of the British conciliatory commissioners to America and their efforts to negotiate a peace had proved an utter failure, and there was now no reason to delay the execution of the instructions Clinton had received. He therefore issued the following orders:

Head-Quarters, Philadelphia, June 16, 1778.
Lieutenant-General Kniphausen and Major-General Grant will cross the river to-morrow at 4 with the following regiments: Yagers, mounted and dismounted, Queen's Rangers, Hessian Grenadiers, Second Battalion New Jersey Volunteers, Maryland Loyalists, Volunteers of Ireland and the Caledonian Volunteers. All waggons and carts, with the waggons and bat-horses belonging to the general and staff Officers, are to be embarked this afternoon at half-past 3, at the upper coal wharf and to-morrow at 6 all the saddle horses belonging to the general and staff Officers are to be embarked at the same place, except two for the commander-in-chief and one for each of the general Officers. All the Sick that are absolutely unable to march are to be at Primrose's wharf to-morrow morning at 5 o'clock, where they will be received on board the *Active*—Webb, Master.[1]

By this order General Clinton opened his first campaign as commander-in-chief of the British Army in America and the first military movement of the year 1778 with what was virtually a retreat. Between eight and nine o'clock in the evening of June 17 all the artillery, and all the commissary stores of the army which the boats had not carried

[1] From order book of Seventh regiment British foot, Lieutenant-Colonel Alured Clarke, commanding, found on the battlefield of Monmouth, and [1899] in possession of the [late] Hon. John D. Buckelew, of Jamesburg, New Jersey.

away were transported over the river at Cooper's Ferry and the supplies placed in wagons under the protection of the 3000 grenadier and light infantry troops of General Leslie's command. The baggage of the army that had not been taken away by the boats had been placed on New Jersey soil the previous day. After the artillery and stores had been transported across the river, the Queen's rangers were sent over, a watchful guard was set against alarms and all the British troops were ordered to sleep on their arms, ready to resist a surprise.

It was a busy, but quiet night in Philadelphia as the remainder of the army prepared to evacuate the Quaker city where they had enjoyed a winter of gay revelry and freedom from military hardships. The night was clear and lovely and the air balmy and still. It was with great reluctance that the young officers and men of the British line bade adieu to the fair loyalists who had helped so to lighten the dull monotony of a soldier's ordinary life. At three o'clock in the morning of June 18 the order was given for the first of the transports, which contained the remainder of the army, to push off for the New Jersey shore. The navy, under command of Admiral Lord Richard Howe formed a line on the southerly side of the ferry route across the river and so protected the transports from any hostile demonstration. The army crossed mostly in open boats, without the slightest hindrance from Americans on either side of the river. In this way the remainder of the "more than 17,000 effective troops," as Bancroft estimates them, which had been stationed in and around Philadelphia, having marched down toward League Island, crossed over before ten o'clock in the morning to Gloucester Point, four miles below what is now the city of Camden. They made no noise in evacuating the city but at the last moment left in the greatest haste, fearing perhaps that the Americans had heard of their intended departure and would attack them. A lady who saw them leave said "they did not go away, they vanished."[2] One of their number, Lieutenant-Colonel the Honorable Cosmo Gordon, of the Third regiment, British foot guards, the gossip of the day has not allowed us to forget. Stupid, no doubt, from the debauch of the previous night, he slept too late, and when he awoke, after ten o'clock, his comrades had gone over the river and the Americans were entering the city. With great haste he escaped, the last man to leave the gay city, and was taken over the river to his command by an active Tory boatman.[3] At eleven o'clock in the morning of June 18 the fleet of Lord Howe weighed anchor for New York. His flag-ship was the *Eagle*, and the three special commissioners were on the *Trident*. Before sailing they had issued a manifesto to the American people, of which the Earl of Carlisle said, in a letter dated October 23, 1778, " 'Tis a sort of last dying speech of the Commission." The patriot Governor Livingston, of New Jersey, made a kite of the commission's proclamation for his son to play with.

The weather was fine and the wind northerly. Captain John Montresor, the Chief Engineer of the army, went with the fleet, as he had just been badly ruptured. On June 21 the fleet lay off Reedy Island, but left there the following day, and after sailing three hours was becalmed.

On June 18, just before noon, the Hessian grenadiers with General Knyphausen in command, took the right of

[2] Du Simitiere to Colonel Lamb, November 24, 1778, in Leake's *Memoirs of the Life and Times of General John Lamb*, p. 213.

[3] This is the same officer of whom it was said in the British House of Commons, February 2, 1775: "Mr. Cosmo Gordon was against any compromise or lenient measures with America until she has entirely submitted." (Force's *American Archives*, Fourth Series, Vol. I, p. 1547). He was the officer who, early in the morning of June 23, 1780, received a rose from Miss Susan Livingston, daughter of Governor William Livingston, probably as a pledge of protection of her father's house, Liberty Hall, Elizabeth Town (Sedgwick's *Life of William Livingston*, p. 352), and who, for his conduct the same day at the battle of Springfield, was tried by General Court Martial August 22, 1782, and finally acquitted. (The trial of the Hon. Col. Cosmo Gordon of the Third regiment of Foot Guards for neglect of duty, London, 1783). He afterward shot and killed his accuser, Lieutenant-Colonel Edward Thomas.

the marching column, and advanced six miles that day to Haddonfield, on Cooper's Creek in old Gloucester County. General Alexander Leslie's force brought up the baggage and supplies and turned them over to General Knyphausen an hour after that officer arrived in Haddonfield. The Fifteenth regiment of British foot, which had been posted at Billingsport, also marched up and joined the main army. During the after part of the day the rest of Sir Henry Clinton's troop reached the vicinity of the village of Haddonfield.

The following order was issued by Sir Henry Clinton that evening at Haddonfield:

Head Quarters Haddenfield
18th June 1778

The Commanding Off'rs of Corps will strictly inform all others relating to Discipline and good Order, and it being the General's Intention to have the Army as amply Supply'd as there Situation can admit of, he desires it may be understood that he is fully determined to execute upon the spot every man detected in marauding or who shall quit his company upon the March, or shall be found beyond the outposts of the Camp without Permission.

All Persons who have Permission to follow the Army are Immediately to give in their Names to the Late Town Major of Philadelphia specifying their Country and by whom Recommended.[4]

General Carrington says of this movement from Philadelphia across New Jersey, and with great truth, "It was no temporary diversion, to entice Washington from his stronghold to a combat in the field, but it was a surrender of the field itself to his control." And again he remarks, "the moral effect of the evacuation was in Washington's favor."[5]

The British fleet off Philadelphia at this time consisted of fifty-seven transports and merchantmen, and with these boats was the squadron of war vessels and armed ships hereinbefore mentioned, expected to act as convoys to the transports. On these boats had been placed a large quan-

---

[4] Lieutenant-Colonel Clarke's order book.
[5] Carrington's *Battles of the American Revolution*, p. 412.

tity of stores, gathered at Philadelphia and the country contiguous thereto, and some of the baggage and heavy ordnance of the army. A portion of the Hessian cavalry, with two Anspach regiments, about 1000 men,—not considered very reliable if they had to march through an open country,—were placed on the transports. It appears that many of these men had formed tender attachments during the winter and it was expected that they would desert at the very first opportunity, if placed with the marching column. When the time arrived for them to embark, many of those who had married Philadelphia maidens concealed themselves until the fleet and army had departed. Hessian documents state that they had shown their inability to march.[6] It was estimated by the Earl of Carlisle that 3000[7] of the miserable Tories of Philadelphia, men, women and children, justly indignant at the British under whose protection they had placed themselves, left with the boats to try their fortunes in some other part of the country. It must have been sad indeed, to see those refugees in such numbers voluntarily exiling themselves upon the approach of the patriots whom they probably knew so well; yet they had reason to fear that the protection papers they held would be considered merely as proofs of their disloyalty and only serve to bring punishment upon them.

On Friday morning, June 19, Sir Henry Clinton, with the Third, Fourth and Fifth brigades of the British line, left Haddonfield, passing in front of General Knyphausen's command. The army proceeded only six miles, as far as Evesham[8] and went into quarters, it having rained very severely all the afternoon and night. Another portion of the army, marching up the King's Highway from Haddonfield, over the North branch of the Penisauken Creek, through Ellisburg and through great forests of gnarled chestnut trees and swamp maples, encamped that night in

[6] Manuscript journal of Quartermaster Johann Heusser of the Fusilier Regiment von Lossberg.
[7] This number is also stated in the German records.
[8] Now Evesboro, in Evesham township, Burlington County.

and near the Friends' Meeting House in Moorestown, Burlington County. They plundered the inhabitants of their household goods, their grain, horses and cattle in that section of the State at every opportunity. It was with the greatest difficulty that the quiet people thereabouts were able to conceal anything of value. They succeeded, however, in concealing in Deer Park Swamp a number of horses, cows and sheep. General Knyphausen with his Hessian grenadiers and the First and Second British brigades remained behind in Haddonfield that day.

It may be mentioned here that when Clinton's advance, consisting of the brigade of General Leslie, with the Hessian yagers in front, came within sight of the little village of Evesham, a little party of the New Jersey militia made an attack on the British light infantry. It was sudden and unexpected, but there is no record in British journals of the effect produced. In this encounter two houses in the village were burned and Captain Jonathan Beesley of the First battalion Cumberland County militia was severely wounded by a yager sharpshooter and fell into British hands. He was a brave and gallant patriot and thought more of duty than of his personal safety. The English officers carried him to headquarters and then demanded of their wounded foe such information as he had of the condition, situation, and probable movements of Washington's army and especially of General Dickinson's forces, which they knew by this time were gathering just in front of them. Captain Beesley deliberately refused to answer any of their questions or to give any information which might endanger his country's cause. He died on the evening of that day in the house owned and occupied for many years by Hinchman Haines, now deceased. The house is still standing [1899] near Evesboro, Burlington County. Captain Beesley was buried that same night with all the honors of war, for General Clinton said, "he was a brave man and should not be treated with indignity." His body was afterward removed to the Friends' burying ground at Haddonfield.

As the guards were fixed on the night of June 19 the parole was "Jersey" and the countersign "Brunswick," showing that they had that town still in mind as the route they expected to take to the seaboard.

The orders for the march were then issued:

Head Quarters, Evesham 19 June, 1778

. . .   .

The troops to be under arms to-morrow morning at 4 o'clock and to take up the same Orders of March by the right as this day. They will receive Orders to move off their ground from his Excellency Lieut. Gen'l Cornwallis.[9]

In the early hours of Saturday morning, the British column began to move toward Mount Holly under the direct orders of Lord Cornwallis. It still rained furiously and so continued until the middle of the afternoon and the storm was followed by intense heat. The seven miles to Mount Holly, marching about a mile an hour were finally covered and the column halted in order that the remainder of the troops might come up. One gill of extra rum was ordered to be issued to each soldier that night from the Commissary store headquarters. General Leslie directed in orders, "the advance sentries on no account to allow any soldier to pass the outposts, unless parties with arms on duty, as the enemy has patrols all around to take up stragglers." This statement shows that the British light troops were already feeling the effective nearness of the Jersey farmers and their rifles.

General Clinton spent Sunday, June 21, at Mount Holly and the army again tried to plunder, but found that the citizens had removed most of their valuables. Before leaving, however, they destroyed the iron works, the main industry of the village, and the dwelling houses of Colonel Israel Shreve[10] and Peter Tallman.[11]

[9] Lieutenant-Colonel Clarke's order book.
[10] Commanding officer of the Second regiment of New Jersey Continental line.
[11] Chairman of the Committee of Observation of Burlington County.

Referring to this wanton act Sir Henry Clinton said in general orders at Crosswicks June 23, "The Houses of Mr. Shreve and Mr. Tallman having been burnt this morning, the Commander-in-Chief will (if the destruction of the houses was intentional) give a reward of 25 guineas to any one who will discover the Person or Persons who set fire to the above Houses, so that they may be brought to the Punishment due to acts, so disgraceful to the army. The Commander-in-Chief gives notice that any Person that may hereafter be found committing such Disorders will be delivered to the Provost Marshall for immediate execution."[12]

In this connection, and calling attention to the bad conduct of one of these British regiments, it is well to insert here the morning orders, June 21, of the Seventh regiment British foot, also called the Royal Fuzileer regiment:

No Regiment having been formerly more Conspicuous for its Discipline than the Royal Fusileers, Lt. Col. Clarke is the more Mortif'd at observing the great Irregularity and excesses that have been committed within these few days—and as nothing is more Disgraceful in a Corps than such humiliating Proceedings he flatters himself the Officers will Exert themselves to the utmost to prevent its happening again, and he Desires the Soldiers may understand, that he is Determined to Punish with the utmost Severity any man or follower of the Reg't who shall be Detected in Marauding or Stragling without the limits of the Encampment. When the Reg't comes to its Ground after a march an Off[r] is to remain with each Comp[y] till the hutts are finished and to report there being so to the Commanding officer then in Camp. The Men are to put their black Stocks into their Knapsacks every morning when they are to march with a clean false collar fixed to it so as they may be put on at a Minute's notice. The lace of the Mens Hatts to be well Clean'd against Evening Roll calling and the Hatts to be well Cocked.[13]

Soon after daylight June 21, General Knyphausen's division, with the stores and baggage, left Haddonfield and, marching by the Chester meeting house of the Society

[12] Lieutenant-Colonel Clarke's order book.
[13] *ibid.*

of Friends on the Moorestown road, joined General Clinton at Mount Holly soon after nine o'clock in the morning. That night a terrific thunderstorm took place and the roads became very heavy.

The order was then issued for the march of June 22. It was in these words:

Head Quarters, Mount Holly, June 21st '78

The following Corps are to be under arms at 3 O'clock to morrow morning and are to March in the Order in which they are mention'd: 90 Mounted Hessian Yagers, and all the Dismounted, the Queen's Rangers, an Off'r and 20 Pioneers, 1st Battalion Light Infantry, 60 Pioneers with 2 waggons of the Engineer's intrenching tools, Queen's Light Dragoons, British Grenadiers, Hessian Grenadiers, 2 12 Pounders and 1 Howetzer, Brigade of Guards, 3rd Brigade British, 3 Battalions of the Fourth brigade British, 6 Pontoons, the Remainder of the Engineer's intrenching Tools, bat horses of the Army, Baggage of the General Offr's and of the army, according to the line of March, Cattle, 5th Brig^e British, Havendon's[14] Troop of Provincial Cavalry are to be under the Command of Brig'r Gen'l Leslie.—One Battalion from the 4th Brigade to flank the Baggage on the left, Lt. Col. Hallem Corps will flank it on the right, Lt. Col. Vandike's Corps will March in the center of the Baggage: the remainder of the army will receive their Orders from Lt General Kniphausen.[15]

On June 22, the entire force, now reunited, marched seven miles in the rain from Mount Holly through Slabtown to Black Horse, now Columbus, Burlington County. More than forty-eight hours passed before the last man of the British Army had left the village of Mount Holly.

Major-General Philemon Dickinson's New Jersey Militia and Brigadier-General William Maxwell's New Jersey Continentals had, as Clinton himself said, "destroyed every bridge on the road" and as the country through which the British force had to pass abounded in many little streams it was necessary to keep a full corps of engineers constantly busy repairing the means of pas-

---

[14] Captain Richard Hovendon of Hovendon's Pennsylvania light dragoons.
[15] Lieutenant-Colonel Clarke's order book.

sage over these streams and over the marshes. In this severe toil, in the heat and in the storm, the skilled officers and men suffered greatly. Over Cooper's Creek, Moor's Creek, Ballybridge Creek, Ancocus Creek and Bird Creek entirely new bridges or causeways had to be built. Much of the roadway was very narrow and the sand very deep through which the wagons had to pass.

To a superficial observer it may seem that Sir Henry Clinton's march was exceedingly slow, but when we think of the heat, the rain, the enormous baggage train and other impedimenta, the bad roads, the numerous creeks just referred to, the annoyances made by the little bands of Jerseymen always near them "harassing and impeding their motions so as to allow the Continental Troops to come up with them," breaking down bridges, blowing up causeways, filling up wells of water along the route, we must conclude that Clinton was doing all that a good soldier could to press to his journey's end with the vast caravan which it was necessary to move with so much caution.[16]

British reports afterward complimented Sir Henry Clinton for voluntarily assuming this heavy encumbrance. They called it foresight and wisdom, because he knew he would pass through an unfriendly country and could not count on obtaining supplies. He knew that his march would be delayed by the patriot militia of the State, and, therefore, he thought proper to carry all his necessities with him.

[16] *The New Jersey Gazette* of July 1, 1778, says that on June 22, twenty-seven British grenadiers were captured and sent to Trenton for confinement and thirty-six soldiers were sent to Princeton.

CHAPTER VII

WHILE all was excitement in Philadelphia over the evacuation of the city by the British soldiery, General Washington, being fully impressed with the idea that a move toward the great harbor was to be made in a few days, called his general officers together June 17 to a council of war at his quarters at Valley Forge. He had already formed in his own mind a plan of operations, but, as was his custom, he asked the opinion of his subordinate general officers as to the best method of procedure in case the British crossed the Delaware River. The following questions were propounded, to which he desired answers in writing the next morning:

I. Whether any enterprise ought to be undertaken against the enemy in their present circumstances?

II. Whether the army should remain in the position it now holds, till the final occupation of the city, or move immediately towards the Delaware?

III. Whether any detachment of it shall be sent to reinforce the brigade in the Jerseys, or advanced towards the enemy to act as occasion shall require, and endeavor to take advantage of their retreat?

IV. If the enemy march through Jersey, will it be prudent to attack them on the way, or more eligible to proceed to the North River in the most direct and convenient manner, to secure the important communication between the eastern and southern States?

V. In case such measures should be adopted, as will enable this army to overtake the enemy in their march, will it be prudent, with the aid which may reasonably be expected from the Jersey militia, to make an attack upon them, and ought it to be a partial or a general one?

All the answers of the nine general officers present at the council, were received at about nine o'clock on the morning of June 18 and read by General Washington. Among these we may state that Major-General Lee, Major-General von Steuben and Brigadier-General Duportail thought it almost criminal to hazard a general engagement at that time with such a brilliant and well-appointed army. Brigadier-General Wayne and Brigadier-General Cadwalader appeared to be strongly in favor of making as bold a demonstration as possible on the enemy and punishing them in every way and at every point. Major-General Lafayette was inclined to adopt the opinion expressed by General Wayne, but did not press it very strongly in his communication. General Greene said everything should be undertaken to injure the enemy that could possibly be attempted and if this led to a general fight, then fight it out.

It was scarcely daylight on the morning of June 18 when George Roberts left the Middle Ferry, on the Schuylkill River, where he had crossed from Market Street, Philadelphia, and putting spurs to his bay horse dashed along on the road to the encampment on Valley Creek. He was accompanied by some light horse from an American scouting party which had been hovering some days within sight of the city. In the early dawn they had seen the bustle on the other side of the river and with their glasses had observed the crossing of Clinton's battalions over the Delaware River. About noon Captain Allen McLane of the Delaware partisan company of foot marched his men to the floating bridge at the Middle Ferry and so entered the city. He had with him a few light horse and as they galloped with drawn swords through Second street with about a hundred men in the party he succeeded in capturing a captain, a provost-marshal, one of the army guides and thirty enlisted men. This he did without any loss to his own command. Afterward a little party of British were picked up at the corner of Ninth and South streets. When Captain McLane reached the center of the city, he hastily wrote to General Washington giving him an idea of the probable movement of the British troops as understood by the patriots of Philadelphia, and informing him of the condition of the city as they had left it. This was despatched by an express rider to Valley Forge.

All was wild commotion in the tents in the American encampment at half-past eleven o'clock in the morning when George Roberts and his little party of mounted men reined up at Potts' house at the Forge. All the soldiers were glad at the prospect of any change from the place where they had endured such suffering, and they were ready and eager for a grand chase across the Jerseys to stop Clinton.

The question of attacking the enemy in New Jersey was now the only pertinent one to be decided and acted upon. In less than three hours most of the official answers on which General Washington's officers had studied and labored during the past night were rendered valueless. The impression among the American soldiers was, that now by a bold stroke some measure of success might be gained against a foe which voluntarily gives up a city without a battle for its possession and takes a hasty flight across an open country in which it will be compelled to act entirely on the defensive.

General Washington immediately issued the following orders to Major-General Lee, a portion of which, as will be seen, had been previously prepared:

Head Quarters, 30 May, 1778

SIR:

Poor's, Varnum's, and Huntington's brigades are to march in one division under your command to the North River. The quartermaster-general will give you the route, encampment, and halting days, to which you will conform as strictly as possible, to prevent interfering with other troops, and that I may know precisely your situation every day. Leave as few sick and lame on the road as possible. Such as are absolutely incapable of marching with you are to be committed to the care of proper officers, with directions to follow as fast as their condition will allow.

Be strict in your discipline, suffer no rambling, keep the men in their ranks and the officers with their divisions, avoid pressing horses as much as possible, and punish severely every officer or soldier, who shall presume to press without proper authority. Prohibit the burning of fences. In a word you are to protect the persons and property of the inhabitants from every kind of insult and abuse.

Begin your march at four o'clock in the morning at the latest, that it may be over before the heat of the day, and that the soldiers may have time to cook, refresh, and prepare for the ensuing day—I am, &c.

Go. WASHINGTON.

P.S.—June 18th.—The foregoing instructions may serve you for general directions, but circumstances have varied since they were written. You are to halt on the first strong ground after passing the Delaware at Coryell's Ferry,[1] till further orders, unless you should receive authentic intelligence, that the enemy have proceeded by a direct route to South Amboy, or still lower. In this case you will continue your march to the North River, agreeably to former orders, and by the route already given you. If my memory does not deceive me, there is an advantageous spot of ground at the ferry to the right of the road leading from the water.

ORDER OF MARCH AND ROUTE OF THE ARMY FROM CAMP
VALLEY FORGE TO NEWBURG ON THE NORTH
RIVER OPPOSITE FISHKILL

Poor Varnum Huntington	1st	Lee	Coryells
1st Pennsa 2d do Late Conway	2nd	Mifflin[2]	Sherard
Woodford Scott No. Carolina	3d	Marquis	Coryells

[1] New Hope, Pennsylvania, to Lambertville, New Jersey.

[2] It was announced in orders, May 26, 1778, that Major-General Thomas Mifflin was permitted by the Continental Congress to repair to and serve in the army, and to take command of the division lately in charge of Major-General Benjamin Lincoln. He reported at Valley Forge May 19. On the fourth day of June, Lieutenant-Colonel Francis Barber of the Third New Jersey regiment was made the adjutant-general of his division. The Continental Congress passed a resolution June 11, directing General Washington to make inquiry as to the conduct of General Mifflin in the office of quartermaster-general, and if the distresses of the army appeared to be chargeable to his misconduct to order a court-martial. General Mifflin undoubtedly had to ask for leave of absence in order to obtain material to answer the charge. It does not appear that he ever took command, because Brigadier-General Anthony Wayne led the Second division of the army.

Glover ⎫			
Patterson ⎬ 4	deKalb[3]	Easton
Larned ⎭		

Weedon ⎫			
Muhlenberg ⎪			
1s Maryld ⎬ 5	Stirling	Coryells
2d do ⎭		

The Detachmt under Colo. Jackson to move to and take posses-sion of Philadelphia and prevent plundering & any abuse of Per-sons. Van Scoicks Regiment to replace the 8th Pennsylvania Regt in the Pennsylvania Brigade—The 2d State Regiment of Virginia to replace the 13th Regiment in Scott's Brigade—Park of Artillery to be attached to the Several Divisions Equally and march with them.

The 1st & 2d Divisions to move the morning after Intelligence is received of the Enemy's Evacuation of the City.

The 3rd & 4th Divisions the morning after these, & the 5th Division the morning succeeding—every day's march to begin at 4 o'clock, A.M. at furthest.

Go. WASHINGTON.

1st, 3d & 5th Divisions by Coryell's Ferry & thro the Clove by Smiths.

To Coryell's and Cross	3 days
Halt	1
White House	1
3 miles beyond the Cross Roads	1
4 miles beyond Morristown	1
Halt	1
Pompton Bridge	1
Sufferans	1
Near Smith's Tavern	1
Halt if necessary	1
Newborough	1
	— 13

2d Division by Sherard's Ferry and Sussex Court House.

To Sherard's Ferry and Cross	3
Halt	1
Union Iron Works	1

[3] The Fourth division was commanded by Major-General the Baron John De Kalb. This officer was taken sick in camp at Valley Forge in the early part of May 1778, and in July he was removed to Philadelphia. He, there-fore, took no part in the battle of Monmouth.

Halket's Town 1
Sussex Court House 1
Halt 1
4 M. beyond Col. Martin's 1
Warwick 1
5 M. beyond Chester 1
Halt if necessary 1
Newborough 1
— 13

4th Division by Easton and Sussex Court House.

To Easton 3
Halt 1
Crossing 1
6 miles beyond Carrs 1
Sussex Court House 1
Halt 1
Then as in 2d Division 5
— 13

Regard to be had to the convenience of Water as well as distance.[4]

During the afternoon of June 18, the commander-in-chief issued these additional instructions for the next day:

ORDERS RELATIVE TO THE MARCH FROM VALLEY FORGE,
JUNE 1778, AFTER GEN. LEE'S AND GEN. MIFFLIN'S
DIVISNS HAD MARCHED.

The Army is to March to Morrow & till further Orders in the following Order.

The Marquis De LaFayette is to lead with	Woodford's Scotts N'th Car'a	Brigades
The Baron De Kalb next with	Glovers Pattersons Learneds	Brigades

The Artillery Park and spare Ammunition

Lord Stirling with	Weedons Muhlenbergs 1st Maryland 2d Maryland

[4] The *Lee Papers*, Vol. II, pp. 406-8, Collections of the New York Historical Society.

The disposition for the baggage of the army to be as follows:

The Commander in Chief's Baggage is to march in the front of the column of Waggons—The Adjutant General's, Paymaster General's Engineers Muster Master General Auditor of Accounts The Baggage of the Marquis De La Fayettes DeKalbs Division the Baggage of Lord Stirlings Division and then the Waggons of the Quarter Master Generals Department Flying Hospital & lastly the Comy & Forage Master General's Waggons—The whole Baggage to fall in the Rear of the Column of Troops. The Genl officers commanding the Grand Division to appoint such guards upon the baggage as shall be necessary for the Security thereof—They will also, appoint a party of Pioneers to move in front of the Columns, to assist the Artificers in repairing Bridges and bad places in the roads.

There will be a party of Artificers to go in front & rear of the whole, to mend Bridges and repair the Broken Carriages; which will take their Orders from the Q.M. Genl.

The sub Inspectors are to assist the Quarter Master General in regulating the order of March, encampment and planting of Guards and to accompany and follow his Directions accordingly.

Go. WASHINGTON.

NOTE—the Light Horse is to March in front and upon the Right flank a days and encamp in the Rear of the Troops o Nights.

The new guards will form the advanced guards of the army and the old guards the rear guard. Each regiment will send out a flank guard on the right flank in the proportion of a sergeant and 12 men to every 200 men.[5]

Special instructions were also issued by General Washington to Brigadier-General Anthony Wayne:

SIR:

You are to proceed with the first and second Pennsylvania regiments,[6] and the brigade, late Conway's, by the direct route to Coryell's Ferry, leaving a proper interval between your division and General Lee's, so as to prevent their interfering with each other. The instructions given to General Lee, are to halt on the first strong ground after passing the Delaware at the said ferry, until further orders, unless he should receive authentic intelligence, that the enemy have proceeded by the direct road to South Amboy, (or

---

[5] *Lee Papers*, Vol. II, p. 410.

[6] This is probably a clerical mistake for "brigades," for General Wayne certainly commanded Mifflin's Second Division on the march.

still lower); in this case he is to continue his march to the North River.

Given at Headquarters, this 18th day of June, 1778.

Go. Washington.[7]

Instructions were also sent to Colonel Daniel Morgan, who was then posted with his riflemen at Radnor in Delaware County, Pennsylvania:

Head Quarters, Valley Forge, 18th June, 1778.

Sir:

I am informed this morning, that the enemy's rear are evacuating the city. You will immediately send down a small party of horse under a good officer, on this side, in order to ascertain the matter, or to gain intelligence. The result of his inquiry you will transmit as soon as possible, and hold yourself in readiness to join this army on the first orders.

I am, sir, your very humble servant,

Go. Washington.

Verbal orders were immediately given Major-General Benedict Arnold, although he was still disabled by wounds (his thigh bone having been broken at the battle of Saratoga), to enter the city of Philadelphia with Colonel Henry Jackson's regiment, about four hundred Continentals, and take command of it. He started at once to assume this duty, accompanied by Lieutenant-Colonel Tench Tilghman, aide-de-camp of General Washington, and his own aides, Majors David S. Franks and Matthew Clarkson. Brigadier-Generals John Cadwalader, Joseph Reed and Henry Knox, and Colonel Stephen Moylan also went with him to Philadelphia.

Immediately upon his arrival there Arnold dispatched the gallant Captain McLane over the river into New Jersey. In disguise, he passed through the British camp at Haddonfield that same night and the next day reported their situation and condition.

General Reed says: "the city exhibited a new and curious scene; some gloomy countenances, but more joyful

---

[7] Ford's *Writings of George Washington*, Vol. VII, p. 70.

ones. Shops shut up and all in great anxiety and suspense."
General von Steuben, who was at York when he heard that
the city had been evacuated, started immediately for
Philadelphia. He found the city in a most deplorable condition and the filth everywhere about him made even this
old soldier's stomach rebel at the thought of eating and
drinking. He started immediately up the river for Washington's Army.

At this time Philadelphia was the most influential city
in the young republic. It had been the seat of the new government and its society contained decidedly the most cul-
tured people in the country. The old Quaker families
residing there and the wealthy and educated adherents of
the English church made a social force which had a potent
influence upon all the neighboring communities.

On the morning of June 19, General Arnold received
instructions from the commander-in-chief. This order gave
him great discretionary power in governing anew the abandoned city.

The same day General Arnold caused a proclamation
to be issued to the people of Philadelphia and had it
posted in various parts of the city. This bulletin recited
the Act of Congress, which had been passed two weeks previously, in relation to the proper government of the city,
and ordered an inventory of all merchandise to be made
immediately, so that it might soon be ascertained what
would be needed for the use of the army and what might
belong to some of the fugitive loyalists.

The Tories who remained in Philadelphia suffered
greatly from the persecutions of their patriotic neighbors.
For a time this ostracism was very severe and nothing was
too violent to be inflicted upon the despised loyalists. This,
of course, was directly contrary to the wishes and orders
of General Washington. At one time twenty-five persons
were indicted under the laws of the State for having
offered aid to the enemy. On the fourth day of November,
1778, Abraham Carlisle, a carpenter by trade, and John

Roberts,[8] a miller, both members of the Society of Friends, having been tried for treason, were found guilty of furnishing secret aid to the British, and were publicly hanged. Carlisle had been in commission under General William Howe to give permission to all persons to pass the British lines during their occupancy of Philadelphia, and many patriots had suffered vile imprisonment on what was known to have been his report. Roberts had been one of the men who guided the British troops to General Lacey's position at Crooked Billet. During the late summer and fall, after the battle which is herein described, the people of New Jersey, especially in that portion of the State contiguous to Philadelphia, entered on the same kind of abuse and persecution, and seventeen men were brought to trial and found guilty of treason. Governor William Livingston [of New Jersey], however, "from motives, as he thought, of policy," pardoned each one of these as soon as condemned. Actuated by the same feelings, he also went to Philadelphia, and tried to save the lives of Carlisle and Roberts, but in vain.

When General Wayne was at Mount Holly, New Jersey, during the latter part of February and in March, he had with him Colonel Israel Shreve's Second regiment of the New Jersey Continental line. This organization remained in New Jersey after General Wayne returned to Valley Forge and it was principally employed about Burlington, Mount Holly and as far down as Haddonfield in stopping supplies from going into Philadelphia. This they succeeded in doing to some extent.

We have already noted that General Maxwell had been ordered on Thursday, May 7, to leave the main army and with his New Jersey brigade march for Bristol and Dunk's Ferry and so cross the Delaware River to Burlington to be joined by Colonel Shreve's regiment at Mount Holly. Within three hours after the brigade was ordered on this

[8] Copy of warrant for arrest of John Roberts, *Pennsylvania Magazine*, Vol. XXIV, No. 1, p. 117.

tour of duty, it was ready to march; but a very heavy rain began that day at noon, and the movement was delayed by orders until the next day.

On May 11, recruits enrolled from several of the county militia organizations in New Jersey, and embodied in an organization known as New Jersey State Troops, for nine months' service, were ordered to join the New Jersey Continental regiments in the field. The greater part of these men reported at Mount Holly before June 5.

A considerable detachment of New Jersey militia, familiar, as it was, with partisan warfare, had been called out about May 1 by Governor Livingston, under the law of April 14, 1778, for a thirty days' tour of duty. This detachment was relieved in June by a second contingent which was now engaged in watching the advance of the British Army. "The Militia of New Jersey were in the highest spirits and almost to a man in arms." Major-General Philemon Dickinson, of Trenton, New Jersey, was in command of these battalions of New Jersey State troops and militia under orders to annoy the British in their march in every possible manner. He was in Burlington County when he was joined by the Continental troops under General Maxwell, who had been ordered to co-operate with him in any plan which seemed best to them for annoying the British.

This was the state of the military forces in New Jersey when at three o'clock in the afternoon of June 18, Major-General Charles Lee marched from Valley Forge with the brigades of General Huntington, General Poor and General Varnum. After the trials of the terrible winter, it is remarkable that in four hours after orders were issued a portion of the American Army was on the march. It shows that Washington was ready for the movement and that he had his force so well disciplined that they acted promptly. At five o'clock General Wayne left with his own command, the First and Second Pennsylvania brigades and the brigade lately commanded by General Conway. Colonel

Morgan's command joined Wayne before he crossed the river. The orders both Lee and Wayne received were, to march toward Coryell's Ferry, now that point on the river between New Hope, Pennsylvania, and Lambertville, New Jersey, and to halt on the first strong ground after passing the Delaware River.

These divisions of the army proceeded three miles beyond the bridge over the Schuylkill River, and camped for the night, General Lee, of course, in supreme command of the six brigades. What must have been the feelings of General Lee as he started from Valley Forge, knowing well for the first time that his "plan" of March 29, 1777, to the British leaders had been utterly ignored or forgotten, and that his letter to General Washington of June 15, 1778, was incorrect and valueless?

It was just after daylight on Friday, June 19, when the main army broke camp and left Valley Forge, under the immediate command of General Washington. They marched by the York road to Doylestown and that night pitched their tents in three divisions, one on the ridge near the Presbyterian church, one on the road to Coryell's ferry ten miles distant, and the third division on the westerly side of Main street in the village. General Washington had his marquee near the residence of Jonathan Fell, a short distance east of the village, and the headquarters of the army that evening were at Doctor Sherman's.

Colonel Philip Van Cortlandt of the Second New York regiment was left at Valley Forge in command. He had there nearly 3000 sick or disabled men. However, he soon sent 2500 of them to Philadelphia, and kept with him about 500, still too feeble to leave the camp hospitals.

All day Friday it rained heavily and this hindered not only the corps under Washington's command, but those which preceded it, the divisions of Lee and Wayne. But the spirits of the men, notwithstanding the storm, were greatly elated over the escape from the dull monotony of camp life, and every man felt a strong incentive to push rapidly toward the British and, if possible, deal a bold stroke for liberty.

The two advance divisions just referred to, reached the river bank late on Friday night and on Saturday afternoon and evening, crossed the Delaware River as ordered, at Coryell's Ferry, and after marching three miles, quartered at Amwell, in Hunterdon County, New Jersey.

General Washington had his headquarters at Buckingham, on Saturday, June 20, and issued orders that night for a gill of spirits to be served out to each man "if the commissariers are provided."

He also wrote an official letter to Major-General Horatio Gates, who was in command of the Northern army at Peekskill, apprising him of the movements of his army and those of the enemy.[9]

[9] Ford, Vol. VII, p. 70.

CHAPTER VIII

THE main army, under Washington's immediate command, having been greatly impeded in their march by the heavy rains, crossed the Delaware River at Coryell's Ferry (now New Hope, Pennsylvania) to Lambertville, New Jersey, and at Howell's Ferry, somewhat over three miles above, during the afternoon of Sunday, June 21, and the early morning of the next day. These ferries were by road about thirty-three miles from Philadelphia and forty miles from Valley Forge. The baggage of the army was brought over the river the same morning and the troops remained near the Delaware River all day Monday, General Washington being engaged writing the report of his movements to Congress. He also issued the following instructions to his subordinate officers:

Headquarters, Coryell's Ferry, June 22, 1778.

Field returns are to be made this afternoon under the immediate inspection of the Brigadiers and officers commanding brigades, who are to be responsible for their exactness. These returns to comprehend those men only who are actually on the spot fit for duty in time of action, among which the guards will be included. The unarmed men to be distinguished from the others.

The soldiers will have their arms well cleaned, and afterwards carefully inspected, together with their ammunition, by their respective officers.

The tents and heavy baggage, if there be any, will be separated from the Army for some days. The officers will content themselves with a few necessaries during that time. The Quartermaster-General will make his arrangements accordingly. He will give orders respecting the movement of the separated baggage. None but invalids and men unfit for the fatigues of a march are to go as guards to the baggage.

Intrenching tools are to be assigned to the brigades in due proportion, and delivered to the care of the Brigade Quartermasters. When circumstances will permit, the artificers and pioneers will advance before the van-guard of the Army and repair the roads with fascines and earth, instead of rails, which serve to cripple the horses.

The Quartermaster General will fall upon some method to have straw equally and regularly distributed to the men when they arrive at the ground of encampment, to prevent confusion and waste.

On a march the Major General of the day will pay particular attention that the column advances in compact order, and not so fast in front as to fatigue and distress the rear.

The Brigadier of the day, with the officers ordered to remain in the rear, will see that everything is properly conducted there; the guards kept to their duty and all damage to the fruit trees prevented, of which the whole road hitherto exhibits such shameful proof.

Commanding officers of companies will see that their men fill their canteens before they begin the march, that they may not be under the necessity of running to every spring and injuring themselves by drinking cold water when heated with marching.

Each brigade is to furnish an active-spirited officer and twenty-five of its best marksmen immediately. These parties to join Colonel Morgan's corps, and continue under his command till the enemy pass through the Jerseys, after which they are to rejoin their regiments without farther orders.

The general will beat at 3 o'clock in the morning, and the Army march at 4 o'clock precisely.—The Quartermaster General will communicate the order of march and the route, and will acquaint the Major Generals with their respective commands.

AFTER ORDERS: The following brigades, during the march, are to compose the right wing of the Army, and to be commanded by Major General Lee's, Woodford's, Scott's, North Carolina, Poor's, Varnum's and Huntington's.—1st Pennsylvania, 2d Pennsylvania, late Conway's, Glover's, Learned's and Patterson's, are to compose the left wing, and to be commanded by Major General Lord Stirling.

The second line is to consist of 1st and 2d Maryland, Muhlenberg's, Weedon's and Maxwell's, (when it joins) and to be commanded by Major General the Marquis de La Fayette.

The Army is to march from the left. The Quartermaster General will furnish guides. A Field officer is to take charge of the baggage guard. If the weather should prove very rainy in the morning, the troops are not to march; in any case, if they march the tents are to be left standing, and when they dry the baggage guard is to strike and load them in the wagons.—Lieutenant Colonel Coleman will take command of the baggage guard.

The officers and twenty-five men from each brigade who are to be annexed to Colonel Morgan's corps are to be sent to his quarters early to-morrow morning about a mile in front of the Army. The two Light Infantry companies in the North Carolina Brigade will be attached to Colonel Morgan's corps instead of the twenty-five there mentioned in the first order of this day.

Lieutenant Colonel Barrett is appointed Bringer-up, vice Lieutenant Colonel Coleman.[1]

General Lee was still writing to General Washington and proffering his advice. He wrote a letter of this kind June 22[2] and Washington received it soon after he had reached the New Jersey side of the river. Governor William Livingston of New Jersey, had written from Princeton to General Lee giving him all the information that he had been able to obtain from Major-General Dickinson, and other trusted Jerseymen, of the movements of the British the previous day.[3] Lee forwarded this communication to Washington, with his own letter just referred to.

On Tuesday, June 23, the entire American Army was at and near the village of Hopewell in Hunterdon, now Mercer, County, about fourteen miles from Trenton and eight miles from Princeton. General Washington had his headquarters at the house owned by Joseph Stout, Jr. The same morning Lieutenant-Colonel Marinus Willett of the Third New York Continental regiment, then stationed at Fort Stanwix, appeared at Hopewell with a letter from Major-General Gates, then at Peekskill, giving a return of the men, ammunition and stores he had under his control. Desiring to see active service, Colonel Willett, with Washington's permission, joined General Scott's staff, as a volunteer aide-de-camp.

Information was received during the day from General Arnold concerning the condition of Philadelphia and the enrolment of volunteers for General Cadwalader's detachment, to join the main army. Colonel Henry Jackson's

[1] General Edward Hand's orderly book, p. 285.
[2] Lee Papers, Vol. II, p. 411.
[3] ibid., p. 412.

Continental regiment was also ordered to march to Washington's command.

The latest knowledge of the movements of the British Army came to General Washington by a letter from Colonel Stephen Moylan of the Fourth regiment Continental dragoons. This letter was brought by General Joseph Reed, and supplemented, of course, by the statements of Reed himself, who had seen the enemy. Both these officers had left Philadelphia for Washington's Army on June 22.

The American Army remained at Hopewell all day Wednesday, June 24, disposing of their heavy baggage, cleaning their fire-locks, placing themselves in the best light marching order and preparing two days' extra cooked rations. It is quite evident that General Washington, now within a day's march of the Raritan River, was reserving his strength for the probable, if not the intended, battle.

At three o'clock in the afternoon of June 23, Brigadier-General John Cadwalader, who had distinguished himself in the Battle of Princeton, January 3, 1777, as the gallant commander of the three battalions of Philadelphia Associators, left Philadelphia with Jackson's Continental regiment, about 400 strong, and nearly a hundred militia, which had been organized by General Arnold at a meeting of the inhabitants of that city, held the previous day. This contingent carried to the American Army a new supply of cartridges, which the troops greatly needed. These cartridges had been made by the deft fingers of patriotic women in Philadelphia during the four days previous, using, for paper wrappers, it is said, some of the sermons on defensive warfare by the famous minister Gilbert Tennent, preached during the French war for the purpose of enlisting men for that struggle. These sermons had been stowed away in Benjamin Franklin's printing room and were brought forth to wrap the ammunition to be fired on the plains of Monmouth.

Brigadier-General John Lacey was also very busy in

enrolling some volunteers from the militia regiments of Colonels Watt and Smith of Cumberland County and from the company of Captain Pugh of Bucks County, Pennsylvania. These volunteers marched under Cadwalader. Colonel Thomas Procter's Fourth regiment, Continental artillery, and the invalids sent from the hospitals at Valley Forge, with some small parties of Pennsylvania militia, replaced the above detachments in guarding the City of Philadelphia and in preserving order there.[4]

On the day General Cadwalader left Philadelphia he wrote to the Commander-in-Chief, and the same night General Washington sent by an express rider a letter written by Lieutenant-Colonel Hamilton to General Cadwalader, in which he manifested a great desire to know every movement of the enemy.

On June 23, the following order was issued by General Washington:

Headquarters, Hunt's House, June 23, 1778.
The troops will cook their provisions and in every respect be in the greatest readiness possible for a march or action very early in the morning.

When the general beats, the Army is to be put in immediate readiness to march; on beating the troop, the march begins.

[4] General Knox to his brother, William Knox:

"Hopewell Township, New Jersey,
"4 o'clock A.M., 25th June, 1778.
"The enemy evacuated Philadelphia on the 19th. Lucy and I went in, but it stunk so abominably that it was impossible to stay there, as was her first design. The enemy are now at Allen Town, about ten miles southeast of Princeton, and we are about six miles north (of) Princeton, so that the two armies are now about nineteen or twenty miles apart. We are now on the march towards them, and their movements this day will determine whether we shall come in close contact with each other. We have now very numerous parties harassing and teasing them on all quarters. Desertion prevails exceedingly in their army, especially among the Germans. Above three hundred German and English have deserted since they left Philadelphia. Had we a sufficiency of numbers, we should be able to force them to a similar treaty with Burgoyne; but, at present, have not quite such sanguine hopes. If general actions had no other consequences than merely the killed and wounded, we should attack them in twenty-four hours. But the fate of posterity, and not the illusive brilliancy of military glory, governs our Fabian commander, the man (to whom), under God, America owes her present prospects of peace and happiness."

The wings and the second line are each to furnish two Captains, three subalterns, three Sergeants, three Corporals, and one hundred and seventeen privates for guard daily, till further orders.

The Commissary of military stores will deliver our arms to-morrow agreeably to the returns signed by commanding officers of regiments or corps, who will send very early to the Artillery park for such numbers as are wanting to complete their men now on the ground fit for duty.[5]

And on the twenty-fourth this order was promulgated:

Headquarters, Hunt's House, June 24, 1778.

Officers are on no account to be absent from their encampment, and are to be particularly vigilant to prevent their men from straggling.

The troops, in point of provision and every other respect, are to be held in constant readiness for moving when the general beats, which will be the signal for marching.

The commanding officers of corps are to make accurate returns of the axes, tomahawks, and such other tools in possession of their corps.[6]

On the top of a hill overlooking the village of Hopewell the late Colonel Joseph Stout had built a large and imposing dwelling. When General Washington reached Hopewell, he took possession of this building for his headquarters. At nine o'clock in the morning of June 24, while the sun was in eclipse,[7] a council of war was called by him in this house.[8]

[5] General Edward Hand's orderly book, p. 287.
[6] *ibid.*, p. 288.
[7] Spark's *Life of David Rittenhouse*, Vol. VII, First Series, American Biography, and Barton's memoirs of David Rittenhouse, p. 275 and Appendix, p. 591. The last reference shows that Rittenhouse at the College in Philadelphia, assisted by John Lukens, Owen Biddle and the Rev. Doctor William Smith, saw this eclipse and made the published record of their observations.
[8] The first house on this site was erected in 1706 by Jonathan Stout, one of the first settlers of Hopewell. In that dwelling the Baptist church of Hopewell was organized April 23, 1715. The property came into possession of Colonel Joseph Stout, and when the congregation of the Baptist church desired to build a meeting house in 1747 Colonel Stout wished to have them erect it on a high hill on his farm. The congregation decided to build in the valley, where the church now stands, and Colonel Stout, taking offence, declared that he would build a larger house for himself than their proposed church. This he did in 1752, making it forty-five feet front and thirty-five feet deep, five feet

All the general officers attended this meeting. General Washington having, as usual, formed his own opinion of the situation and what was the best line of conduct to pursue, asked the judgment of his compatriots as to whether it was advisable to hazard a general engagement with the British forces. He informed them as to the latest position and strength of the enemy and the force which he could bring against them. General Lee[9] again vehemently urged that a comparatively small detachment, if any, be sent to aid General Dickinson and General Maxwell in their operations on the enemy's flanks, while the main column take up the march toward the Hudson River. He said he thought it would be better to build a bridge of gold for the use of the British Army than to attack or in any way hinder the passage across the country of a force so well-disciplined; that if, as he supposed, the armies were about the same in numerical strength, to risk an engagement with the enemy would appear to him very criminal. He thought the late alliance with France would be a more effective step toward independence than any act of the army, however bold it might be in conception, and that it would be better not to hazard any engagement at present. He did not doubt that if a partial demonstration were made, it would soon become a general one with an enemy so well prepared for battle. As General Lee was the oldest

larger each way than the church. It occupied a fine position overlooking the Hopewell valley. The first story was divided into four large rooms, separated by a wide hall. The council of war was held in the southeast room. This room had a large fireplace and its walls were entirely covered with wood panel work. The front southwest room was occupied by General Washington and the room in the rear by General Lafayette. Colonel Stout died in 1767, and the house was bequeathed to his son, Joseph Stout, Jr. It was conveyed to Wilson Stout in 1789, to John Weart, Sr., in 1799, bequeathed to his son, John Weart, in 1822, and in 1851 to Spencer S. Weart, by whom it was taken down in 1853 and replaced on the same site by a new dwelling, much of the same material being used in its construction. The farm was afterward owned by Spencer A. Weart, a son of Spencer S. Weart.—From notes in the family record, furnished by the Hon. Jacob Weart, of Jersey City, N.J.

[9] In a dwelling a quarter of a mile down the hill from the house where the council of war was held, General Lee had his quarters on the night of June 23, 1778. In this house David Stout resided.

of the major-generals in rank and was thought to have had great military experience, his counsel at this time was very weighty and many of the younger generals followed his expressed opinion. He seems to have been strenuous in his efforts to give the enemy an uninterrupted march across the State; but there were others, such as General Greene, General Lafayette and General Wayne, who were in favor of sending a large force instantly to annoy the British, and to follow this detachment with the whole army in easy supporting distance. General Lafayette said it "would be disgraceful and humiliating to allow the enemy to cross the Jerseys in tranquillity." At last it was decided to send 1500 men to reinforce the parties now harassing the left flank and rear of the British column. Very reluctantly General Lee assented to this compromise, and unwillingly signed the written opinion of the Council; General Lafayette and General Greene signed it because, forsooth, they thought it the first step only toward the accomplishment of their wishes, and General Wayne, always eager for a fight with his country's foes, declined flatly to affix his signature because he believed that a strong force should be sent to annoy the enemy and, if circumstances were favorable, let it lead to a pitched battle. So thoroughly impressed were Generals Greene, Lafayette and Wayne with the idea that the Council had not gone far enough in their opinions as expressed in writing to General Washington, that they each sent him a letter giving more fully their own views on this important matter. General Lafayette in his communication also represented the opinions of General von Steuben and General Duportail.

It does not appear very clear to the military student of today why Washington was accustomed so often to call his officers into council. He certainly was an officer of experience, as much so as many of them, he was accustomed to assume responsibility, he had rare decision of character. He may have wished to explain his own views to his subordinates and hear and weigh their objections, if any; he may have wished those on whom he depended to understand the situation as he knew it and so to act promptly and intelligently as a unified force; he may have wished to show them that he had confidence in their firm support when the crucial moment arrived. But it is doubtful, as we look at it today, whether any one of the councils held in this campaign, contributed substantially to the success of the movement in New Jersey.

It is quite certain that General Washington had matured in his own mind a plan for the campaign. He knew well that the patriotic people demanded of him as bold a stroke against the enemy as prudence would allow. No opposition of General Lee could change what he saw clearly to be a duty, that the army of Great Britain should not be allowed to make a holiday march across the State. It does not appear that the judgment of General Lee, who had seen much of foreign wars, embarrassed General Washington's mind a moment. In a prompt and practical way he began to carry out his own views, supported, as he now knew he was, by those upon whose opinions he relied. And this he did in the full realization of his own personal responsibility, regardless of strong and open opposition.

As soon as the Council adjourned, as if in compliance with some of its recommendations, General Washington sent out Colonel Daniel Morgan with his corps of riflemen, six hundred strong, to attach themselves to General Maxwell's brigade and operate on the enemy's right and rear.

Cautious yet enterprising, and relying on his own opinion of the situation, General Washington detached Brigadier-General Charles Scott, later on in the day, June 24, with 1440 chosen men to annoy the British left and rear. This force included the splendid regiments of Continentals, First New Hampshire, Colonel Joseph Cilley; Ninth Pennsylvania, Colonel Richard Butler; First Virginia, Colonel Richard Parker, and Fourth Maryland, Lieutenant-Colonel Samuel Smith.

General Washington relied greatly on the exertions of

Major-General Philemon Dickinson, that patriotic New Jersey soldier who commanded her militia, and his confidence was not misplaced. He wrote General Dickinson some instructions from Hopewell at half-past four in the morning of June 24 and received from him the next day a statement of the manner in which he had disposed of his force.[10] This force was composed of detachments from sixteen organizations of State troops and militia, and it was commanded by some of the most zealous and efficient officers in the service.

He also dispatched that reliable officer, Major-General von Steuben, to ascertain, if possible, the exact position and intentions of the British Army. He hoped in this way to obtain the opinion of a skillful soldier and one accustomed to viewing with an experienced eye the movements of the armies of Europe. It was a rare compliment to von Steuben's soldierly judgment.

On the morning of Thursday, June 25, General Washington moved his entire army from Hopewell, leaving their tents behind, and proceeded about seven miles to Rocky Hill,[11] Somerset County, and Kingston,[11] Middlesex County. He dispatched from Rocky Hill a third detachment of 1000 selected men, under command of Brigadier-General Anthony Wayne, to harass and impede the march of the British Army. This detachment included Brigadier-General Enoch Poor's splendid brigade of Continentals. Major-General the Marquis de Lafayette was sent forward with General Wayne under orders to take command of all the troops hovering around the advancing column of the foe. Lieutenant-Colonel Alexander Hamilton, of Washington's staff, accompanied Lafayette for the purpose of keeping his chief well informed of the progress of events. General Washington had his headquarters at

[10] *Lee Papers*, Vol. II, p. 413.
[11] Five and a half and three miles northeast of Princeton, respectively, and two and a half miles apart. Kingston is ten miles east of Hopewell.

Kingston on the night of June 25, and he gave the parole as "Monmouth," showing that he had given up the idea of Brunswick as the destination of the enemy.

General Washington gave the following instructions to General Lafayette on placing him in command of the advance corps:

SIR:

You are immediately to proceed with the detachment commanded by Gen. Poor, and form a junction (as expeditiously as possible) with that under the command of Genl. Scott. You are to use the most effectual means for gaining the enemy's left flank and rear, and giving them every degree of annoyance. All Continental parties, that are already on the lines, will be under your command, and you will take such measures, in concert with Genl. Dickinson, as will cause the enemy the greatest impediment and loss in their march. For these purposes you will attack them as occasion may require by detachment, and, if a proper opening shd be given, by operating against them with the whole force of your command. You will naturally take such precautions, as will secure you against surprise, and maintain your communication with this army. Given at Kingston, this 25th day of June, 1778.

Go. WASHINGTON.[12]

The advance detachments numbered now over 5000 men and constituted a command much larger than the ordinary force often assigned in continental times to a major-general. General Lee by right should have been offered this command as the post of honor, but his opinions expressed at the Council and afterward more pointedly to his friends, that all these plans must come to nought and that defeat, perhaps utter rout would befall the American Army in the near future, made General Washington hesitate and at last give to another the position nearest the enemy. General Lee said he was well pleased to be free from all responsibility for a plan which he was sure would fail. General Lafayette accepted the place with enthusiasm, and riding by the side of General Poor he left the main army for the purpose of attacking the enemy with

---

[12] Ford's *Writings of George Washington*, Vol. VII, p. 73.

the advance continental and militia regiments—the whole force of his command.

While General Washington was still at Kingston a splendid white horse was brought to his quarters and presented to him with the compliments of William Livingston, the war Governor of New Jersey. General Washington rode this horse into the Battle of Monmouth where he fell, exhausted by the heat.

The main army left Kingston for Cranbury soon after sunset of Thursday, June 25. A small detachment of the Fourth regiment New Jersey Continental infantry, Colonel Ephraim Martin in command, was left behind in charge of the heavy baggage of the army.

CHAPTER IX

THE night of June 22 was spent by the principal part of the British Army at Black Horse, now Columbus, and around Mansfield, Burlington County. The orders of General Clinton in the morning were from Black Horse and those at sunset for the march of the next day were dated at Mansfield.

The following is a copy of the orders:

> Camp at the black horse June 22nd 1778.
>
> The Troops will immediately send to the Provision Park mess head Quarters for the day's Provisions, the one fresh, the other salt and rum to the 24th Inclusive.

> Head Qts Mansfield 22nd June '78.
>
> The army will march to-morrow in two columns, Gen'l Leslie's corps reinforced by Havendon's Dragoons forming the Van Guard of the left Column will be ready to March at 4 o'clock. The first Division will form the left Column and will be ready to march at 3 o'clock in the same order as this day. His Excel[y] Gen'l Kniphausen's Divisions led by the Second Light Infantry form the right Column and will be ready to march at 4 o'clock, it is to move as soon as the first Division is off their ground. The Right column will pay every attention to the right flank, the Provincial troops will have the same Station as in the Day's March and the Baggage will move in the same Order as this morning.[1]

In the march of June 23, Lieutenant-General the Earl Cornwallis had command of the First Division, and Sir Henry Clinton and his staff were with Cornwallis.

The necessity for pushing forward the great force with its immense baggage and supply train seemed more urgent every hour. As General Clinton saw for the fourth time this great train of fifteen hundred wagons[2] start out on the journey, it is said,—with what truth cannot now be

---

[1] Lieutenant-Colonel Clarke's order book.

[2] General Knyphausen to Frederick II, Landgrave of Hesse-Cassel, July 6, 1778.

determined,—that for a moment he had it in mind to order
the whole thing destroyed. It seemed a terrible encumbrance and he longed to rid himself of its responsibility.
But the thought that this would appear to his men a sign
of weakness, aroused his military pride and he resolved
to push it through to the seaboard with all the skill he
could command. Had General Clinton destroyed his baggage and all the loot of the army at this time he would
undoubtedly have been able to fall upon the army of
General Washington with terrific energy and effect. Had
he possessed the great decision of character necessary to
do such an act, a week later, instead of decamping in the
night from a battle-field on which he had been worsted,
he might have punished the American Army so severely as
to have secured an early peace.

Besides this vast train of baggage, the large number of
loyal camp followers who had to be protected by the troops
made an additional encumbrance. Of these followers the
women constituted the most troublesome part. On May
26 General Clinton had in orders "permitted commanding
officers of companies to take two women per company"
with them on the march, provided that they were "known
to be good marchers—as no carriages will be allowed for
them or their baggage." Although he had thus been precise
as to the number and qualifications of these women nearly
every day on the march he was compelled to make some
reference to them in his orders.

On June 16 he says "If any Reg't has more women than
allowed, the Commanding officer is Desired to send them
down to the ships, if he can Possibly get an opportunity;
if not, they are to march with the army, but by way of
Punishment, will be allowed no Provisions." The next day,
"The women of each Regm't to march at the head of it,
under an Escort of a Non-Commiss'd Officer & 6 men who
will take Care that they do not go out of the road on any
account." On June 18 he ordered "The Women of the
Army always to March upon the flanks of the Baggage of

their Respective Corps, and the Provost marshal has Received positive orders to Drum out any Women who shall dare to Disobey this Order." Again on June 23 he was compelled to revert to the same subject: "Many of the women who were sent on Board the Transports from Philadelphia, being at Present with the army, the Commanding Officers will give in returns of such women in their respective Corps, and they will specify by whose Permission those Women rejoyned the Army."[8]

These women apparently were not under the control of the officers in command and are said to have been perfectly lawless and to have gathered up much of the stolen property on the line of march. Von Elking, the German historian, in speaking of this party remarks, "A soldier of to-day could have no conception of such a procession."

On the march of June 23 the military execution took place of Drummer John Fisher of the Twenty-eighth regiment British foot, who had been captured badly wounded, June 20, had been tried and found guilty of deserting and bearing arms in the rebel service.

Very early in the morning of June 23 General Leslie entered Bordentown with his advance corps, consisting principally of the Fifth British brigade and the Hessian yagers, and, marching through the village passed out on the road to Crosswicks. As they approached Watson's Ford they found the Jersey militia guarding it and the floor-boards of the bridge removed. The Jerseymen had also raised the draw, erected some little redoubts and were prepared to defend the ford for a short time. The remains of these entrenchments between the high ground and the creek, south of White Horse, can still be seen [1899]. A little skirmish with the Sixteenth British regiment light dragoons ensued just at dawn, the Jerseymen being under strict orders to harass but not to give battle to the enemy. During this affair four men were killed and several badly wounded, and the militia moved off under the pressure of

[8] Lieutenant-Colonel Clarke's order book.

superior numbers and the near approach of an overwhelming force. Brigade Major William Gamble of General Dickinson's staff received a gunshot wound in the breast during the skirmish. As a strategic point a very competent military critic says, "The position at the draw-bridge is an excellent one, as is the line of Crosswicks generally on either side for defence. The only chance for an attacking force, if the whole line was held, would be above Groveville, and then only by the simultaneous destruction of all the dams on the creek, the threatening of several points and the crossing of one in force. At the draw-bridge with artillery the militia could have been held sufficiently back to repair the crossing." During the day a forage party went up on Black's Creek to Lewis Mills, took all the bread-stuffs in the building and then burned it. Passing on toward Crosswicks by a road south of the creek General Cornwallis found the roads thereabouts encumbered with felled trees, and a part of Maxwell's New Jersey brigade firing at his marching men from every point which offered the slightest concealment. General Maxwell had sent all the baggage of his brigade, in charge of Lieutenant John Shreve of the Second New Jersey regiment, to the barracks at Trenton and his force was now in light marching order, and able to annoy the enemy greatly at this point. At last it became so unpleasant, that Lieutenant-Colonel John Graves Simcoe, with the Queen's rangers, was sent forward to disperse the rebels. This he was able to do after some time and the Americans retired to the shelter of a wood on the north bank of the Crosswicks Creek. The sluices of this creek had been closed below and it was not fordable at this place. From the appearance of the American force in that position Sir Henry Clinton judged that they were about to give battle, so he formed his men in order to resist an attack and ordered up his batteries and cavalry. He found also that the draw on this bridge had been raised, although the bridge had not been entirely destroyed as was intended. The militia tried hard to complete its destruction before the enemy reached it. In cutting away the sleepers of the bridge a young patriot named Job Clevenger, of the First Burlington militia, lost his life, being shot in the head with a musket-ball and falling into the creek just as the little skirmish commenced. The British engineers were now called to the front and under the protection of some light artillery the bridge was repaired.

Captain Charles Stevenson, with a company of light infantry, had been posted on the left of the flanking party. Simcoe formed his corps behind the meeting-house, and under the protection of Lieutenant Alexander McLeod's detachment of the Forty-second regiment British foot and three pieces of light artillery, the dragoons dismounted and so passed over the bridge. The First battalion of light infantry then crossed over to pursue the Americans. This they did gallantly for some distance, receiving severe fire at times from the retreating troops on the right. In this little skirmish a musket ball struck Captain Charles Stevenson of the Queen's rangers, a very gallant and at this time conspicuous officer who was reconnoitering the bridge and the position of the Americans, and inflicted a bad wound in his left breast, which was thought at the time to be mortal. He recovered, however, and was among the first to enter Crosswicks with the reconnoitering party, only to be shot by Private Caleb Shreve of the Burlington County militia from the cellar window of a house in Crosswicks.[4] The report is that four of the British were seriously wounded in this little affair, and it is known that Colonel Elias Dayton of the Third New Jersey Continental regiment had his horse shot from under him.

The British encamped that night around Crosswicks and their column extended out on the road to Gibbstown, now Ellisdale, in Monmouth County.

[4] This house was on the southwest corner of the road leading from the Quaker meeting-house to the bridge and the road leading from Bordentown to what is now the village of Ellisdale.

Sir Henry Clinton spent the night at the house of Mrs. Bunting in Crosswicks, and there is a tradition in her family, confirmed by papers still preserved, that the British commanding general became intoxicated during the evening. The description of the mishap which occurred to him is copied from these papers and is believed to be correct:

But she (Mrs. Bunting) was not allowed to indulge in her sad reflections for many moments before she was summoned to the room below to supply bucket, clothes and all things necessary to remove the mud from the august person of the British General. He, it seemed, had an attack of nightmare caused by the carouse of the evening, and probably imagining that the Yankees were upon him, had started from his bed, and rushing through the door, which was opened on account of the heat, dashed down the hill, and before the astonished sentinel could decide whether he had seen a ghost or not, his noble commander was floundering knee deep among the mud and mallows of the little creek. The plunge awakened him, and his loud outcries brought officers and soldiers rushing from their tents in full expectation of finding themselves attacked by the Rebel army. The shouts and curses, the confusion, the rushing here and there of half-dressed men, formed a scene at once alarming and ridiculous. But the cause being at length discovered, the discomfited General was led back to his quarters, and with Mrs. Bunting's aid was cleansed, and half stupified as he still was, placed again in the clean, comfortable bed which he had occupied. Order was restored in the camp and silence reigned unbroken till reveille aroused the slumbering host.[5]

Whether this be true or not, the order for the march on June 24 was issued in Clinton's name on the night spent at Crosswicks. It was in the following words:

Head Quarters, Crosswick, 23rd June 1778.

The Army will march tomorrow morning.

The Corps of Brigadier Gen'l Leslie will if possible join the Division at Crosswick at six o'clock. The 2nd Division under the Command of His Excellency Lt Gen'l Kniphausen will begin its march at 4 o'clock, the 1st Division will be in readiness to march at six o'clock in the same order as this day.[6]

[5] Woodward's *History of Burlington*, p. 28.
[6] Lieutenant-Colonel Clarke's order book.

[87]

In compliance with this order the troops of General Cornwallis and General Knyphausen crossed Crosswicks Creek at Walnford, on a bridge of their own construction, early on the morning of June 24; the former marched to Allentown about four miles, encamping at "Eglinton," the homestead of Robert Montgomery, at Cabbage Town,[7] and Knyphausen's men went to Imlaystown and camped in a wheat field of Peter Imlay's farm. These little villages were about three miles apart. During the day General Leslie brought up his light troops from Bordentown to Imlaystown.

Again during this short day's march the British found the bridge over Doctor's Creek torn up. The troops of Generals Maxwell and Dickinson were still swarming in front of the enemy and the performance of the previous day had to be repeated by the Queen's rangers and the light infantry battalions. The light batteries of the British were this day brought actively into service.

A gentleman who was with the New Jersey militia in these little skirmishes said in a letter published at the time: ". . . the Militia saved in my opinion Trenton and the country adjacent from rapine and desolation. In short their conduct during the whole time gave me the most pleasing ideas of the strong love of liberty which is natural to the human soul. Surely while the farmers of the country are induced by the mere fondness of freedom to leave all their domestic concerns at this season of the year and undergo the hardships of a soldier's life—to suffer the severest fatigues and with pleasure face every danger, I say while this continues Americans must and will be free."

James McHenry, a Secretary of General Washington, wrote of these little affairs with the British: "Thirty or forty were killed in the different skirmishes with our militia and flying parties."

The afternoon and evening of June 24 were excessively

---

[7] Now Canton, a mile northeast of Allentown, in Upper Freehold Township, Monmouth County.

warm; not the slightest breeze tempered the heat on the weary march.

It was now necessary for Sir Henry Clinton to determine which of the two routes to New York it would be better for him to take. One road led to the Raritan River, to Amboy and across Staten Island, and the other by Monmouth Court House, Middletown Point and Sandy Hook. He charged Lieutenant-Colonel Simcoe to procure him intelligence of the exact whereabouts of Washington's Army and its movements through some of his loyal Jersey troopers and their refugee friends who followed them, and this Simcoe essayed to do immediately. During the night of June 24 all the information of this nature that Clinton needed was obtained for him, and two Monmouth County men from Simcoe's regiment were selected as the guides for the army during the rest of their march in New Jersey. It was evident at this time that General Washington expected Clinton to attempt the passage of the Raritan River, and he knew that Clinton's rich baggage train would be a grand prize for the poor Continental sufferers of Valley Forge. Sir Henry Clinton, however, suspected that General Gates was marching down the Hudson River toward Brunswick to meet him. Consequently, he determined to take the road leading to the hills of the Navesink and so frustrate, if possible, the plans of the American officers, and carry out with more expedition the orders of his Majesty, the King.

A change in the order of march was now made, and General Knyphausen, with the Hessian mercenaries, who had constituted the rear guard, and the Second Division in charge of the heavy baggage and stores of both divisions, were placed on the advance and Lord Cornwallis and his splendid division, freed from all impedimenta, took the left of the column.

Sir Henry Clinton spent the night of June 24 at Allentown and issued his order for the march of the next day. This is the text of the order:

[89]

Head Quarters Allen's Town June 24th 1778.
The Baggage to be loaded and the Army to be in readiness to move at 4 o'clock to-morrow morning. The 1st Division will march by half companies from the left in the following order—Brigadier General Leslie's Corps, consisting of the 5th Brigade and Hovendon's dragoons, pontoons and Baggage, Cattle, 4th Brigade, 3rd Brigade, Guards, Artillery, Hessian Grenadiers, British Grenadiers, Queen's Dragoons, Light infantry, Corps of Yagers, Allen's Corps to flank the Baggage of the left; the Army will receive one day's fresh and one day's salt Provision as soon as they come to their Ground. The women to march with the baggage according to this day's order.[8]

In this way the march of June 25 was made. Along a space of nearly twelve miles there followed in close succession all the soldiers of Clinton's Army, foot, horse and artillery, provision train, baggage, army wagons, numerous private carriages, a large number of bat-horses,[9] bakeries, laundries and blacksmiths' shops on wheels, large hospital supplies, boats, bridges, magazines,—withal a crowd of female camp followers and "every kind of useless stuff." With this immense train it required the best of generalship to ensure the safety of the column, which Clinton himself thought was "vulnerable."

At a very early hour General Knyphausen gave his order to march and his heavily equipped veterans started on the road to Monmouth Court House. Soon after five o'clock in the morning the remainder of the army were on the march. The advance halted on the roadway about four miles from Monmouth Court House,—while Sir Henry Clinton made his headquarters at the Rising Sun Tavern, six miles farther south.

It has been thought that Sir Henry Clinton made his great mistake on this day and that when a clear and easy retreat was really all he desired, he should have taken the short march to the Raritan. He certainly had not perfectly correct information of the position of the entire American

---

[8] Lieutenant-Colonel Clarke's order book.
[9] In the British Army, a horse for carrying baggage belonging to an officer or to the baggage trains.—*Cent. Dict.*

force for in after years he replied to his critics as follows: "Gates in front beyond the Raritan; Washington in the rear and left behind the Millstone Creek, with the Fords of the Raritan on his left to join or be joined by Gates." General Gates was not with his troops at this time "in front beyond the Raritan," but on his way from Peekskill to White Plains, New York.

General Washington said that Clinton's movements had the "air of design." Possibly Washington did not fully appreciate the difficulties under which Clinton labored and, therefore, his march seemed slow. General Greene, it seems, agreed with General Washington that Clinton was anxious to draw the American Army toward Mount Holly where in the "lower country" he could have a good opportunity to use his artillery and his horse to advantage and then, perhaps, by a quick movement with his light troops gain the hilly country in Somerset and Morris Counties. The vast encumbrance in Clinton's train was not then fully appreciated and General Washington, declining what he thought Clinton's seeming challenge, and confident of his ability to check him later, tarried at Hopewell to give his men some rest.

During the day of June 25 the American Continentals from Washington's Army hovered around the British column in greater numbers than before. Especially was this the case in the rear of their column. General Cadwalader with the Pennsylvania militia, and Jackson's Massachusetts Continental troops had come up, reported to General Lafayette and took part in capturing stragglers and marauders from the British Army. General Scott was also there with his selected brigade, and Lieutenant-Colonel Anthony Walton White's detachment of the Fourth regiment of Continental cavalry, kept close on the British rear, a target for the ribald abuse of the women camp followers of Clinton's Army. Lieutenant Wickham, of the Queen's rangers, while patrolling with a small force, captured two countrymen who thought from their green uniform that they were troopers of Light Horse Harry Lee. After telling all they knew about the movements of the American Army they were astonished to find themselves hustled off to the British headquarters under guard.

No modern writer explains the situation at this time with more accuracy than the eminent battle historian General de Peyster, and his language is here quoted: "Washington was nearer to Brunswick, could move on interior lines through a denser, friendly population, where he could find supplies. If Clinton, who had to carry his food with him, still prosecuted his march to Brunswick he might find himself in a cul-de-sac with the Raritan in front; the South River and extensive and impassable marshes extending for miles southward; to his right Lawrence Brook, then a much more important stream, embarrassing his immediate communications; while Washington could come in on his left flank and rear. . . . In this position Washington expected to hold him until the Northern Army, under Gates, could be brought down from the Hudson, to prevent the escape of the British, until the militia could be assembled from every quarter. Thus between his own army, that of Gates and the militia, Sarotoga might be repeated and Clinton be swarmed out—Burgoyned."[10]

All day of Thursday the twenty-fifth the British Army was continually harassed and had to defend itself against Colonel Morgan's riflemen operating on its right flank, General Maxwell's Continental Jerseymen on its left flank and General Scott's detachment with the troops from Philadelphia constantly assaulting its rear guard. Just in front of General Knyphausen's division was General Dickinson's Jersey militia, now joined by a new party of levies under Brigadier-General Nathaniel Heard, of Middlesex County, and they were doing all they could to destroy bridges and check the progress of the army. The Hessian records speak of the great heat of this day and

[10] General de Peyster in the "Affair of Freehold" in *Old Times in Old Monmouth*, p. 60.

Present appearance of the house of Thomas Tomson, Senior, four miles west of Freehold, on the Smithburg turnpike. This house was used by General Clinton as his headquarters on the morning and afternoon of June 26, and by General Knyphausen prior to the battle. It is now owned and occupied by Charles M. Higgins.

PHOTOGRAPHED AUGUST 12, 1926, BY W. S. M.

say that nearly one-third of their troops were so overcome as to fall by the roadside.[11] Withal, swarms of mosquitoes attacked these soldiers and their faces were swollen with the poisonous sting.[12]

General Clinton issued this order that night from the Rising Sun Tavern for the march of June 26: "The army will march to-morrow morning at 4 o'clock in the same Order as this Day."[13]

According to orders General Knyphausen marched his Hessian troops a short distance, hardly four miles, on June 26, and encamped just beyond the Monmouth Court House. At ten o'clock in the morning the rest of the army, greatly overcome with the heat, came up to the village of Freehold by the road from Crosswicks and the Rising Sun Tavern. This road crossed what is now [1926] the farm of the estate of James B. Vredenburgh to where the Presbyterian Church now stands in Freehold and enters the Main street at the point where Henry L. Jones now resides. The British Army pitched their tents on each side of the road by which they had travelled.

The army then stretched out in a long line from West Freehold to the junction of Dutch Lane Road and what is now the road to Marlboro. The headquarters of the Commander-in-Chief were established in the stone dwelling of Thomas Tomson, Sr., four miles west of Freehold. He spent the day of June 26 in this house, leaving there late in the afternoon.[14]

About five miles to the rear of the British column General Lafayette was quartered at Robin's Tavern, and from

[11] Johann Heusser's manuscript journal.
[12] Ewald's *Belshrungen* [*Belehrungen*?], Vol. II, p. 352.
[13] Lieutenant-Colonel Clarke's order book.
[14] Mr. Tomson built the house in 1765 and he was occupying it at this time. It is still standing and now [1926] owned by Charles M. Higgins. Some of the general and staff officers of the British Army remained in the Tomson house the night of June 26, much against the wishes of the patriot owner, and tradition tells us that they had a drunken carnival and dance that night. It was with difficulty that many of the officers could attend to their military duties the next day. [This house has been known since then as "General Knyphausen's headquarters."]

this post he was directing the operations of his select corps, which, though almost starving, were still watching the movements of the British, with the eager desire and firm intention of attacking them the next morning.

During the day there was much skirmishing between the Hessian yagers and the American advance troops. At times this looked very serious and the Queen's rangers were ordered into service on both flanks of the yagers, whose guns had no bayonets, so as to prevent a sudden assault of the Continental light troops.

Up to this hour it would appear that Clinton did not wish Washington to think he was running away, nor that he had the slightest fear, but never once did he act as if he were desirous of battle.

This order was issued for the next day:

Head Quarters, Monmouth Court House 26 June '78.
The army will remain to-morrow in its Present Position.—One Day's Salt and one Day's fresh Provisions will be issued to the Army early to-morrow morning.[15]

The night of June 26 was very rainy and sharp lightning and heavy thunder prevailed until nearly daylight.

General Clinton remained in the Tomson house until late in the afternoon of June 26 and then moved two miles and a half nearer Freehold to the house of William Covenhoven. He made his headquarters at this house until his army vacated Freehold at midnight after the battle. It appears that his retinue sorely abused this house and its occupants during their stay in it.[16]

The position of the British Army at this time was one of great strength, so much so that even Washington asserted that "it was too strong to be assaulted with any prospect of success."

The extreme right of the army, held by the Hessian sol-

---

[15] Lieutenant-Colonel Clarke's order book.
[16] Affidavit of Mrs. Elizabeth Covenhoven, seventy-five years of age, wife of William Covenhoven, in *New Jersey Gazette* of August 12, 1778. [The house is still standing at the western edge of Freehold, is in excellent repair, and is owned by the estate of William Moreau, 1926.]

Present appearance of house of William Covenhoven, now owned by the estate of William Moreau, on western edge of Freehold, on the Freehold and Smithburg road. This house was General Clinton's headquarters on the night of June 26 and until midnight of June 28.

PHOTOGRAPHED BY W.S.M., SEPTEMBER 17, 1926

diery was at the junction of the roads leading to Middletown Point and to Colt's Neck, Holmdel and Shrewsbury and was on the edge of an extensive tract of woodland. A low swampy bottom fully protected a considerable part of the left side of the army. General Washington said, "Their right flank lay on the skirt of a small wood while their left was secured by a very thick one, a morass running towards their rear, and their whole front covered by a wood, and for a considerable extent towards the left, with a morass."[17] The left of the army lay along the road leading from Allentown to Monmouth Court House and four miles west of the court house. The British Army had marched some sixty-seven miles since leaving Philadelphia, and the American Army, then at Englishtown, had passed over more than eighty miles since they had abandoned the cantonment at Valley Forge.

On account of the rain and heat, the British remained inactive in their tents after ten o'clock Friday morning and all day Saturday, June 27, except for sending out a few foraging parties who plundered the neighboring farms of supplies of food, grain and hay and, by way of amusement, pulled down the bell in the court house and demolished the steeple of the English church. The picket guards, however, were well established, and during the day the soldiers were engaged in cleaning their arms, the intense heat and occasional rain making a quiet and listless encampment. The British officers felt that at any time by a quick march of sixteen miles they could reach the high ground about Middletown and then be secure against attack. It is not easy to explain why they did not make the march on June 27, regardless of the heat. A strong physical exertion and the great object of the march would have been attained. The delay of Sir Henry Clinton looks to us today almost as if he courted a fight. He certainly lost forty hours of valuable time when he might have saved his

[17] Sparks' *Writings of George Washington*, Vol. V, p. 424.

army from an inopportune engagement and his baggage from danger.

Sir Henry Clinton issued orders on the afternoon of June 27 to break camp before dawn of the following day, press as rapidly as possible on the Middletown road to the coast and take the strong position there which could so easily be defended. The parole for the night was "Berwick" and the countersign "Coblentz." The following was the order for the march:

Head Quarters Monmouth Court house 27 June 1778.

The Army will move to-morrow morning. The 2nd Division under his Excellency Lt. Gen'l Kniphausen, will march at 3 o'clock and the 1st Division at 5. The Baggage of the whole Army will go with the second Division, except the Bat horses of the 1st, which may march with it. The Baggage of the 1st Division will follow that of the 2nd in the order which they have hitherto moved. 27th Regim't to join its Brigade before the hour of march to-morrow morning. Colonel Innis, Inspector Gen'l of the Provincial Forces will follow the Light Infantry of the 2nd Division, with a Corps of safe Guards, Consisting of a Detachm't of Dragoons and 150 of Chalmers's Corps; the Corps of yagers, will join Lt. Gen¹ Kniphausen to-morrow to take such situation in his line of march as his Excellency shall think Proper to order.

If any disorderly People attempt to force the safe Guards, or to Plunder where they are Posted, the Guard is to make them Prisoners, and to fire at them if they should attempt to resist them.[18]

The night of June 27 was very hot and no breeze from the woods or from the not far distant ocean relieved the intense deadness of the air. A heavy thunderstorm came up in the night, worse even than the storm of June 26. The pickets of the British Army, however, were on the alert, as they had been instructed to keep close watch. The whole army lay on their arms. A deserter had been brought into headquarters and he had said to Clinton, "the rebels are extended along our left flank and are very numerous."

During the passage of the British Army through Monmouth County they burned the residences of Doctor Thomas Henderson, Peter Forman, General David For-

[18] Lieutenant-Colonel Clarke's order book.

man, Benjamin Covenhoven, George Walker, William Solomon, David Covenhoven, Garret Vanderveer and David Clayton.

Doctor Nathaniel Scudder, the patriot physician, soldier and statesman, the only member of the Continental Congress who gave his life in battle for the liberty of his country, wrote July 13, 1778, to the Honorable John Hart, the Speaker of the New Jersey House of Assembly: "Great plunder and devastation have been committed among my friends in this quarter, but through the distinguishing goodness of Providence my family and property escaped and almost in a miraculous manner."

Doctor Thomas Henderson, the physician of the country around Monmouth Court House,[19] says in the *New Jersey Gazette*, after giving a list of the names of the owners of the dwelling-houses burned, as just enumerated (the house of Benjamin Van Cleave also being added),—"John Benham's house and barn they wantonly tore and broke down so as to render them useless. It may not be improper to mention that my own and Benjamin Covenhoven's houses, adjoined the farm and were in full view of the place where General Clinton was quartered. In the neighbourhood below the court house they burnt the houses of Matthias Lane, Cornelius Covenhoven, John Antonidas and one Emmons; these were burnt the morning before their defeat."[20]

[19] Doctor Henderson was afterward a member of the Continental Congress. He was the man who appears hereafter in this narrative as the "countryman," giving Washington information of General Lee's retreat.
[20] See letter dated Monmouth, July 18, 1778, in the *New Jersey State Gazette* of August 5, 1778.

CHAPTER X

THE details of all the movements of the British forces, with a settlement of the question whether Sandy Hook or Amboy was the route determined upon by Sir Henry Clinton, were sent by General von Steuben and received by General Washington June 25 at Kingston, a little village three miles northeast of Princeton. General von Steuben also gave some important advice to General Scott. General Washington gave immediate orders for a night march, without the heavy baggage, toward English-town and Monmouth. At nine o'clock in the morning of June 26 they arrived at Cranbury[1] in a very heavy rain storm, and this, with the extreme heat, made farther marching impracticable without entailing great suffering on the men. The American Army, therefore, remained near Cranbury all day, though some detachments advanced to take new and more favorable positions against the enemy.

During June 25 and June 26 General Lafayette wrote very frequently to General Washington informing him of the movements of his command and the position of the British Army. The first of this series of letters was written at Cranbury at half-past nine in the evening of the twenty-fifth, although the document is not dated. General Lafayette was at that time somewhat worried lest he could not reach and attack the foe. His rations were running low and rum seemed necessary for the fast and early march he had ordered for the morrow. The march, however, was begun about four o'clock in the morning of the twenty-sixth, although he remained in Cranbury until five o'clock to write another letter to Washington. He had in the meantime received instructions from his chief to press on rapidly and overtake the enemy. General David Forman,

[1] About ten miles southeast of Kingston.

of Monmouth County, was now with Lafayette to give him all possible information about the roads of the country he knew so well. Lafayette was filled with military ardor and hoped to deal a sharp blow at the enemy. He evidently wished to feel before he engaged in battle that Washington and the main army were near for his support. Lafayette rode on two miles to Hightstown and after seven o'clock he wrote again to General Washington.[2]

At the noon hour, June 26, Hamilton wrote Washington a letter from Robin's Tavern. At that time the American Army had halted, under sore distress for food, with the rear of the British Army only four miles in advance of them on the road toward Shrewsbury. Hamilton was then exerting himself to the utmost to procure intelligence which might be of use to the cause.

General Lafayette came up to Robin's Tavern and he also began to write to Washington at half-past four. The main army had then reached Cranbury. Colonel Morgan was still annoying the foe on their right flank and General Dickinson's militia was harassing them on their left.

Hamilton wrote his second letter of the day to his Chief from the same tavern at four o'clock in the afternoon. This letter added little to the information then well known. He knew that the British Army had reached Monmouth Court House and had encamped. The hostile forces were then seven miles apart. While he was writing this letter some instructions came from Washington to Lafayette, Hamilton read them and closed his letter by informing Washington that the advance detachment would march toward Englishtown[3] at three o'clock in the morning of June 27.

It was half-past ten that night when General Lafayette began his fourth letter of the day to Washington. He must have been greatly fatigued for he dated his letter the

[2] Lafayette spelled the name "Ice Town" in his despatches. It is situated about a mile and a half south of Cranbury.
[3] Ten miles east of Cranbury.

[99]

twenty-eighth instead of the twenty-sixth. He said little more than to reiterate the statement of Hamilton that the detachment would move forward at an early hour the next morning.

Before leaving Kingston General Lee became convinced that he was allowing the young French officer to occupy too long the post of honor nearest the foe, and his jealous heart and professional pride began to assert themselves. He spoke constantly to those about him of the wrong that was being done him by allowing Lafayette so great a command. He began also to feel that his military reputation would suffer if a junior officer were allowed to hold such an important place in the movements of the campaign and he regretted his first decision in declining the honor. It is also said that Major-General Lord Stirling showed some disposition to interpose his claim. In talking with his friends General Lee coupled the name of Lord Stirling— and he might also have said Major-General Greene—with the assertion that great injustice was being done by General Washington in neglecting older and more experienced officers; but the opinions which Lee had so often and so forcibly expressed rendered him unfit for the important service to which Lafayette had been assigned. At the same time, Lee now wished to escape from his unfortunate position even by accepting a duty which he felt would result disastrously. At last on the evening of June 25, General Lee requested General Washington to place him in command of the advance corps. Of course the commander-in-chief was much vexed at this turn of affairs at such a critical time, but, by a singularly false estimate of Lee's character, he immediately instituted a plan to please him. He wrote to Lee[4] from Cranbury the next morning proposing an expedient by which he could favor him and yet not wound the feelings of Lafayette. This plan was for Lee to join Lafayette with two more brigades and then by virtue of his rank assume command of the corps, without

[4] Ford's *Writings of George Washington*, Vol. VII, p. 75.

detaching Lafayette from the force now under his control. General Washington also followed this letter to Lee with one to Lafayette[5] advising him of what he had done and expressing the wish that this plan would not interfere with any desire he had to annoy the enemy. Had not General Lafayette been a devoted friend of Washington, this change just on the eve of battle could hardly have taken place without causing an unpleasant scene. But neither at this time, nor ever afterward did General Lafayette show himself other than the true soldier and the close friend and admirer of General Washington. By this correspondence and these orders a young officer, as General Greene said, with "great thirst for glory," whose whole heart was in the impending contest was supplanted by one who, though greatly his superior in experience, was thoroughly opposed to the movement he was under orders to make immediately.

General Lee was now ordered in command of the division of General Lafayette, but with instructions from General Washington to allow Lafayette to carry out any plan he had formed to damage the enemy. The brigades formerly commanded by Generals Scott and Varnum were ordered to accompany General Lee and join the advance division. The brigades of Maxwell and Wayne which had been following the rear and flanks of the British were ordered up from the Rising Sun Tavern, about six miles from Allentown, where they had rested, and were directed to report to General Lee near Englishtown. This they did promptly on the morning of June 27. This command had come to General Lee through the kind courtesy of General Lafayette and that officer had good reason to think that General Lee would carry out the plans then being executed. From that hour, however, Lafayette's plans were ignored.

General Lee saw very clearly that General Washington and his dashing young French assistant might, perhaps,

[5] *Lafayette's Correspondence*, Amer. ed., Vol. I, p. 180.

severely punish the distended column of the British, and the glory of such an action would not only win the applause of the country, but would prove that his advice at the council board was not the best for the cause. Perhaps, too, he was actuated by a desire to be in the very advance himself, where only by his own orders could distress be given to Sir Henry Clinton. And if, perchance, any vigorous orders were issued to him by General Washington, perhaps he thought he would carry them out in his own way, and, by dilatory action or by inaction, give the British the march "on velvet"[6] which his own policy approved.

It was clearly a mistake in General Washington to supplant the young and enthusiastic Lafayette, who was eager to fight and who had under him lieutenants who knew well how to fight, by an officer who did not believe it was proper to attack the British on their transit through the Jerseys.

The precepts found in the *Art of War* are very pertinent to the action of General Washington in reference to General Lee. "To commit the execution of a purpose to one who disapproves of the plan of it, is to employ but one-third of the man; his heart and his head are against you; you have command only of his hands." "An unwilling commander, it is said, is half beaten before the battle begins, therefore an officer who is in favor of the measure is to be preferred for the execution of it to one who disapproves of the plan; and one who volunteers to carry it out is to be preferred to either, supposing the qualifications of all three to be on a par in other respects."[7]

During the afternoon of June 26 General Washington was impressed with the fact that General Lafayette had placed his division too far to the right to command the aid of the main army in case of necessity, and that it would be better for efficient service that he take position more

6 Clinton in *Anbury's Travels*, Vol. II, p. 382.
7 Jomini's *Précis de l'Art de la Guerre.*

to the left and nearer to Englishtown; so he ordered this
to be done, and at a very early hour on June 27 Lafayette
took the new position as directed by Washington.

CHAPTER XI

DURING the whole day of June 27 General von Steuben was reconnoitering the enemy. This he did very closely and reported all he saw during the morning to General Washington. After sending this communication, he continued his investigations during the afternoon, but as he approached the encampment of the Hessian grenadiers, he was discovered and nearly taken prisoner. In his eagerness to escape he lost his hat. He would doubtless have been shot had it not been for General Knyphausen who recognized him and prevented it. During the evening he was directed to attach himself to the division under General Lord Stirling.

On Saturday, June 27, the force under General Washington's immediate command marched at sunrise on the Cranbury road to within five miles of Englishtown, at which village General Lee was posted with his advance corps. Here General Lee received an order from Washington to halt his column. General Washington had his headquarters at Penelopen, now Manalapan. Englishtown was five miles by road from Monmouth Court House. All the various detachments sent out by General Washington soon after crossing the Delaware River had reported to General Lee, except Colonel Morgan's Virginia riflemen who were still on the British right flank at Richmond Mills, now Blue Ball, three miles from Freehold, and General Dickinson's New Jersey militia, who were on their left flank.

During that day the American Army cooked two days' rations and in every way prepared themselves for the issue of a fight, which they knew was imminent.

That night orders were issued at follows:

Head Quarters, Penelopen, 27th June 1778.
As we are now near the Enemy and of consequence Vigilance and Precaution more essentially necessary the Commander-in-chief

desires and enjoins it upon all officers to keep their Posts and their soldiers compact, so as to be ready to form and march at a moment's warning, as circumstances may require.

The drums to beat on the march. When the rear is to come up, a common march; to quicken the march, a grenadier march. These signals to begin in the rear under the direction of the brigadier of the day, and are to be repeated by the orderly drum of every battalion from rear to front. An orderly drum to be kept ready braced with each battalion for this purpose. When the whole line is to halt for refreshment the first part of the General will beat, and this to be repeated by every orderly drum down to the rear.[1]

It does not appear that any of these signals on the batter-head of a drum were obeyed during the march, and in the retreat and battle of the next day. It was, perhaps, too late to familiarize the various corps with these orders.

The parole of the American Army the previous night had been "Lookout" and the countersign "Sharp and keen," and these were good mottoes to bear in mind all day of June 27.

It may not have been strictly a military necessity for General Washington to fight the British Army, but it was clearly a political necessity. France had acknowledged the independence of America and it might have been possible for America to wait until French troops and French sailors could be at hand to give efficient aid. But it was far better that the Americans should strike a strong blow for themselves when so good an opportunity offered, for even an attempt to punish the royal army would show that the Americans were still struggling to be free and were not content with simply keeping an army together without any aggressive movement, waiting for a foreign nation to help them. In addition to this, it was necessary for General Washington, if he would not sink his military reputation into obscurity and drop out of public sight as a leader in this fearful struggle for a young nation's life, to promptly exert himself and show that the army at least had confidence in its chief and would follow where he led

[1] Washington's order book, in the Congressional Library.

the way. It was unavoidably necessary, if he would retain the support of the patriots at home and in the field, to prove the falsity of the insinuations made in Congress and the charges of incapacity arising in jealous army circles. General Washington must assume the responsibility of risking an engagement although some of his general officers had advised against it. He must seek a fight, and this was the time to do so. The soldiers of the army felt that Washington had the necessary confidence in his own ability to command, and he had full confidence in their ability to execute any operation against the best troops in the world, if properly led. He knew that he could bring his entire army, foot, horse, artillery, regulars and militia, into service for direct attack and he was well assured that Sir Henry Clinton could not take from a safe line of retreat more than one-half his force; the other half, being necessary to protect his baggage train, must act entirely on the defensive. In this state of affairs it was important that Washington should show that he did not fear to offer battle to the formidable Briton. Twice on New Jersey soil he had punished their detachments, and must he now by inaction efface the glory of those victories? After the cabals at Valley Forge and the professional advice of General Lee at the council of war, it would not do to allow the soldiers drilled by von Steuben to shrink from a bold assault. Indeed, he was eager for the hour to pit his drilled regulars, full of patriotic ardor, against the British veterans.

Very soon after noonday, June 27, General Washington called General Lee to his headquarters to inform him that he had determined to assume the responsibility of attacking the British column the next morning. He desired Lee to prepare to strike the enemy at the first favorable opportunity. While General Washington was giving General Lee his instructions he sent for General Lafayette, General Maxwell, General Wayne and General Scott to come to his quarters. These officers instantly complied and they heard the commander-in-chief direct General Lee to attack the rear of the enemy on the morrow with his select division, promising to support him promptly with the main body of the army. The chief did not specify that the object of attack should be a mere rear guard or covering party, but even if they were the very flower of the British troops he wished the picked force of the American Army to engage them promptly. The full meaning and intention of these orders all the officers, except Lee, it appears, fully understood and agreed to. General Washington then made two requests—one, that on this occasion they should for the day waive their respective dates of rank and fight at any point where it was deemed most desirable by General Lee—and the other, that General Lee should hold a conference with the general officers of his division during the afternoon and arrange some of the necessary details of the attack. As they were leaving, General Washington remarked that General Maxwell was the oldest in commission and perhaps should have the preference in the attack, if he so desired, although as many of his troops were recruits and there was a great scarcity of cartouch boxes in the brigade, as shown in the returns, perhaps some other brigade would have to be placed on the advance. At all events he thought an attack, if begun by a "picked corps would probably give a very happy impression." Upon Washington again urging a conference for the purpose of forming a plan of attack on the enemy, General Lee named five o'clock in the afternoon at his quarters.

At the appointed hour Generals Lafayette, Maxwell and Wayne dismounted at Lee's quarters and they had a few moments' talk together. General Lee said, that at present the numbers and exact situation of the enemy were mere conjecture, that the country thereabouts had not been carefully reconnoitered and that if they formed any precise plan for the next morning the least unexpected event might embarrass, distract, and lead them astray. Any plan now agreed upon might in a moment become invalid. In his judgment it seemed best to move cautiously and rely on the vigilance of his officers and the prompt obedience of the men whenever it was found desirable to make any movement which the circumstances might require. In the meantime, each of them must hold his force subject to march at a moment's warning. General Lafayette expressed the desire to be with General Lee on the morrow, and Lee said he was gratified that Lafayette wished to do so and it should be as he desired. He then entreated them to avoid all disputes about rank, as General Washington had suggested, as it might happen that the oldest officer in rank might be ordered on the left and his junior on the right and he expected to be obeyed; that if they felt aggrieved at his orders they must comply with them first and complain afterward.

While he was thus talking, General Washington, who had ridden over to Englishtown and was on his return to his own quarters, having just passed over the bridge of Wemrock Brook and being in sight of General Lee's camp, sent Lieutenant-Colonel John Fitzgerald of his staff to Lee to direct him so to draw up his troops on the ground on which he was posted, that he might be prepared at any time that night to repel an attack. Washington told his aide to say to Lee that he did not think it probable that an attack would be made but, the enemy being very near, it was not impossible. He directed General Lee to keep his force on their arms during the night and to send word to General Dickinson and Colonel Morgan informing them how he wished them to cooperate with his division the next day. Washington also expressed the hope that Lee's generals had been in conference and had agreed upon such plans as would make a successful attack. Colonel Fitzgerald rode rapidly up the hill to General Lee's tent and found him with the general officers already stated. He called Lee out of his quarters and gave him General Washington's orders. General Lee said he thought from what he knew of the British commanders that they would not let the night pass without making an attack on him, and that although his men were greatly fatigued he would before dark put them in the very best position to receive an attack. General Lee went back into his tent and the conference ended. No plan whatever had been agreed upon; he had assumed to himself the entire control of the movement without informing his generals of any proposed disposition of his force.

It does not appear that during the night of June 27 he made the slightest effort to possess himself of such information of which, as he confessed at the council, he was ignorant and which certainly he sorely needed. Surely during the next ten hours he could have ascertained for himself the strength and situation of the hostile camp and even had maps made of the contour of the land on which the engagement had been ordered and must of necessity take place. A prudent, patriotic general would have tried to obtain these facts.

As General Maxwell mounted his horse to leave General Lee's quarters a young officer touched his hat and asked leave of absence the next day to visit his brother who was dying at the tavern at Black Horse, now Columbus, New Jersey. "Yes, yes," was the answer of the bluff old general, "it happens very well for you, Major Howell, we'll have a hot fight tomorrow." The officer felt the rebuke in the consent thus given by his veteran commander and he staid by his men through all the fight on the hot day that followed. This soldier, but twenty-four years of age, was Major Richard Howell of the Second New Jersey Continental regiment, in after years the distinguished Governor of the State.[2]

As soon as his guests had gone, General Lee left his quarters to make some disposition of his division before sunset. He was, therefore, absent when General Scott came

[2] The brother referred to was Lewis Howell, the surgeon of the regiment, who died at the tavern mentioned, June 29, 1778, the morning after the battle, soon after Major Howell was able to reach his bedside. They were twin brothers.

to his tent at half-past five, having evidently a wrong impression of the hour of the conference. But later in the evening General Scott called again, and Lee repeated what he had already stated to Lafayette and the other officers. He said he had no other orders for him and only wished him to comply with such requests as regards rank as he had just expressed to him.

By General Washington's direction Lieutenant-Colonel Hamilton wrote a letter to General Lee late in the evening of June 27 directing him to detach a party of observation to lie very near the enemy.[3]

This letter was taken by Captain-Lieutenant Edward Dunscomb of the Fourth New York regiment, an officer of General Lee's guard, and delivered to Captain Evan Edwards of General Lee's staff about half-past one in the morning of June 28. General Washington at that time apprehended from some information he had received, that the British would decamp during the night and he wished General Lee to detail from six to eight hundred men as a party of observation to give the very first intelligence of any movement, to skirmish with the foe, to stop their march, if possible, and give time for the army to come up to the conflict. This letter was but an order, in the same line of direction that Lee had already received, to attack the enemy as soon as they began to march. The orders which Washington wished sent to General Dickinson and Colonel Morgan were in accordance with his plan to give the enemy a blow.

By direction of General Lee, Captain Edwards immediately wrote instructions to General Dickinson informing him what General Washington desired and expected him

---

[3] Hamilton's testimony at Lee's court-martial, p. 11. Hamilton said he did not keep a copy of this important official communication; it does not appear among the papers of General Lee published by the New York Historical Society; it is not in the "Official and other papers of the late Major-General Alexander Hamilton, compiled from the originals in the possession of Mrs. Hamilton," nor in the *Works of Alexander Hamilton,* edited by John C. Hamilton.

to undertake in conjunction with orders which he had just given General Lee. He wrote also to Colonel Grayson that he had selected him to command the "party of observation" suggested by General Washington. Captain Mercer, by authority of General Lee, sent a messenger to Colonel Morgan to advance with his troops near the enemy and attack them when they moved. He gave him discretion how to act, except that he must not so expose his men as to render them incapable of acting with General Lee should he at any time during the day require their services.

During the early hours of the night of June 27 the sentinel near George Washington's headquarters challenged a gentleman who evidently did not have the countersign. To the officer of the guard, when he approached the sentinel, this man introduced himself as "Doctor Griffith, chaplain and surgeon in the Virginia line, on business highly important with the commander-in-chief." The officer said, "No, Sir, no, impossible—intensely engaged; my orders are positive; the General cannot be seen on any account." In persuasive tones Doctor Griffith said to the officer, "Present, Sir, my humble duty to his Excellency and say that Doctor Griffith waits on him with secret and important intelligence and craves an audience of only five minutes' duration." When General Washington learned that the reverend doctor was so very anxious for an interview at that unseasonable hour, he directed that he be admitted. The conference was very brief, but it was said at the time that Doctor Griffith warned the commander-in-chief of the probable conduct of General Lee on the morrow from information which had come to him from trusted friends and patriots. He did not mention the names of those who had given him this information, but he begged the general to be on his guard the next day against the bad conduct of those on whose military skill he was obliged to depend for the execution of his orders. Doctor Griffith left a deep impression on the commander-in-chief and the next day proved that the warning was timely.[4]

[4] Doctor David Griffith was the surgeon of the Third regiment of the Virginia line and he also acted as chaplain of General Weedon's brigade. In after years he was the pastor of Christ Church, in which General Washington worshipped in Alexandria. He died in the city of Philadelphia on August 3, 1789, and was buried the next day in Christ Churchyard in that city, having lived a life of ardent piety, great learning and most exalted patriotism.

CHAPTER XII

THAT portion of the old county of Monmouth on which the battle was fought is a somewhat elevated table land about one hundred and seventy feet above the ocean. In the northeastern part of the county are the highlands of the Navesink. The village of Middletown is situated on the highest ground with the most uneven surface around it of any land in that portion of the State. That part of the county near Sandy Hook and Middletown was infested with Tories during the Revolutionary period and it was the great objective point in New Jersey for forage parties to plunder the inhabitants and make off across the harbor in safety to New York.

The village of Monmouth Court House or Freehold[1] was situated nearly in the central portion of the county. In the year 1778 it contained about forty houses. The two most prominent buildings in the village were the court house, on what is now Main Street, and the old English church still standing, in front of the station of the Pennsylvania Railroad on Throckmorton Street. Besides these public buildings the village had a blacksmith shop, a wheelwright's shop, two taverns, two school-houses, three stores and about thirty dwelling houses.

Between Monmouth Court House and Englishtown the main roadway of the county passed over three ravines or morasses and near the old Tennent Church and graveyard.[2]

---

[1] "In old times when Freehold is spoken of the township is generally meant. The present town of Freehold had no existence until 1715 when the court house was built here, and even then and down until the Revolutionary war Freehold village was called the Monmouth Court House."—James S. Yard in his *Old Times in Old Monmouth*, p. 248.

[2] This church, erected in the year 1751, was named after the great but eccentric preacher, William Tennent who, for many years had been a great power for good in the church and in the community. He died in 1777, the year previous to the battle and so was not a witness to the conflict around his own dwelling and near the edifice which had resounded

A stream, now called Wemrock Brook winds across the battle-field, runs through the west ravine and branches off toward Hartshorne's Pond.

Much of the ground in the year 1778 was covered with dense woods, some of it with thick briars and heavy underbrush, and a part of it was open and in fine cultivation. The soil itself, the very best in the State for farming purposes, was, in the month of June, fully covered with the promise of an abundant harvest.

In a critical study of the Battle of Monmouth the historian and the reader must give great care to the exact positions of the various bridges, causeways, roads, defiles, hills, morasses, and ravines. It is at times very perplexing to localize all these features of the battle-field with any certainty. The topography of the ground has undergone and is now undergoing such changes that it is often quite difficult to ascertain the various points referred to by participants in the battle. Scarcely a single definite name is given in history to any of the various localities.

Also, there is another hindrance to the careful study of this important engagement. General Lee seems to have assigned and reassigned his general officers to different detachments from the ones they commanded in the march from Valley Forge across New Jersey. For instance, General Wayne first had command of the First and Second brigades of Pennsylvania Continentals, and Conway's brigade, constituting Mifflin's Second Division; it is often called his detachment. Afterward he was assigned to another detachment, consisting of two brigades, and still later, to three regiments of selected troops. General Scott was in the field in person, but he did not take charge of his own brigade of Virginians. Most of them were in the detachment of Colonel William Grayson. Writers on the battle often confound General Scott's brigade with Scott's detachment. Brigadier-General Varnum was not present in

with the tones of his matchless eloquence. He was buried under the central aisle of this historic building. [see frontispiece.]

Monmouth Court House
FROM THE PAINTING BY MRS. CARRIE A. SWIFT, OF FREEHOLD, N.J.

the fight, yet his name, associated so closely with his brigade, leads many map-makers, as well as writers, to speak of and note him as at certain places in person. Colonel John Durkee, and, later, Lieutenant-Colonel Jeremiah Olney commanded Varnum's Rhode Island brigade.

On the eve of the battle it is well to note the exact force which the American chieftain could bring on the fighting line. From a return dated on the day of the battle, we find that under General Washington's immediate command were 665 commissioned officers and 7,159 enlisted men, in all 7,824 soldiers. Add to this 6,000 men under General Lee, and we have an active force of more than 13,000 men.

It is somewhat difficult to determine the exact available strength of General Lee's division at this time. No return of the number of troops in this division was ever filed in the War Office and Lieutenant-Colonel Robert H. Harrison, General Washington's military secretary, says that no report thereof was made by General Lee. Lee himself said that he had thought he had 4,100 men, but afterward discovered he had considerably less. Lieutenant-Colonel John Brooks, Lee's adjutant-general, who must be considered good authority, makes this statement of the force:

Brigadier-General Scott's detachment,	1440 men,
Brigadier-General Wayne's detachment,	1000 men,
Brigadier-General Maxwell's brigade,	900 men,
Brigadier-General Varnum's brigade, between 300 and	350 men,
Brigadier-General Scott's brigade, less than	300 men,
Colonel Jackson's detachment,	200 men.

This statement would make—say about 4,190 men. He quoted General Maxwell as authority for his own brigade and Lieutenant-Colonel Olney for General Varnum's brigade. General Wayne corrected this list by making Maxwell's brigade 1,000 men, Varnum's brigade 600 men, Scott's own brigade, which included also a small detachment from General Woodford's brigade, 600 men, Butler's and Jackson's regiments 400 men, and, with the men connected with the twelve pieces of artillery and the little squad of light horse, in all about 5,000 men. Lieutenant-Colonel Laurens, an aide to General Washington, considered the division to be 5,000 men, and Lieutenant-Colonel Alexander Hamilton, another of his aides, stated them to be 5,000 rank and file, with Colonel Morgan's 600 riflemen and General Dickinson's 800 militia subject to his orders for cooperation. Lieutenant-Colonel Harrison, just mentioned (and he had such knowledge as would make him correct), thought Lee's forces amounted to 5,000 men exclusive of the corps under Colonel Morgan. Certainly, taking Lieutenant-Colonel Brook's statement, virtually General Lee's idea, if we include Colonel Morgan's riflemen and General Dickinson's militia, both of which would have responded to orders intelligently issued, General Lee had nearly 6,000 men whom he could have brought into action, and these men were fully equal numerically to the force which Sir Henry Clinton could bring to bear offensively against him,—exclusive of the Hessian contingent guarding the baggage.

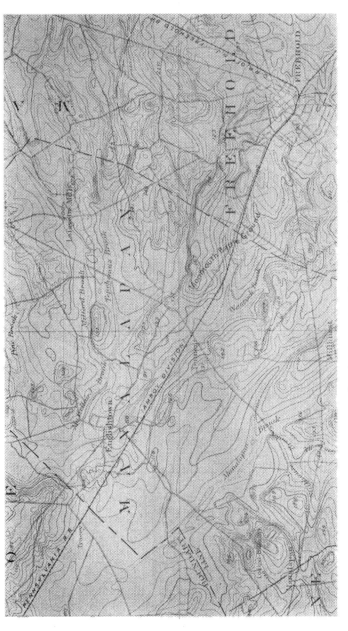

Map Showing Monmouth Battle Ground

CHAPTER XIII

IT was about three o'clock in the morning of June 28 when Colonel William Grayson with his Virginia Continental regiment was ordered by General Lee to assume command, as senior officer, of a detachment from General Scott's own brigade and General Varnum's brigade, with four pieces of artillery under Lieutenant-Colonel Eleazer Oswald of the Second regiment Continental artillery, amounting in all to 600 men, and prepare to march without delay. His men immediately broke camp on the heights back of Englishtown, leaving behind their packs and many of them their coats, and Colonel Grayson reported himself to General Lee for further orders. He was then directed to proceed toward Monmouth Court House by way of Englishtown and General Lee told him that he would meet him at the latter village. It was just six o'clock when this advance detachment entered the little town and Colonel Grayson rode off to find General Lee. He was there, as he had promised, and he directed Colonel Grayson to advance on the old road by way of the meeting-house toward the court house and to keep him constantly informed of his march and what he learned of the movements of the foe. General Lee's adjutant-general, Lieutenant-Colonel John Brooks, at this time handed Colonel Grayson a copy of so much of Lieutenant-Colonel Hamilton's letter of the previous day as directed Lee, by Washington's order, to detach a "party of observation" as a check to a possible night attack. At that hour it could hardly be called even a formal compliance with General Washington's instructions. It was too late then to take position against an assaulting column at night, for the morning had dawned and the British, without thought of an encounter with General Lee's division, were just awaking in the fierce sunlight of a sultry Sabbath morning. But in this way General Lee selected Colonel Grayson's detachment as the party which General Washington desired to march toward the enemy at least five hours previous. This was the way he obeyed the first order of the day.

Unfortunately Colonel Grayson was detained some considerable time at Englishtown waiting for a suitable guide, but one was at last furnished him in the person of Brigadier-General David Forman of the New Jersey militia. This gallant officer had greatly distinguished himself at the Battle of Germantown and he was the chosen leader of the patriot bands in Monmouth County, which had all they could do to protect their homes during the long war from the incendiary attacks and murderous assaults of the pine robbers and armed Tory refugees of the New Jersey coast.

At half-past four in the morning General Dickinson, ever vigilant and active, who had been watching all night in the woods, sent one of his staff officers to General Washington and to General Lee, to inform them that the enemy were in motion. This information was correct. The forward movement was the one which Lieutenant-General Knyphausen had received orders from Sir Henry Clinton to make at daylight on Sunday morning. It was of the greatest importance to the British Army that the baggage train which Knyphausen guarded should be pushed on beyond the ridges on the Middletown road at the very earliest moment. This message came into the hands of General Lee just at five o'clock and was in accordance with the instructions which General Dickinson had received the previous evening from General Lee, through Captain Mercer, to inform him of the first movement of the British toward Middletown, as he proposed to make an immediate attack. Captain Mercer had impressed the idea on the mind of General Dickinson that it was of vital importance that his information should be perfectly authentic and promptly transmitted, that Lee would depend upon receiving it and that the result of this after movements would be governed strictly by what he heard from him. General Dickinson had replied to Captain Mercer that General Lee might be assured his Jerseymen would bring him the best and most reliable facts and that he should have the information at the earliest possible moment.

Although orders were issued at five o'clock to be ready to march it was not until seven o'clock that General Lee's division was fairly started on the road to meet the enemy. They left in their camp the sick, the lame, and all those who appeared to be worn out with the marching hitherto, as well as some soldiers in charge of the baggage, in all about four or five hundred men. At seven o'clock General Wayne's detachment, General Scott's detachment, General Maxwell's brigade and Colonel Jackson's detachment marched in the order thus given. Receiving his order at five o'clock to be in readiness to march, General Maxwell reported himself ready very soon thereafter to General Lee in person. Lee was greatly surprised that he had not started and told him he must now take the rear of the column. Immediately returning to his brigade he gave the order to march, filed out into the main road and found himself and his command even then in advance of both General Wayne's and General Scott's detachments, contrary to his instructions. Colonel Jackson's detachment, following after Scott's detachment, continued in their rear, instead of behind Maxwell's men as they had been ordered.

It may be noted here that General Lee was, as he confessed, almost an utter stranger to the names and faces of the commanding officers of the respective corps, and that he did not know the designations of his command as they marched off to do battle under his generalship.

As Colonel Grayson's detachment was leaving Englishtown, Captain Evan Edwards of General Lee's staff came into the village and reported that the enemy had disappeared. After marching a little over two miles General

Lee, through an aide, had ordered Colonel Grayson to move cautiously, but soon after, Captain Edwards came up and directed a more rapid advance. This, of course, was in compliance with the report Edwards had just brought in. Grayson's detachment had passed the old meeting-house, crossed the bridge at the west ravine[1] and was ascending the hill beyond when the six light horse-men who accompanied him, a little distance in front, espied General Dickinson and his New Jersey militia engaged in a little skirmish with the enemy.

Just before this skirmish with the British troops General Dickinson had sent his aide to General Washington, as we have already noticed, to inform him that the enemy had left their camp ground and had commenced their march toward Middletown. On the way to General Washington the aide had given this intelligence to General Lee. Washington immediately ordered all the troops with him—called by him the main body of the army[2]—to march by the same

[1] General Carrington in his work on the *Battles of the American Revolution* speaks of the west, middle and east ravines. He is entirely correct and exceedingly explicit in this description. The same titles will be used in this work to designate these ravines.

[2] "Field Return of Troops under the immediate command of his Excellency Gen'l Washington.

"Ponolopon [Manalapan] Bridge
June 28, '78

BRIGADES.	COLONELS.	LIEUT. COLONELS.	MAJORS.	CAPTAINS.	SUB-ALTERNS.	SERGEANTS.	RANK & FILE PRESENT FIT FOR ACTION.
Woodford		3	2	9	30	46	385
North Carolina	2	2	1	7	16	28	369
Poor		3	2	16	37	57	639
Huntington	2	2	3	14	22	80	509
1st Maryland	2	1	2	9	47	72	657
2nd Maryland	2	2	2	9	17	41	529
Muhlenberg	2	4	2	13	35	80	575
Weedon	3	2	3	15	56	59	449
1st Pennsylvania	3	3	2	9	14	46	352
2nd Pennsylv[a]	2	2	1	10	20	51	401
3rd Pennsylv[a]		3	4	10	22	56	343
Glover	3	3	1	19	37	61	512
Larnade	1	1	2	12	21	42	294
Patterson	2	2	2	19	34	69	357
Total	24	33	29	171	408	788	6,371

"ENDORSED—Field Return 28th June 1778   "ALEX[R] SCAMMELL,
"Exclusive of detachment under General Lee &c."   "Adj't Gen'l

road as had been travelled by Colonel Grayson's advance detachment. He also sent word by his aide, Lieutenant-Colonel Richard K. Meade, to direct General Lee to relieve his men of their packs and blankets, but this had already been done by Lee's order. Washington also told Lieutenant-Colonel Meade to say to General Lee in the most distinct manner that he "desired he would bring on an engagement, or attack the enemy as soon as possible, unless some very powerful circumstance forbid it, and that he would soon be up to his aid."[3] This order, it will be noticed, was not peremptory. It was quite evident to Meade, however, that General Washington was anxious to bring on a general engagement and that he intended to support General Lee's division with all his force as soon as General Clinton developed his plans for the battle.

The discretion which General Washington gave General Lee in the order, Lee afterwards took advantage of, and although no one but himself saw any "powerful reasons" against making an attack, he could plead that discretionary power, which he afterwards did, as an excuse for his conduct.

Lieutenant-Colonel Meade mounted his horse and rode toward Englishtown. He passed through the village, but General Lee had left there soon after eight o'clock. At last Meade found him not quite a mile distant on the road toward the meeting-house. Here he learned that Lee had obtained new information through Captain Benjamin Walker, aide to Major-General the Baron von Steuben, who had informed him that the British had not yet marched. Von Steuben, it is believed, had seen only the rear guard of the enemy and had concluded that the main body had not yet started as previously reported by General Dickinson. This information, however, caused General Lee to halt his command. With some hesitation, now that the situation had apparently changed, Colonel

---

[3] From Meade's testimony at Lee's court-martial, p. 11.

Meade gave the orders with which General Washington had intrusted him. Lee replied that he "would endeavour to answer his intentions."[4] At the same time General Lee was very angry because the information he was receiving was so contradictory. The next moment, however, fearing that he was pushing Colonel Grayson's men too hastily into great danger he sent back for General Wayne, gave him a few timely instructions and, relieving him from his own detachment, directed him to gallop up to the advance guard, the post of honor, and take command.

There was a delay at this point of nearly half an hour and during this time General Dickinson's militia was engaged in annoying the British pickets. This little skirmish of the militia of New Jersey was the very opening scene in the Monmouth battle. These farmer boys were then engaged in harassing the outposts of the Fortieth regiment of British foot and a detachment of the Seventeenth regiment of British light dragoons, who were attempting to conceal and cover the withdrawal of the army. It was a daring act for these undisciplined yeomen to pit themselves for one moment against the very best troops of Britain. But for some time they sent irregular volleys among the red-coats. In the end, however, they were compelled to give way and General Dickinson, seeing Colonel Grayson's detachment approaching, sent word to him to support his retreating column. Grayson instantly complied, taking his own Virginia regiment forward with quick step, and Lieutenant-Colonel Oswald followed with one of his field-pieces. When Colonel Grayson reached the top of the hill the enemy, no doubt apprised of a well-disciplined force approaching, had fled and were even then out of sight. This was shortly after eight o'clock and General Lee was just leaving Englishtown. Captain Edwards came up to Grayson's detachment during Lee's absence and told Colonel Durkee, the senior officer, to post his troops in the

---

[4] Lee's defence at his court-martial, p. 201.

best way possible on an eminence nearby until he could inform General Lee what was occurring at that point. Colonel Durkee did so and meeting General Lee with General Wayne on the highway they all rode to the west ravine together. In the meantime, Colonel Grayson returned to the main road and General Dickinson accompanied him. Upon reaching that point, still very high ground, they met General Lee and that part of his division which had just been witness to the closing scene of Dickinson's skirmish. On the ride down the hill General Dickinson had expressed the opinion to Colonel Grayson that the enemy would send two columns after General Lee's division, one on the right and the other on the left flank, and that he had better not advance farther until he informed himself fully of the present situation of the British troops. He thought it well for himself to "shuffle it out with his militia"[5] on the left and annoy them as much as possible. He also told General Lee when they joined him half an hour afterward what he thought of the situation.

Annoyed, as he said, by false alarms and contradictory intelligence, General Lee accosted General Dickinson with considerable warmth, as being the first cause of his mental confusion. The same kind of information was still coming to Lee every moment, first that the enemy were retreating, then that they were on the American flank, and then that they were about to attack the advance line. General Lee told General Dickinson that, being a Jerseyman, he had been told to look to him for the most reliable intelligence and he would like to know why and by what means such uncertain information was brought to him. General Dickinson, naturally irritated by Lee's tone and manner, replied with equal spirit, that his advices were frequent and perfectly consistent and he asserted confidently that the enemy were still near the Monmouth Court House. Gen-

---

[5] Grayson's testimony at Lee's court-martial, p. 41.

eral Dickinson closed the conversation by saying, "General Lee, you may believe or not, but if you march your party beyond the ravine now in your rear, which has only one passage over it, you are in a perilous situation."[6]

General Dickinson made a slight mistake here. He thought he had struck the advance party of the British Army returning to engage the Americans, whereas it was only one of their flanking parties. Captain Lord William Cathcart had brought an order to Lieutenant-Colonel Simcoe to "take his Huzzars and try to cut off a reconnoitreing party of the enemy (supposed to be M. Fayette) who was upon a bald hill not far from his left." In this skirmish, although of brief duration, two huzzars and three men of the light infantry battalion were wounded. One of the former died afterward in the hospital, the English church, in the village. Captain Philip Snook of the First Hunterdon County regiment, and Captain Moses Estey of the Fourth Hunterdon County regiment, New Jersey militia, also received severe wounds.

It must be noted here that the right and left of the retreating British became the left and right flanks of the same troops as they faced toward the American advance and afterward marched in pursuit of the troops of General Lee falling back to another position.

While on the march with the main body of General Lee's division, General Maxwell determined to take the position in line to which he had been assigned in orders and he halted his brigade for a few moments to allow General Wayne's detachment and General Scott's detachment to pass him. General Wayne did so and General Scott had just saluted General Maxwell when Captain Mercer dashed up and directed Maxwell to march his brigade by the Covenhoven road toward Craig's Mills, now called Baker's Mills,[7] at which point Captain Mercer told him he would strike a direct road leading to Mon-

[6] Lee's defence at his court-martial, p. 205.
[7] John Craig's mill was near his house. See p. 155.

mouth Court House, and to remain near the forks of the road until further orders were sent him. Captain Mercer gave General Maxwell a rude tracing on paper which mapped out the roads in that direction as nearly as he had been able to ascertain them. This sketch General Maxwell took with him. The order which he had received from General Lee by the hands of Captain Mercer was in consequence of the information which Lee had received from General Dickinson's scouts, who reported that the enemy were still at Monmouth Court House and that it was possible that they might endeavor to come in on the American rear at Englishtown by the upper road. General Maxwell immediately complied with General Lee's orders and marched half a mile up the road where he was halted by Lieutenant-Colonel Meade, one of General Washington's aides, who, as a favor to General Lee, carried an order to General Maxwell to march his brigade back and take his position again in the column. General Maxwell brought his command back to the old road and waited a long time at the junction of the roads near the meeting-house before the detachments of General Wayne and of General Scott came up and passed him. As soon, however, as this was done, he again took position on the left of the column. By this time Colonel Jackson's detachment, as will hereafter be seen, had been ordered by General Lee (General Wayne's aide, Captain Benjamin Fishbourne conveying the order), to take position on the extreme advance, and General Lafayette had received a written order from General Lee by Captain Mercer, to put himself at the head of Wayne's and Scott's detachments.

Two long halts had already been made between Englishtown and the meeting-house, the first consuming nearly an hour and the second quite half an hour. This delay in advancing toward the enemy was very damaging to any plans which General Washington had ordered General Lee to execute. A month after these events and in reference to these halts General Lee said, "The first halt I made, in consequence of the advice I received from General Dickinson of the whole force being ranged in battalia, was censurable. I must do his Excellency the justice to declare, that he never gave me, directly or indirectly, such orders—they would have been unworthy of a man many thousand degrees his inferior in understanding."[8]

While General Maxwell was making the little diversion with his brigade which has just been noticed, a considerable body of men was observed on the left of the column and somewhat to the rear and report flew along the line that this was a party of the enemy. But the alarm was soon over when Colonel Frederick Frelinghuysen emerged from an orchard with his own battalion of Somerset County militia and the Middlesex County militia regiments of Colonels Henry Van Dike and John Webster. As soon as General Lee became aware that they were patriot troops he despatched them on the same detour upon which he had sent General Maxwell's men and had them posted on a high hill looking toward Craig's Mills. In this way Maxwell was relieved from this duty.

Still, as General Lee remained near the bridge over the west ravine, the only place which General Dickinson told him was passable for artillery, all kinds of information was brought him by Monmouth farmers and other patriotic men who were anxious to do some service to the cause. But their opinions were unmilitary and although often correct, as has since appeared, were not technically stated and so were misunderstood. Why did not General Lee even then send out officers on whom he could rely to obtain certain facts that he needed, regardless of Dickinson or of zealous countrymen, and in this way partly repair his neglect of the past twenty-four hours? To make any effective movements at this time he needed the most authentic information.

General Wayne was now in command of General Scott's

[8] Lee's defence at his court-martial, p. 201.

own brigade, not his detachment, and also General Varnum's brigade, the force which up to this time had been in charge of Colonel Grayson as senior officer. When General Wayne assumed direct charge of these troops one brigade was on each side of the bridge spanning the west ravine.

But a short distance behind them was the detachment formerly commanded by General Wayne and the detachment now commanded by General Scott. This force was in charge of General Lafayette. Although he said he considered himself a volunteer, so anxious was he to meet the British grenadiers in battle, that General Lee looked to him during the day to execute one of his most important movements. General Lafayette had this day taken a hurried breakfast at the house of Joseph Story, two miles from Englishtown, and had hastened up to this advance column with the eager desire to take a prominent part in the battle he saw was impending.

About this time General Lee and General Wayne ascended the hill on the east of the ravine for the purpose of reconnoitering the enemy, if possible.

An order was soon after issued by General Lee, and carried by Captain David Lennox, Wayne's aide-de-camp, who was accompanied by Captain John Mercer, Lee's own aide, directing Colonel Richard Butler, of the Ninth Pennsylvania Continental regiment, to march this splendid organization to the extreme right, and ordering Colonel Henry Jackson's detachment, which consisted of his own regiment and Lee's regiment of Continental infantry, Lieutenant-Colonel William S. Smith commanding, on the extreme rear of Lee's column, to join Colonel Butler's force. While Colonel Butler's command was coming with rapid step to the right of the division the Colonel rode forward to meet General Lee and General Wayne. He was instructed by them to keep his party as much concealed as possible, and General Wayne directed him to attack the British wherever he happened to meet them.

With a sergeant's guard in front, and as many soldiers on each flank a little in advance, and marching the right of platoons by files, Colonel Butler led his men directly toward the British, posted at the court house. Seeing him start off with these tactics General Lee changed the order and directed him to march from the center by files. In this way they advanced some distance, but finding it inconvenient, Butler returned to his own assignment of marching order. They marched on the road to Forman's Mills, passed the pond now known as Hartshorne's pond[9] and the mill there, and came out in the elder William Wikoff's fields. There was much wooded country on the left of the roadway but on the right there appeared considerable cleared ground. Colonel Butler was obliged then to skirt the left road as closely as possible.

Colonel Jackson's detachment, being furnished with a guide, started on what was afterwards thought too rapid a march for so warm a day to join Colonel Butler on the advance. In this way they marched what seemed to General Wayne and Colonel Jackson about four miles until they saw the court house in the distance and the enemy near it. This was just at the time when the main body of Sir Henry Clinton's army was passing out of sight toward Middletown, with their left just beyond the Allentown road. General Lee, who had then come up to Butler's detachment, ordered General Wayne's advance troops to form in front of a wood while he took observation of the enemy. Having done this, he ordered the whole of the advance guard to move forward and at the same time Colonel Butler and his party were detached from the advance and moved more to the left, out of direct sight of Colonel Jackson's men.

[9] Edmund Williams of Shrewsbury bought this grist mill and land adjacent to the pond in 1777 and owned it until 1801.

CHAPTER XIV

SIR Henry Clinton was impressed with the idea that General Washington and the American Army, which he thought numbered 20,000 men, did not desire to fight his brave grenadiers and fierce Hessian auxiliaries, but that the plunder of his army stores and the capture of his baggage train was the grand object of their rapid march in the past forty-eight hours.

In his manuscript notes Clinton says, "Washington, so little desirous does he seem to have been of risking a general action, had passed the South river and put three or four of its marshy, boggy branches between his army and that of the British."

The British Army had passed a night without alarm and General Knyphausen moved his division of Hessians and loyalists, with General Grant's brigade, which had the special charge of the stores, the bat-horses, the wheel carriages, and the personal baggage, soon after four o'clock in the morning of Sunday. The British camp around the court house was noisy that Sabbath morning with the shouts of the team drivers, the confusion incident to getting the boisterous camp followers on the march at so early an hour and the stern commands of the German officers as they drove their heavily-laden men into line. When this train was fully on the march it extended over more than eight miles. Sir Henry Clinton gave his order at eight o'clock for the rest of his command, except a small covering party, to follow by the route taken by General Knyphausen and try to gain the higher ground near Middletown sixteen miles distant, by way of "a plain" as Clinton said, "near three miles in length and about one mile in breadth." The location of this plain is now somewhat obscure, but it must be the ground between what we know as the east ravine and Briar Hill.[1] He had with him the very flower of the soldiery of the crown in the division under the immediate control of Lieutenant-General the Earl Cornwallis. In this division were the Third, Fourth and Fifth brigades, British foot, the First and Second battalions of British grenadiers, the Hessian grenadiers, the British foot guards, the First battalion light infantry and the Sixteenth regiment of light dragoons. Although in the order of the previous day they were included among those who were to join Knyphausen's division, it appears that the Second battalion light infantry and the Queen's rangers were also with Cornwallis' division during the day of June 28.

Sir Henry Clinton well understood his position. General Lee, as it appears, had not posted himself at all about the topography of the country, but Clinton knew what ground, made up of ravines and marshes, lay between him and his foe. He had his spies and scouts at work on Saturday and the country around the court house was fully mapped out for his information. Late the previous night and early in the morning of June 28 he had learned the proximity of Washington's entire army and began to think that vigorous exertions were necessary, but still he believed that General Washington "after having always hitherto so studiously avoided a general action would not now give in to it against every dictate of policy." He could only suppose that his views were directed against his baggage. He says that he knew Washington had come up with his whole army, estimated at about 20,000 men, with which was also the northern division under General Gates. It seems somewhat strange to us today that Clinton was so misled as to suppose that so large a force as he imagined it simply wished to sack the baggage and plunder the provision train, rather than to strike a strong blow for freedom. With Clinton's mind clearly astray as to the intention of the Americans, with his attention fully concentrated in

[1] About two miles east of the court house.

great anxiety upon the safety of his train in Knyphausen's division, and upon this alone, what a happy opportunity presented itself for a bold, sharp attack, such as General Washington desired, upon the long extended column of British troops!

In consequence of the contradictory reports that reached General Lee, the brigade named after General Varnum but under command of Colonel John Durkee of the Fourth Connecticut regiment and the brigade of General Scott, passed and repassed the bridge at the west ravine several times. This bridge is often spoken of in sketches of the battle as the "long causeway" and is near the late residence of John I. Conover. General Lee remarked afterward, in reference to these movements at the bridge, that he was "teased, mortified and chagrined" by these "little marches and counter-marches, from one hill to another, over the ravine as it gave an awkward appearance to our first manoeuvres."[2] When General Lafayette came up with his detachments to the bridge where General Lee was, Lee determined after a brief conversation with him, that he would act regardless of alarms and the strange intelligence he had been receiving from countrymen that heavy columns of the enemy were advancing on the right and then that they had not marched at all, that the main body of the foe had marched northward and that those left behind at the court house were merely a covering party. General Lee told one of these self-appointed couriers to go about his business and not bring him any such reports. Lee then decided to go forward and find the enemy, see for himself what their situation really was, and govern himself accordingly. Lieutenant-Colonel John Laurens, of Washington's staff, who had been reconnoitering with some light horse, and Lieutenant-Colonel the Marquis Francis de Malmedy, General Lee's aide-de-camp, gave him some trusty intelligence just at this time and he sent out some of his staff to urge on the immediate advance of his division.

[2] Lee's defence at his court-martial, p. 204.

Colonel Grayson's regiment and Lieutenant-Colonel Oswald's battery again assumed their positions in the marching column. The route was then eastward from the west ravine, marching in platoons of sub-divisions, about two miles without making a single halt, crossing on the way a piece of low ground, covered with much thicket. This was what will be called herein the "middle ravine." Every effort was made in this march to keep as concealed as possible. General Lee instructed Lieutenant-Colonel Oswald to keep his guns in the woods and as much out of sight as he could, because he did not yet wish the enemy to know that he had any artillery. This he was able to do and having pulled down some fence he was in good position to sight his two pieces of artillery at the foe.

When General Lee's troops arrived at the edge of the open fields near and in sight of the court house, they were halted and began to prepare for an attack. A deep morass which we will call the "east ravine" began on the open ground near the court house and extended some distance to a heavy wood on the extreme left of the American advance. This ravine is not now as clearly defined as it was in the Revolutionary period. General Lee was not at all aware of this dangerous ravine, and his guides had not thought to tell him of it. General Knox first informed him of its existence, and Lee simply remarked, "that he was not sufficiently informed of the ground before that he came on it, and that the morass was a disagreeable circumstance but that he would endeavour to make the best of it."[3] The enemy were clearly to be seen near the court house and from appearances they consisted of some light dragoons with several detachments of foot soldiers supporting them. It was certainly not the main body of the British Army and could only be considered to be a covering party to the main column and to the baggage train which was known to be on the advance toward the coast. The British, both cavalry and infantry, did not appear to be arranged in

[3] Knox's testimony at Lee's court martial, p. 179.

very soldierly order and this fact rather astonished the American officers at first sight. However, they moved toward the left as if to make a dash at General Lee's advance troops.

General Lee and General Wayne passed out some distance toward the front and carefully reconnoitered the situation. General Lee was at this time in considerable personal danger, but to all who saw him he appeared cool, self-possessed and brave.

An immediate order was then sent to Colonel Richard Butler, who had halted with his Ninth Pennsylvania regiment at the cross-road which led from the court house to Amboy, to move forward and attack the enemy. He prepared to obey with great alacrity notwithstanding the heat was becoming intense and his men were suffering greatly. Colonel Grayson's detachment with Patton's regiment Continental infantry, Lieutenant-Colonel John Parke commanding, were then marched on toward Colonel Butler's line as a supporting force. When they reached his position the skirmishing had already begun. On being asked by General Lee how many men General Wayne's new command would consist of Captain Mercer replied, about 550 soldiers. General Lee thought this was not enough. Colonel Henry Jackson's detachment would have been ordered to accompany Colonel Butler's command, instead of Lieutenant-Colonel Parke's regiment, had they not been short of cartridges, having only fourteen rounds per man. The sergeants of Colonel Jackson's detachment under the charge of one of General Lee's staff officers were ordered to collect a cartridge each from the rest of the troops near them and so make up the deficiency. This took some time, and Colonel Jackson, therefore, did not go instantly forward to Butler's new position. General Wayne then ordered him to support Lieutenant-Colonel Oswald's two guns which were pushed to the front in the woods on the left. This was promptly accomplished. It was difficult to move artillery and ammunition wagons over the rough and miry road, but Oswald succeeded at last in getting his guns in a good position. While Oswald was doing this and before Colonel Jackson's men had arrived he was unsupported in his advance by any infantry and was so uneasy about it that he begged Lieutenant-Colonel Laurens to apply to General Lee in his name for troops to cover his battery. Before this could be done, Jackson's men appeared.

General Lee noticed a regiment in the distance (probably Butler's), and supposing it was the enemy, detached Lieutenant-Colonel Jeremiah Olney, Second Rhode Island regiment of General Varnum's brigade, to go out and attack them. They soon discovered the mistake and the regiment was then ordered by General Lee to the support of Lieutenant-Colonel Oswald's battery according to the request conveyed by Laurens. In the attempt to secure the position several men were killed and wounded by the shot from the British batteries. Colonel John Durkee, Fourth Connecticut regiment, who commanded Varnum's brigade, was severely injured in his right arm so that he lost the use of it entirely. His suffering was so great that he was obliged to turn over the brigade to Lieutenant-Colonel Jeremiah Olney of the Second Rhode Island regiment. Major Simeon Thayer of the Second Rhode Island regiment lost an eye by the windage of a cannon-ball and Second Lieutenant Nathan Weeks of the same regiment was killed.

General Lee was now very confident that his movements had been correctly made and that the capture of the British party would soon be accomplished. He told Lieutenant-Colonel Jeremiah Gilman of the First New Hampshire regiment to inform General Washington that he was in hopes of cutting off all the rear guard of the enemy. This confident message Gilman delivered to the commander-in-chief about a mile west of the meeting-house and General Washington, of course, received the impression that all was going well at the front.

The Queen's rangers, a partizan corps organized in
America for the British Army and commanded by the gallant Lieutenant-Colonel John Graves Simcoe, had again
formed in line on the northwest side of the open field and
between the American troops and the court house building.
They were supported by the Sixteenth regiment, light dragoons, which formed part of the rear guard of the army.
This position was near Hartshorne's pond a short distance from the elder Mr. Wikoff's house. The light horse
of the American troops, being very few in number, were
kept concealed for the present in the woods at the rear,
while the foot soldiers were wheeled to the right, so as to
face the British line. The infantry detachments of the
enemy were somewhat to the rear of the rangers and to
General Wayne they hardly appeared within fair supporting distance. At a glance Wayne supposed the dragoons
to be about three hundred in number and that there were
fully twice as many infantry troops. When Colonel Butler's regiment passed well up on the right of General
Lee's force, about a quarter of a mile in column from the
center, they received a scattering discharge from the firearms of the two flank companies of the rangers. A file of
Butler's men fired a terrific volley in return, although they
had been instructed to reserve their fire, and then they
attempted to push rapidly forward. This fire of the Ninth
Pennsylvania regiment caused the severe wounding of
eight of the Queen's rangers, among whom was their commander himself, who received a musket-ball wound in his
arm; his horse was injured, frightened and ran away with
him.[4] After this the dragoons gave way and hurried
through the village of Freehold "in great disorder and
confusion," as General Wayne considered, but, as Colonel
Butler thought, in "regular order." Colonel Butler's men
followed them to a point near an orchard on the left of

[4] The Monmouth Battle Monument in the Borough of Freehold is erected
on ground which was the theater of this little skirmish at the opening of
the battle.

the roadway toward the court house. General Wayne was informed by Captain Thomas Langhorne Byles, Third Pennsylvania battalion, who had been watching the British from close quarters, of the exact position and surroundings of the rangers and he expressed the opinion that if Wayne or General Lee wished to make a bold attack on the foe, now was the time to do it. Butler's men were then posted in a clump of woods a little space to the left of the retreating enemy. In taking this new position, with some artillery and detachments of infantry on their flanks, the movement, so near the British, was performed in good order and in correct military style.

As soon as General Wayne was fully apprized of the result of Colonel Butler's advance, he sent Captain David Lennox of his staff to inform General Lee that the British had fallen back and then halted, and that he desired more troops to be sent to the front. When General Lee was informed of what had happened he merely replied to Captain Lennox that it was a customary movement of retreating troops and that General Wayne need pay no very great attention to it. But soon after this General Lee sent Captain Mercer to General Wayne to direct him to advance his command and attack the rear of the enemy and prevent them if possible from retreating to the main body of the army or from obtaining any reinforcement. Colonel Henry Jackson's detachment, strengthened also by Patton's regiment Continental infantry, Lieutenant-Colonel John Parke commanding, had not at this time come up nor had Lieutenant-Colonel Oswald's battery. General Wayne said to Captain Mercer, on giving him the order just referred to, "send me a cannon and I will engage to stop them." The guns he wished and an additional force were at that moment near at hand and soon after the force reported to him.

Colonel Jackson's detachment was again ordered to report to Colonel Butler and Lieutenant-Colonel de Malmedy of General Lee's staff was sent to guide them to the part of the field where he was posted. It seemed to Colonel Jackson quite a mile and a half to the left in front, but could hardly have been much more than half that distance. Colonel Jackson's command took a very quick step and soon came within one hundred yards of Colonel Butler's men just as General Wayne directed him to march his gallant force out of the edge of the wood, through a small orchard to an open plain where the enemy then seemed to be forming. This was some five hundred yards away on Colonel Jackson's right flank. Colonel Jackson then called out to his party with a design to inspire them, "My lads, if there are any of you who have not a mind to go into action, now is the time for you to fall out." Just at this moment a cavalryman rode up in great excitement and begged Colonel Jackson, with many strong expletives, to form his men instantly or they would all be cut to pieces by the British light horse. Jackson's Massachusetts men then wheeled into line and formed, Colonel Butler being also in position about three hundred feet to their left. But the American light horse, a few of which were then protecting each flank of Wayne's detachment, seemed to be the particular object of attack for the Queen's rangers and the light dragoons who, when they saw them, charged violently to within forty yards of Colonel Butler's line. Here they received a severe volley into their ranks, and with a discharge of their horse-pistols they galloped off. After ten minutes' halt at this position both regiments wheeled into divisions under Colonel Butler's orders and marched across the open field, still keeping the same respective distance apart as before. At this very moment (Sir Henry Clinton says it was about ten o'clock in the morning), the Americans could hear the cannonading going on between Oswald and the enemy. Captain Thomas Seward of the Third regiment Continental artillery thought the covering party of the British had ten cannon, one twelve-pounder and nine six-pounders. The British artillery fired a dozen rounds at General Wayne's men as they crossed the open ground and one of the shots took off the arm of one of Jackson's men. Colonel Butler then took his regiment into a wood near by and Colonel Jackson marched his detachment obliquely to the left under cover of the same piece of woods. This brought some of the men on the low ground of the east ravine, the left flank in a morass and the right under a hill. At this time Colonel Grayson's own regiment was posted directly in the rear of Colonel Jackson's detachment. Colonel Butler noticed that the British troops were apparently withdrawing and again he sent word to General Wayne by Captain Byles that it was a good time to strike the enemy. Butler's troops then crossed a small morass, three-quarters of a mile north and east of the court house, and General Wayne, coming up at this time, ordered them to advance and place a piece of artillery on a little hill in their front. This was done. The British gunners had just set fire to a barn in front of their lines, and the burning of this building made a conspicuous object on this part of the battle-field. In descriptions of the battle in after days it served well to locate the various skirmishes.

It was now clearly the plan of General Lee to surround the rear party or covering detachment of the enemy which appeared in his front and apparently removed some distance from the main body. He said that if this was all or nearly all of their rear guard, instead of pushing them too hard and obliging them to fall back on the main body, he would rather press them a little and keep them occupied in front while he himself, with a considerable portion of his force, would seek to find an intermediate space between them and the main portion of the British column, which was unprotected, and thus be able to take the whole of their rear guard prisoners. He felt confident that he could do it. It is quite clear that General Lee wished only to make a slight demonstration and that he never had in mind any direct attack on the British forces. Instruction was then given General Wayne not to push them too impetuously, lest the covering party fall back on the main body, nor to force a portion of the main body to come back to the relief of the covering party, but to affect shyness and diffidence rather than confidence, to keep them amused and make them halt. To have General Wayne attack too precipitately would "subvert that plan and disappoint his intentions."[5] He proposed to manoeuver rather than to fight. While General Wayne made a feint of attacking, Lee intended to have General Varnum's brigade press the enemy on their right flank with General Scott's own brigade as a support, expecting—(it is strange that he expected, since he had kept up no line of couriers)—that Colonel Daniel Morgan's corps would come up somewhere on the American right and press the British on their left flank. General Lee then intended to put himself at the head of the column of troops, with General Scott's detachment in the lead, and marching through a close wood on the left push his force between the two bodies of the British troops and thus capture the whole of their covering party. Could this have been done, he said, "the enemy would have been caught in a forceps." General Lee gave all his orders for these movements as if assured of complete success. He believed at that time that the rear guard of the enemy was but little, if any, more than 1500 men and all British reports show that this was a correct estimate at the time. Had he handled his command promptly, General Lee might have executed his plan successfully. But the parts of his division were not working in harmony and he was trying to carry out his ideas without imparting to any of his subordinates his ulterior designs. This was a very difficult thing to do at that time with men who held opposite views as to what was best to do, and it is not to be wondered that he failed. He had not, withal, the influence over his officers and men that an officer should have who has such an important command in the front of

[5] Edward's testimony at Lee's court-martial, p. 189.

the army. This subtle power must be possessed by a commander who expects to execute with success any plan he may have formed.

General Lee's division was now in position, with its right flank covered by a small wood in front of the village. The right of the British force opposed to Lee's men was at this time at the juncture of the cross-roads leading to Shrewsbury and to Middletown; their left flank, at which point their light horse was concentrated, was extended to the open field close to the village.

In pursuance of the general plan of General Lee, to capture the covering party of the British, Lieutenant-Colonel Oswald was ordered to the front with his guns to fire on the enemy. For a short time he had Colonel Jackson's detachment as a support but this was removed and Lieutenant-Colonel Malmedy reported the fact that Oswald's battery was without cover. As the British light dragoons, which had just received Colonel Butler's fire, were moving off, Oswald sent four or five cannon shot to hurry them along, and then Captain Thomas Wells of the Third regiment of artillery limbered up the pieces while Oswald explored the nature of the east ravine. As soon as this was thoroughly understood, the artillery was passed over a causeway of the ravine into a field of grain, and another cannonade commenced. It was now quite evident that the enemy had brought into action more guns than Oswald commanded and their fire was, therefore, more severe. In this engagement the American battery lost two matrosses[6] killed and several wounded. Two of their horses were also killed and the men were falling by the wayside utterly prostrated by fatigue and the intense heat. By this time one of their guns had become entirely disabled and all the round shot had been expended. On his rear Oswald observed Varnum's brigade and he fell back

[6] *Matross.* Formerly, one of the soldiers in a train of artillery who were next to the gunners, and assisted them in loading, firing, and sponging the guns. They carried firelocks, and marched with the store-wagons as guards and assistants. *Cent. Dict.*—Ed.

under its cover, taking with him his large ammunition wagon, which up to this time had not followed him over the causeway,—it being thought unsafe.

About this time Captain Edwards, who had been off with two light horsemen on a reconnaissance, again reported to General Lee that the enemy were retreating. General David Forman also gave his opinion of the situation of the enemy and offered to guide a column of Lee's troops by a road to the left which would bring them in front of the retreating rear-guard of the British. General Lee said to General Forman in a petulant manner, "I know my business," and did not accept his offer; but Captain Mercer was sent out to explore the road and to see if artillery as well as infantry could move along the road to the left, then concealed from view. He went some distance along the route, saw the place where the neighboring farmers told him two thousand of the British had spent the previous night and had just broken camp and gone toward the village. Captain Mercer thought the road was practicable and so reported. Captain Edwards was then instructed by General Lee to take Varnum's brigade, and two pieces of artillery and guide them around on the right of the enemy. He did so, taking them as far as he had reconnoitered, and then, strange to say, left them, and went over to join General Wayne's command.

General Lee's confidence must have been great when he said to Dr. James McHenry, General Washington's Secretary, "Inform his Excellency that the enemy do not appear to well understand the roads; that the route he was then on cut off two miles; that the rear of the enemy was composed of 1500 or 2000 men; that he expected to fall in with them and had great certainty of cutting them off." He then gave McHenry a hasty idea of the present position of the two forces, described how he himself intended immediately to take a detachment by a short route, and get in between the two bodies of the enemy. "Say also to him," he added, "that the enemy are constantly changing their front, which is a usual thing with those who retreat."[7]

General Lee was nearly correct in his estimate of the force in front of him at that moment. He was fully impressed with the success of his plans and he had imparted his confidence to those around him. One of his aides said to General Lafayette, "The rear guard of the enemy is ours." General Lee also said to the same officer, "My dear Marquis, I think those people are ours."[8] On leaving Colonel Grayson, after giving him some minute directions, Lee also exclaimed with much animation, "By God, I will take them all."[9]

While General Wayne was pushing on in the advance, General Scott, with by far the largest detachment of General Lee's division, was marching toward the court house. When they came within sight of it and of the enemy near it, they moved out of an orchard, crossed the east ravine and halted. General Scott then directed Colonel Joseph Cilley of the First New Hampshire regiment to form his men in line of battle while he went forward with General Wayne to examine the situation. When General Scott returned to his troops, he ordered them to march from right of battalion, recross the ravine and form on the back of it by the side of a hill covered with a dense wood. This was done and Scott's detachment took post on the left of the other troops of the division. He was not able, however, to bring up his artillery to this position. General Lee then formed what he called "a potence" for the better security of his front and flanks. General Wayne did not think, as he examined the appearance of the hostile force in sight, that it could possibly be over 2000 men, and to him and General Scott they seemed to be moving to gain the higher ground beyond, on the line of the Middletown road.

General Maxwell also marched his brigade, with a few

[7] McHenry's testimony at Lee's court-martial, pp. 89-90.
[8] Lafayette's testimony at Lee's court-martial, p. 17.
[9] Grayson's testimony at Lee's court-martial, p. 45.

light horsemen of the New Jersey militia attached to his command, in the same route taken by General Scott's detachment, keeping in the woods as much as possible, which General Lafayette told him was General Lee's wish. About two miles eastward from the meeting-house the brigade turned into a road on the left and at last came out in a large open field in full view of the court house. General Maxwell led his column in person but he received no orders from General Lee to form his brigade at any particular place. It is quite apparent that all the movements of Lee's forces were loosely made and very uncertain. All the morning Maxwell had been following General Scott's lead without any definite or special orders having been given him. On the open ground he halted his brigade five minutes and found that he had a morass, or what was the east ravine, on his right flank and a very dense thicket on his left. General Scott's detachment was but one hundred yards ahead of him and had already formed as General Maxwell saw the enemy approaching on the extreme right of his position. Oswald's guns were firing at the British as General Maxwell formed his line. It was thought by Maxwell that General Scott would move his men to the right and fill up the intervening space between them. Just at this moment he saw General Scott galloping up to see him and to consult about the situation.

While these movements were being made the enemy had formed on an eminence and were preparing to make a dash at the American light horse. They advanced some distance beyond Colonel Butler's line with the design of luring him on to an attack—which proved effective. The Queen's rangers, about 300 men, with about 200 foot soldiers to support them, again made a charge and the American horse gave way. But General Wayne's command, and especially the Ninth Pennsylvania regiment, still efficient, received them with a well-directed, deadly fire, so that the rangers broke and retreated rapidly. General Wayne shouted to his men to encourage them to rush quickly forward and use the bayonet on the Tory troopers. The support which the rangers expected to get from the British foot failed them in this crisis and they fled from Colonel Butler's fire, broke up the line of the enemy's infantry and put the whole rear-guard into much disorder. Colonel Butler's men pursued them about two hundred yards when three or four pieces of the enemy's artillery opened on them again and they were obliged to stop further pursuit. The halt was made in a slight depression, which was covered with underbrush. Here they remained some fifteen minutes, the enemy's artillery all the while firing at them. The British column seemed after this to be bearing toward the American right and to desire to gain possession of some high ground near the court house. At last they succeeded and as each detachment came up on the eminence it halted and formed. General Wayne sent Captain Byles to bring up Varnum's brigade to his support. He also sent Captain Fishbourne to General Lee to beg for more troops to be sent to him. The Captain came up to General Lee about half a mile in the rear of Wayne's advance, but Lee made no response to the request.

Just at this juncture in the action a curious incident occurred. Lieutenant-Colonel David Rhea, Fourth regiment New Jersey Continental line, was some distance away from his command reconnoitering the enemy. A British dragoon caught sight of him and dashed toward him. Colonel Rhea, observing him about fifty yards distant, drew his pistol and took deliberate aim, but missed the dragoon. With drawn sword and mounted on a fine horse the dragoon dashed directly toward him and the Colonel was compelled to use spurs to his steed and fly abruptly. A barn was in the direct line of his retreat and the Colonel rode around it, then through its open doors and back to his regiment for shelter. As the trooper left the barn a hundred muskets were fired at him but he escaped them all, gave up the chase and took his place in his squadron, unscathed.

After nearly another hour had elapsed, General Wayne, always ready for a fight, again sent Captain Benjamin Fishbourne to General Lee to inform him that the British were retreating, that there was nothing to fear in making a bold advance and to urge him to push on his troops. General Lee was found by General Wayne's aide near an orchard, a mile and a half from the court house. On being informed of Wayne's opinion and wishes he said "pho! pho! it is impossible!" and gave no orders but said he would see General Wayne himself. A short time after this General Wayne saw General Scott, who also had no orders, and they directed Captain Thomas L. Byles and Captain David Lennox to find General Lee and to beg him again in the strongest terms to push on the troops against the enemy. These staff officers rode two miles to the rear and found General Lee with a body of troops retreating before the British. The whole plan had by that time changed.

General Lee afterward laughed at General Wayne's anxiety to push up the troops, quoting him as saying, "that the enemy were precipitately retiring and that then was the time to press them; another instant when they made a halt, he was as fully convinced that it was their intention to attack, and of course a reinforcement was equally necessary." "I could not help being surprised and expressing my surprise that every appearance of retreat in the enemy, and every halt they made, should pass upon him, the one as the effect of fright and necessity and the other as a serious design."[10] General Lee said that General Wayne thought the whole executive duties of the day were transferred to him and that he had nothing to do but make such call for troops as his idea of affairs at the moment indicated. But General Wayne really thought and so stated afterward that General Lee could have brought into action all the troops he had near the east ravine and that at this very time when he needed reinforcements he could have ordered 3000 men into action.

[10] Lee's defence at his court-martial, pp. 222-3.

There was, evidently, considerable dissatisfaction concerning General Lee among his subordinate officers at the front. He did not seem to them to be acting as quickly and effectively as they thought he might. A French officer, Captain Pierre Charles L'Enfant, of the Continental Engineers, seemed surprised at the inactivity displayed and remarked it in General Lee's hearing. Lee replied, "I have orders from Congress and the Commander-in-Chief not to engage."[11]

General Wayne's annoyance at General Lee's want of action cannot easily be described. Fighting man that he was, he felt that if victory was desired it must be earned by the conflict of battle, and, for himself, he was always ready. The glory that the ambitious soldier coveted was in full view of his eager eye and, although obedient, he was irritated by the only instructions he had received, which ordered him merely to feign an attack. He felt, too, that his position required him to fight, fight boldly and without feint, otherwise give way instantly his important post in the formation.

[11] L'Enfant's testimony at Lee's court-martial, p. 112.

CHAPTER XV

THE numerical strength of the rear guard of the British Army opposed to General Lee's division appears to have been about 2000 men. Of this number 300 were light dragoons. Contemporary opinions, however, differed materially on this point and it can only be accounted for by the fact that Sir Henry Clinton, as he says in his report, ordered a reinforcement from the main body of the army to join the rear guard, and that this force, from the various points of vantage of the American officers appeared from time to time in very different numbers.[1]

[1] Lieutenant-Colonel Hamilton thought the rear guard did not exceed 800 infantry and cavalry, if so many, and Lieutenant-Colonel Meade, also of General Washington's staff, thought this was about the maximum; Brigadier-General Forman, of the New Jersey State troops, who was at all parts of the field and should have been able to form a correct opinion, said he judged they did not exceed 1000 men. General Wayne said the enemy increased from 600 to 2000 men while he was looking at them. Lieutenant-Colonel Laurens, Washington's aide-de-camp, who had several good views of the enemy, said they never had more than 2000 infantry, cavalry and artillery, and this was even after they left the village in pursuit of Lee's division. Lieutenant-Colonel Fitzgerald, another of Washington's aides, named 1500 as his highest estimate of their number, and Lieutenant-Colonel Harrison, Washington's military secretary, said he did not see 2000 of the enemy at any time that day, and this number included their cavalry. The Baron von Steuben conceived them to be 1500 infantry and 150 horse. Captain Edwards, aide to General Lee, estimated them at 2000 but could not see to their rear, and Colonel Cilley, of the New Hampshire line, saw about 800 men at first and afterward their number increased to about 2000 or 2500 in sight. General Scott named 2500 soldiers the horse included, and Lieutenant-Colonel Oswald, of the artillery, about the same number. Colonel Butler, of the Pennsylvania line, thought there might be 1500 foot and 200 horse although he saw 500 or 600 other foot soldiers afterward. Captain Lennox, of General Wayne's staff, said 1000 foot, 300 horse and a considerable reinforcement coming up. Colonel Jackson, of Massachusetts, estimated them at 3000, and, like Captain Edwards, did not see to their rear. He supposed there were many more. Lieutenant Colonel Olney, of the Rhode Island regiment, and Captain Seward, of the artillery, gave still higher figures which certainly must have been far from correct. The former named 4000 or 5000 as the first party, with the reinforcement of 2000 approaching; the latter said 800 to 1000 cavalry and from 6000 to 8000 infantry and 10 pieces of cannon, one 12-pounder and the rest 6-pounders.

General Lee told his aide, Captain Mercer, during the fight that he supposed them to be between 1500 and 2000 men, although Captain Mercer considered them 3000 strong.

[147]

General Lee said he made different estimates of their force at different times during the day, knowing that they tried, as he did, to conceal their numbers. He could only infer their strength from their manoeuvers, and then decide what was best for him to do according to the size of their party. He claimed that the British guards, the British grenadiers, the Hessian grenadiers, the British light infantry, the Hessian yagers, the Queen's rangers, and indeed all the British cavalry, with two brigades of British foot, comprised the party directly in his front. Of course this has since been proved fallacious.

Up to this time all the advantage had been with the American arms, and it needed now to be followed up by intelligent orders correctly and enthusiastically executed, in order to inspire the troops to quick action.

Sir Henry Clinton at this time fully believed that the Americans were about to attack the right and left flanks of General Knyphausen's division. He thought his baggage train was the weak place in his column and was fully impressed with the idea that the Americans preferred to plunder his army rather than to give battle to the very flower of the British troops on this continent. He therefore determined to charge the American front with such vigor as to compel them to recall their flanking parties to the aid of their more seriously threatened main column. General Lafayette was the first officer to see this new movement of Clinton and he wished to lead an attack promptly on the British left. He expressed his desire to General Lee and that officer said, "Sir, you do not know British soldiers; we cannot stand against them; we shall certainly be driven back at first and we must be cautious."[2] Lafayette did not like this kind of talk in the very face of the foe and he brusquely replied, "It may be so, General, but British soldiers have been beaten and they may be again; at any rate, I am disposed to make the trial."[3] Then Lafayette

[2] Custis' *Recollections of Washington*, p. 218.
[3] Lossing's *Field-book of the Revolution*, Vol. II, p. 151.

sent word to General Washington that his presence was needed on the field. Twice, also, were messages of a similar nature sent to the Commander-in-Chief by Lieutenant-Colonel Laurens of his staff.

Soon after Lafayette left him General Lee himself began to be impressed with the idea that his plan of getting in between the divisions of the British Army had been completely frustrated by this new movement of Clinton and that he must make some show of interference with the changed plan of the enemy. The British column was then marching directly toward the court house, a movement which threatened the American right flank, and General Lee requested Lieutenant-Colonel Hamilton, who was riding near him, to direct General Lafayette to take three regiments of General Wayne's detachment, then on the center, the Thirteenth Pennsylvania regiment, Colonel Walter Stewart, commanding; the Fourth New York regiment, Colonel Henry B. Livingston, commanding; and the Ninth Massachusetts regiment, Colonel James Wesson, commanding; and some light artillery, Captain Thomas Seward of the Third Continental artillery regiment in command, in all about 800 men, and to march toward the enemy, attack their left flank and cover the right of the army. Colonel Morgan had not reported, as General Lee said he expected he would, and it was quite apparent that if the enemy pushed hard on the American right flank the situation would soon become very dangerous. General Lafayette and his force immediately crossed the east ravine, emerged from a copse and marched for formation near the wooden court house building with their right along a thick wood. Colonel Stewart's regiment marched in column, eight men in front, and took position on the right side of a ravine and a wood with a large open, unbroken plain in front and their right flank leading up to the line of the Middletown road. To the rear of the extreme right flank, as they faced the British, was Freehold village. They were then but six hundred yards from the enemy.

Just at this situation of affairs, some accounts of the battle relate that General Lafayette, mounted on a white horse, a very conspicuous object in battle, advanced with his aides some distance in front of his troops in order the better to reconnoiter the enemy. The British artillerists espied this prominent figure in the scene before them and were just sighting their guns for the party of the distinguished Frenchman, when Sir Henry Clinton's order caused them to desist, and possibly thus Lafayette's life was spared.

Not so fortunate, however, were some of Lafayette's command. Several of his men were killed by the bullets of the British advance and Colonel James Wesson, of the Ninth Massachusetts regiment, was severely injured in the shoulders and back by a shot from the enemy's twelve-pounders. Just at this time General Lafayette was greatly surprised to see some of Lee's troops going quickly toward the village, though this could have afforded little or no protection against any hostile demonstration, the buildings being mostly of wood instead of stone, as was at first supposed. This movement of General Lee's troops had a singular look to the force on the extreme American left flank. To Generals Scott and Maxwell, and Colonels Grayson and Jackson it seemed like a retreat. They watched it carefully with their glasses and the longer they looked the more they began to fear that they themselves would soon be cut off from the main body. This induced them at last to make a retrograde movement through a misunderstanding of Lee's first orders and by reason of his failure to send them any subsequent orders for their guidance.

About this time, half-past eleven o'clock in the morning, a body of fresh troops joined the British rear guard. They had marched that morning on the Middletown road with the main body but were now called back by General

Clinton to reinforce the covering party. This new body consisted of the entire Second brigade of British foot and the Seventeenth regiment of light dragoons. Lord Cornwallis was with this detachment and it was well known that "he never hesitated a moment to accept a battle when the opportunity was given him." This force had no such numbers as some of the American officers imagined, yet they were good troops and marched slowly and in regular order to the support of their comrades near the court house, who had all the morning borne the rattling fire of the American riflemen as well as the terrible heat, made all the more oppressive by the severe exertions of a conflict. Within fifteen minutes they had placed themselves on the right of the advanced corps of the American Army and were rapidly gaining ground. Cornwallis was now in supreme command of the corps resisting Lee's force, and so continued the remainder of the day.

General Lee was quickly apprised of this movement but he made no effort to secure the cooperation of the different parts of his command for the purpose of resisting it.

General Clinton still believed that the baggage train was the plunder which the American Army desired, and from reports which he had received he thought that Colonel Morgan's men might be lurking on one flank and General Dickinson's militia on the other. He therefore considered it wise to increase the size of his covering party and give a severe blow to the troops harassing his rear before all the outside detachments could be called in to support them. He considered from what he had heard from his scouts, that the main army under General Washington, which he thought 20,000 strong, having two marshes to cross, could hardly reach them before he had severely punished their advance. He believed that General Lee could not now bring into the field more than Lord Cornwallis could fully attend to. This was his plan and he intended to put it into execution with diligence, hoping, however, that it might not lead to a general engagement.

The preservation of the baggage seems to have been ever present in the mind of Clinton, whereas he should have dismissed it from his thoughts, called a strong contingent of Knyphausen's division from the charge of it and then have struck a sharp blow for the continued supremacy of Great Britain in the western world.

As already stated, General Lafayette had seen some of General Lee's troops going toward the village, which was behind him, and he was astonished. He also noticed a battery of artillery leaving its advanced post for want of ammunition and, not knowing the cause of this movement, thought it looked like a retreat. He found that but one regiment of his own command, the Fourth New York Continental infantry, Colonel Livingston, had followed him, or, at least, the other regiments had failed to come up. Lafayette was at a loss to know what the movements meant, but in the distance he heard orders being given to troops to post themselves farther back and to go into the woods so as to annoy the approaching enemy. Captain John Stith, an officer of the Fourth Virginia Continental infantry, detailed for duty with Colonel George Baylor's Third regiment of light dragoons, then came up to the rear of General Lafayette's detachment, and desired that Lafayette should be informed that General Scott's detachment had retired from the left flank. This information puzzled General Lafayette still more and he felt that perhaps he had been crowding Colonel Livingston's regiment too closely against the enemy. Just at this time a strong cannonade was being made by the British batteries and one of Colonel Walter Stewart's men lost a leg by a round shot as the Thirteenth Pennsylvania regiment was passing over the open ground. Lieutenant-Colonel Laurens, General Washington's aide, who had been in conversation with General Lee, rode up to General Lafayette at Lee's request, informed him that it had been found necessary to retire to the village and gave him Lee's order to that effect.

Colonel Laurens, who had busied himself all the morning in obtaining information, received a letter about this time from Colonel Fitzgerald, written by Washington's direction, desiring to know the condition of affairs and adding that he was ready to support Lee with the main army. General Lee told Laurens he did not know what to say in reply.

Major Jamair, Lafayette's aide, then carried Lee's order to the commanding officers of the three regiments in this detachment to slowly fall back and form in an orchard on the right of the village. The detachment immediately obeyed the order, and then Major Aaron Ogden, General Maxwell's brigade major, came riding up very rapidly at the special request of General Lee and directed Colonel Stewart to retire to a wood still farther in the rear of the orchard pointed out by Major Jamair. Colonel Stewart marched his men, some on the right and some on the left of the roadway, and the other regiments in the detachment followed in the same order. This, however, was soon found to break the command too much and an attempt was made to keep them more together. They retreated then in some disorder. As these regiments were retiring, Colonel Stewart met General Lee, who was just in their rear near the house occupied the previous night by the British General, James Grant, and asked him to designate the wood in which he wished his men to be posted. Seeing the wearied men, he pointed toward an orchard near by and said, "Take them to any place to save their lives."[4] Afterward Captain Edwards came up to General Lafayette's command and ordered them in General Lee's name to a wood still farther back and on the other side of the ravine.

Lafayette did not like all these movements. He thought he knew General Lee's character and ambition, and he had carefully watched him during the morning, so he sent

[4] Stewart's testimony at Lee's court-martial, p. 47.

word to General Washington that his presence was needed immediately at the front.

As they were crossing the east ravine just back of the court house the British light horse again appeared and Colonel Stewart hastily formed his regiment to receive them; but they soon wheeled off and returned to the large detachment of foot now marching up from the village. About this time General Lafayette found himself alone with Colonel Livingston's regiment, about a quarter of a mile beyond Freehold. Colonel Stewart's and Colonel Wesson's commands had gotten into another portion of the column in the general disorder which prevailed.

So the retreat of Lafayette's detachment was begun and by constant orders to fall back they at last were merged into the column of retreating troops who were making their way back toward the meeting-house.

General Lee said he merely sent General Lafayette the information that General Scott's detachment was falling back, and not that he was to do so too, but he upbraided himself that he had not done so promptly on finding his left had been uncovered.

Colonel Richard Butler, of the Ninth Pennsylvania regiment, was the last to give way from the ground on which he had been contending so well. At the moment he did so the enemy were in his front and on his left and a morass was on his right. The ground on which he was posted was considerably lower than that occupied by the enemy, though not enough to be of any serious danger, but being hemmed in on three sides, his situation was perilous indeed and there was no one near from whom he could obtain orders. General Wayne had gone with General Scott to the edge of an orchard near the village to watch the movements of the enemy. Colonel Butler then summoned the two field officers in his detachment, Major Francis Nichols of his own Ninth Pennsylvania regiment and Major Benjamin Ledyard of the First New York regiment, and they had a brief council. They concluded

Present Appearance of John Craig's House

that it was best to act promptly and Major Ledyard went off some distance in the rear to see, if possible, where the other part of the division had gone. Before he returned, however, Colonel Butler felt compelled to order the retrograde movement, which was somewhat perilous, being so close to large bodies of the British. Butler's men then passed through the east ravine and took the road by the way of Forman's Mills. On arriving at this point they made a long halt to try to refresh the weary soldiers to some extent. On the route there Major Ledyard reported the retreat of all of General Lee's division, and then, after they had rested, Colonel Butler marched his men still farther westward to Craig's house[5] and mill and there found that they were on the extreme left of the main body of General Washington's Army.

Just as General Wayne was moving off the ground in retreat a messenger came riding up to him from Colonel Daniel Morgan, who all the morning had been listening impatiently to the sound of the enemy's cannon while he, without orders of any kind that day, felt it his duty to stay where he had been posted at Richmond Mills, on Squanbrook, one of the streams leading into Manasquan River at least three miles away from the battle-field. General Wayne's only answer to the inquiry of the officer for orders from General Lee was that he could himself see the situation, that the American troops were being drawn off and that Colonel Morgan must govern himself accordingly. It is singular that this hasty remark of General Wayne was in any way misunderstood and that when Colonel Morgan heard it he delayed a single moment to strike the flank of the advancing foe.

Colonel Morgan had with him that day, to guide him if he received orders, the Monmouth County patriots Colonel Samuel Forman, Lieutenant-Colonel Joseph

[5] The John Craig farm and the property where the Craig mill stood is now owned by Samuel Craig Cowart, of Freehold. The farm is about two miles west of Freehold and the house, which is still standing (1926), was built in 1710.

Haight and Sergeant Tunis Forman, of the Second regiment militia.

The orders given Colonel Morgan for the day are found in the following item, incorrectly dated, from General Lee's trial on July 21, page 138:

Major-General Lee produces to the Court a letter from Colonel Morgan, which being read, the part admitted as evidence is as follows:

"Manasquan Brook, June 29, 1778.

"SIR:

"General Lee wrote me yesterday, at one o'clock in the evening, he intended to attack the enemy's rear this morning and ordered me to attack them at the same time on their right flank."

Colonel Morgan, of course, heard the firing, because the day was clear, the artillery was very active and he was near the scene of action. In a biography of Morgan, we find an attempted apology for the singular conduct of this gallant soldier. The excuse cannot be considered of any importance when we know that it was clearly impossible for the Forman brothers and Lieutenant-Colonel Haight who were with him, to lead him astray a single rod in a section of the county so well known to them. Referring to General Dickinson and Colonel Morgan, Graham says, "They had already partially engaged the enemy, when the latter were observed retracing their steps toward Monmouth. Soon after, and while the din of the conflict that ensued was heard in the distance, Morgan received orders to join the army. Unfortunately, he took a route on his return which diverged somewhat from that leading to the field of battle; and from this cause, with the late hour of the day at which he commenced a march of some miles through a broken country, he did not reach the American army till night."[6]

Lieutenant-Colonel Oswald, the artillerist, having suffered much in men and horses killed and by his men falling at their guns overcome by the heat, began to retreat toward the west ravine, with his field pieces. General Lee

[6] Graham's *Life of General Daniel Morgan*, p. 211.

[156]

afterward said that this act caused him great surprise. He said he knew Oswald to be a most excellent soldier and that it must be some very substantial reason that would induce him to retreat before the enemy. General Lee then rode up to Oswald and in a most excited manner asked him why he retired. Oswald replied that he had expended all his round shot, that one piece was entirely disabled and that his heavy ammunition wagon had not yet come up to the causeway on the other side of the east ravine. At this time he could see no infantry on his right or left flank that was in position as his supporting force. It seems strange indeed that even General Lee would allow this state of affairs to remain for a moment. It certainly reflected sorely on his ability to command troops in battle.

As has been stated, General Scott was posted with his detachment on the west side of the east ravine at the edge of a wood about half a mile from the court house and about a hundred yards in front of Maxwell's brigade. When the enemy came so close to the village they passed on General Scott's right flank and almost at his rear. This made his position very precarious as the British seemed to be getting between him and the main body of General Lee's force. He received no orders from General Lee and he could only observe the strange movements of the other American troops without any apparent attempt on Lee's part to carry out the plan he so boastfully said he proposed to lead in person. General Scott then had a conference with General Wayne and also one with General Maxwell, and Scott's staff officer Lieutenant-Colonel Marinas Willett went on some slightly higher ground near by, leaving Colonel Cilley of the First New Hampshire regiment in command, and reconnoitered the enemy. Soon after this, seeing a backward movement on the extreme right, General Scott called out to Lieutenant-Colonel Brooks, Lee's adjutant-general, who was riding within call, and asked him for orders from General Lee. He said he had none and General Scott called his attention to the American troops going off the field in the direction of the court house. After waiting about half an hour General Scott gave the order to retreat by left of battalion in columns and this detachment, after passing through a wood, soon joined the remainder of the division retiring on the old road. They had barely left their post when Captain Mercer rode over to the west side of the ravine with a message from General Lee to General Scott to the effect that there was no need of pushing his detachment more to the left and rear of the enemy, as they were already now in the rear of the enemy's advancing column, but to hold his position until further orders. Just as Captain Mercer was nearing the place where he expected to find General Scott and his men he met Colonel Jackson's regiment and was informed that General Scott had gone. Soon after General Lee had sent Captain Mercer off with this message he also despatched Captain Edwards with the same message to General Scott, so anxious was he that the order should be delivered without mistake or failure. Captain Edwards met Captain Mercer returning, and Mercer told him what he had found out in reference to General Scott's detachment. They both returned to General Lee and told him that General Scott had left the woods where he had been stationed and that the enemy were pushing their force rapidly in that direction. General Lee was very indignant and appeared astonished and disconcerted at this news as he said he was about to go and put himself at the head of his troops on his left flank. He said he could not conceive that General Scott's detachment was in any danger whatever. This action on General Lee's part, it will be remembered, was according to his original plan, although it would seem that he was not very prompt in its execution. General Lee remarked when he heard of Scott's movement that "his orders not being obeyed might or would prove the ruin of the day."[7] It was only seven minutes, Captain Mercer said, after he reported Scott's retreat that he saw

[7] Captain Compston's testimony at Lee's court-martial, p. 162.

General Lafayette's troops on the right already falling back some distance behind the court house.

It appears that General Lee did not know at this time where General Scott's detachment had gone; nor did he attempt to find them. He was asked one day why he did not seek for them, and he pleaded a scarcity of staff officers, that he "was uncertain to what point he was retired and I did not choose to dispatch one of my aide-de-camps on an errand which might prove as fruitless as the former."[8] He thought General Scott culpable in not reporting the cause and direction of his movement, and in this General Lee was certainly right. Whether General Scott had a good reason for moving his command or not, he should instantly have informed General Lee and also notified him of his situation from time to time, and asked for further orders.

When General Scott met General Maxwell he told him that he had seen the American troops retiring on the right and that if Maxwell was obliged to retreat he would send his battery of artillery to report to him. Then he said he would try to get his command over the east ravine, if it was possible before the enemy approached. General Maxwell was well convinced that if he did not get his own as well as General Scott's cannon over the causeway at the ravine and the enemy should make a quick dash on him, he would lose all his guns. He, too, as General Scott had done, called out to Lieutenant-Colonel Brooks, as he rode by, for some orders, but Brooks had none to give him. Maxwell then took his brigade from the open field to the cover of an adjoining wood. Shortly after this General Maxwell gave the order to retreat and his brigade was soon marching in fair style. Several battalions were now pushing rapidly over the ravine and taking the old road back to the meeting-house. Lieutenant-Colonel Brooks again came up to General Maxwell and remarked that the woods then in their front would make a good position from

[8] Lee's defence at his court-martial, p. 226.

which he could cover a retreating force and that if he placed his batteries there they would be able to take an approaching enemy on their flank. General Maxwell's brigade filed through the ravine as the enemy were advancing toward them and in ten minutes not a continental soldier was to be seen in their old position on the left of the army.

Colonel Henry Jackson and his detachment had been posted on the westerly slope of the east ravine with no orders to move forward or fall back and when a heavy column of the enemy advanced toward the American right, he naturally became very anxious about the dangerous position his men occupied. Lieutenant-Colonel Oswald was still keeping up a desultory fire, yet it did not interfere with the march of the British. However, he ceased firing soon after and retreated, as has been stated. Colonel Jackson thought the hill just in front of him rendered his position in the ravine very precarious and he believed he ought to move his command even without orders. Lieutenant-Colonel William S. Smith hoped he would not do it unless he obtained General Lee's orders and it was then agreed that Smith should attempt to find Lee. So he rode off for that purpose. But while he was gone Captain Mercer came near the detachment, as he was searching for General Scott, and Colonel Jackson told him that Scott had gone. After thoroughly reconnoitering the enemy Captain Mercer directed Colonel Jackson, in General Lee's name, to move his detachment to the woods on the left. He did so instantly going through the ravine, which was deep and very miry. Marching from the left this brought Lieutenant-Colonel William S. Smith who had then returned, not having found General Lee, on the lead of the party. This column had to make many short halts to refresh the men, who had had severe marching all day. In this way, from time to time, they marched on until they were merged in the ranks of the grand retreating division.

General Lee then ordered Colonel Jackson, through

Mr. John Clark, an auditor of accounts of the American Army, but now voluntarily assisting him, to form his men against a rail fence to check the enemy's cavalry. Colonel Jackson remarked when he heard this order that his men were greatly fatigued and could not form, but Lieutenant-Colonel Smith still in the advance of the detachment succeeded in getting at least one-half of Jackson's men in line of battle. After a few moments spent at the fence General Lee ordered them again to retire some little distance and form in line behind another fence. Still later General Lee met Colonel Jackson in person and upbraided him, with much profanity, for not promptly obeying his orders, though they were conveyed by a gentleman unknown to Jackson and not in the military line. General Lee himself then ordered the detachment to retire, saying he "meant to effect a retreat." So Colonel Jackson's men were again caught in the current of the retreating column and he heard the soldiers behind him in the other regiments crying out to hasten his slow steps, "Colonel Jackson, march on! march on!"

Colonel Grayson's detachment had been posted well up to the front on the left and had been concealed in a wood. General Wayne, however, had ordered him to take position in the open field, which order caused Captain Mercer to tell Colonel Grayson that General Wayne had no right to command him but that he must look for orders direct to General Lee. Colonel Grayson remarked that he would return to the woods if Captain Mercer so requested, but he did not do it.

While Captain Mercer was watching the movements of the British Colonel, Grayson called out to Colonel Jackson who was in his rear in the low ground of the east ravine to come up and form on his left on Briar Hill, about three-quarters of a mile beyond the court house, but seeing that Grayson had no artillery with him, Colonel Jackson did not think it best to comply with his request. At this moment Colonel Grayson threatened General

Knyphausen's command. The covering party of the British appeared at considerable distance from them, first drawn up in line with the cavalry on their flanks and then moving on the American right toward the court house.

Between the detachment of Colonel Grayson and the enemy a house was on fire and between this fire and a wood on the left the party which had turned back to reinforce the covering detachment of the British column was clearly to be seen. After viewing the situation thoroughly Captain Mercer returned to where Colonel Grayson was riding at the head of his detachment and seeing Colonel Jackson's men retreating over the ravine he ordered Colonel Grayson in General Lee's name to follow in the rear of Jackson's detachment. This was done. Both of these detachments then crossed the ravine and came up to where Scott's detachment was posted on the skirt of a wood on the westerly side of the morass. The enemy was plainly to be seen from this point marching in considerable force. A few moments later and all the American troops on that part of the field were in full retreat. Colonel Grayson halted his men only fifteen minutes, after a two-mile march, in an orchard in front of the house of Mr. Hart. The retreat of this party was in good order, the marching being as good as could be expected in such sultry weather.

CHAPTER XVI

THE American troops had moved away from the court house and from the village of Freehold in some order, but the battalions were crowded so close that General Duportail feared that if the enemy sent their grape-shop among them the havoc would be terrific. General Lee came away from the village with these troops. When he heard that General Scott and General Maxwell had retired he said that obliged him to leave the ground he had chosen and to make the best of a bad bargain, but he took no steps to meet a derangement of his plans. He allowed the retreat to go on without any determined effort to make a stand. In fact, while crossing Mr. Rhea's fields General Forman said Lee urged some of the battalions to make more haste in their retreat. In this way, through a cloud of dust that hid the movements of the troops, over roads only wide enough to accommodate a platoon, the men struggled on their weary way in the heat of that terrible day until they reached a fence by William Ker's [or Carr] house. This was about two and a half miles from the court house. Near this house a halt of nearly half an hour was made by some of the battalions.

General Lee was found by those who sought him near the ravine which was in front and to the left of Mr. Ker's house, and surrounded by a number of mounted staff officers and men. He remained in that place about twenty minutes but during that time gave no special directions and only said that matters were all in confusion. He had no message to send to General Washington by his aide, Lieutenant-Colonel Meade, who found him there, and Meade, strange to say, went toward the court house to reconnoiter the enemy instead of hurrying back to his chief to report the situation.

As Lieutenant-Colonel Marinus Willett, General

Scott's volunteer aide, passed General Lee, he heard him say to those around him, who were discussing the condition of affairs and bemoaning the retreat, "It does not signify, the enemy have too much cavalry for us."[1]

The nature of the retreat up to this time is somewhat difficult to determine. It appears, however, from the statements of various officers who saw the retreat at different times that parts of it were performed in good order, with no apparent straggling, and that other parts were quite disorderly, the men moving along with no system, utterly regardless of their destination, overcome with distress and heat, and the regimental and brigade commands much broken. It does not appear that any general or field officer, excepting Colonel Stewart, saw his own command in any disorder, but always another part of the force. General Scott said the retreat appeared in confusion; the men were running and the horses trotting with the field pieces. General Forman saw much confusion and irregularity among the troops. Colonel Cilley thought they retreated rapidly, and the rear went off on a trot. He thought they must have seen something he did not see. He said he saw nothing which could occasion them to go off in that manner. To Captain Fishbourne the retreat seemed in much disorder and with much scattering. It seemed to be in small parties, although sometimes a regiment or two might be together. Lieutenant-Colonel Hamilton considered the retreat as made in tolerable order, but as chance should direct, without system or design. Lieutenant-Colonel Meade saw the troops a good deal scattered—no order observed. Lieutenant-Colonel Tilghman thought the column was in great confusion and said that a line could not be formed in that situation. They neither kept proper intervals, nor were heads of columns ranged. Colonel Gavion of the Engineer Department said the troops were retreating in great disorder. Captain Mercer did not see troops in disorder until the party was broken up on the hill; he thought all the

[1] Narrative of the military actions of Colonel Marinus Willett, p. 68.

troops in perfectly good order as far as the heat of the weather would permit. Lieutenant-Colonel Olney thought the men were extremely fatigued, but there were few stragglers. All the men he saw kept their platoons and divisions with the greatest exactness. Lieutenant-Colonel Brooks said the retreat from the court house to Ker's house was performed as far as he saw it, with great deliberation and in good order; that in general the troops retired in columns by battalion, some by brigade. Captain Edwards reported that the troops marched in great order and took post regularly except some at the last part of the line which was broken by a charge of the enemy. Lieutenant-Colonel Fitzgerald thought the troops retreated in disorder, some scattered, some in column—but more from ignorance of a place to go to than from the retreat itself. Colonel Stewart said the troops he was with retreated in a disorderly manner and that, on the order being given to retreat, the regiments seemed anxious to move with expedition. Lieutenant-Colonel Laurens spoke of them "as retreating and in disorder." General Washington called it "disorder and confusion." General von Steuben said they were "retreating in great disorder." Lieutenant-Colonel Hamilton wrote, a few days after the battle: "After changing their position two or three times by retrograde movements, our advanced corps got into a general confused retreat and even rout would hardly be too strong an expression." General Knox asked General Lee why the troops retreated from the court house, and he said "he could not tell for he never saw such disorder, for every one took upon himself to give orders without his knowledge."

It is a pertinent fact, as Lieutenant-Colonel Laurens wrote, that "all this disgraceful retreating passed without the firing of a musket, over ground which might have been disputed inch by inch."

We must, therefore, conclude that some parts of the retreating column fell back in as good shape as was possible for even the best disciplined soldiers on such a sultry day, and that in other instances, as was afterward adjudged, the battalions made a disorderly retreat; that the division as an entirety was much broken, but that the men were not wholly panic-stricken.

The numbers of the British seemed the greatest just when they came out of Monmouth Court House and advanced down the highway toward the Americans, then approaching William Ker's house. Up to the time when they reached the village, the covering party, reinforced by a large column under Lieutenant-General the Earl Cornwallis, had been marching with the cavalry on their right flank and in their front. After that they changed their front to the left and marched across the open fields between Freehold and Ker's house in two columns, well closed up, and with their cavalry and light artillery moving between the columns.

The land was more open near the village and beyond it, and, therefore, at this phase of the battle more of the troops of the British Army were in plain view than at any other hour during the day. After this the battle was enacted on low ground, from elevated positions and on the highway skirted with thick woods. In this way no very large numerical force was ever in position at ony one place.

By way of apology for his own lack of soldierly ability, if it is not judged to have been treachery, General Lee told his aides that several of the battalions had retreated without his knowledge and some contrary to his orders. He also said that although this was "extremely unsoldierly he believed it to be a very happy thing for the army as the enemy were so much superior both in infantry and cavalry, in cavalry especially; for had that not been the case that whole detachments at least must have been sacrificed."[2]

Captain Mercer, General Lee's aide, said that Lee ex-

[2] Lieutenant-Colonel Brooks' testimony at Lee's court-martial, p. 171.

pected to meet only the covering party of the enemy but that the British general had his whole force drawn up to receive them. This, of course, was not true.

General Lee afterward said in referring to the retreat, "When I called to mind the several circumstances of this day the only omission with which I can justly upbraid myself is, that I did not, on first receiving intelligence of General Scott's having abandoned the wood on our left, immediately order a retreat on the right."[3]

We must conclude, however, that General Lee's own bad management was the immediate cause of the retreat; that it was not so much the disobedience of his orders which caused it as the absolute want of proper orders at the proper time.

General Carrington in his "historical and military criticism" of this retreat says, "It is to be noticed that there was nothing of the nature of a panic. No commander knew why he retreated only that such were understood to be the orders and that others retreated. . . . General Lee deserves credit for self-possession and a real purpose to bring the men away in safety, when he found he could not handle the division." And again he says, with much truth, "While all narratives agree that the advance of subordinate commanders was prompt and orderly, however blindly conducted and in a direction favorably to success, it is equally clear that General Lee made no adequate effort to concentrate his division, promulgated no definite orders; and in the conducts of his movements and the precipitate retreat, absolutely failed to control his army and keep it in hand. His presence inspired none, discouraged many, and absolutely left the division to work their own way out of confusion, as if there were no officer in general command. A careful examination of the facts seems to exclude the idea that Lee was guilty of any overt act of treason; while it is equally true, that upon the basis of his antecedent opinion, and his expectation of failure, he

[3] Lee's defence at his court-martial, p. 222.

[167]

did not make the proper effort to render that failure the least disastrous possible, and thus fulfill the obligations of high command."[4]

No criticism, in our opinion, could be more correct and none more fully cover the bad condition of the American Army at this juncture.

It may be noted here that up to this time General Lee was defeated, as he had predicted any one would be who attempted to cope with the British light infantry.

General Lee's plan was first to take position on the westerly margin of the east ravine with the village of Monmouth Court House to cover the right flank. This he was unable to accomplish because the village was not built of such materials as would protect the flanks of an army, although there was an apple orchard and some woods near the town. But it was found that the artillery of the enemy on the eastern side of the ravine would command the ground on the western slope, and Lee was therefore obliged to abandon the idea of forming his men there. The giving way of the left flank of the division necessitated the retreat, as he thought, to the middle ravine. General Wayne claimed that it was a good position to hold but General Lee emphatically expressed his professional opinion against it, and thought that to adopt such a course would not only be censurable but criminal. Reports at this time reached General Lee that his right flank had actually been pierced by the British, but after investigation General Duportail assured him that there was no truth in this rumor. Then General Lee asked General Duportail, the chief engineer of the army, to examine the hills back of the middle morass which seemed to them both at first a good place to check the enemy. He made a hasty reconnaissance and reported that he thought the position would answer the purpose. General Lee had a high opinion of the Chevalier Duportail's abilities and said he thought him "a real acquisition to the continent." Nevertheless,

[4] Carrington's *Battles of the American Revolution*, p. 417.

when General Lee himself came to the rising ground he pronounced the position untenable, because, he said, high land on the left and front commanded the position. General Lee at last pronounced it "an execrable position,"— and so the retreat continued.

General Lee, however, with a view to giving the advancing column of the British some slight check at this point, so as to save the lives of the great body of his retreating soldiers, directed Captain Edwards to post some pieces of artillery on a hill near by, and Colonel Stewart's Thirteenth Pennsylvania regiment and Patton's Continental regiment, Lieutenant-Colonel Parke still in command, were ordered to attempt to protect the retreating men. The wood on his right was so insignificant that it afforded slight protection and he felt that if a squadron of the British dragoons attempted to strike a blow on his flank, they would push all his force against that bridge over the west ravine which General Dickinson, six hours previously, had so emphatically impressed on his mind was the only place thereabouts where that morass could be crossed, at least by artillery.

Just at this time one of the residents of this part of the county, Captain Peter Wikoff,[5] of the Second regiment Monmouth County militia, came up, probably not in uniform, and, saluting General Lee, told him that his farm was next adjoining William Ker's, that he was thoroughly acquainted with that section of the country, and asked if he could be of any service to him or to the cause. General Lee said he considered himself fortunate to have such a man near him and begged him to tell him where there was a position near by where his flanks would be protected from the British cavalry and the men could be screened from the intolerable heat. Captain Wikoff showed him a wood south of Ker's house, but General Lee

[5] This officer is often referred to in history and on maps as the "younger Wikoff," to distinguish him from his father William Wikoff, who owned a thousand-acre farm near Briar Hill and who appears as the "elder Wikoff" on maps of the battle.

said that "there was not time to take them there; that
the enemy were pressing too close upon us."[6] Lee asked him
for some other place and then directed Captain Wikoff's
attention to Combs' Hill in the distance. This hill had a
ravine in front and a heavy wood in the rear. To attack a
party posted on this eminence an enemy must come in on
the right after making a circuit of at least three miles. To
attain this position, however, a rough causeway must
immediately be built of fence rails, as the most available
material, because the artillery and the ammunition
wagons could not be pulled through the mire of the morass.
General Lee said there was not time to do this now and
that no time should be lost in getting the men under the
protection of some cover from the enemy and from the
heat. There was a small timber tract somewhat nearer
than Combs' Hill and at Lee's request Captain Wikoff
began immediately to guide the troops in that direction,
with the expectation, as he afterward said, of placing them
later in the day on Combs' Hill. The first part of the retreat was over and the second phase, in somewhat more
confusion, began as they passed away from William Ker's
house. The enemy was now approaching rapidly and
General Lee directed Colonel Stewart, whose regiment,
as we have seen, had been supporting some artillery on the
right, to place his troops, with the Third Maryland regiment, Lieutenant-Colonel Nathaniel Ramsay commanding, on the left of the highway so as to protect the retiring
column and to check the quick advance of the foe. Colonel
Henry B. Livingston, with the Fourth New York regiment, although greatly worn out by the labors of the day
promptly obeyed an order to relieve Colonel Stewart in
the support of the artillery. His command then took
position on each side of the light batteries. Lieutenant-
Colonel William S. Smith's regiment, all that was left of
Colonel Jackson's detachment that had not been worn out
with the heat or caught in the retreating column, was then

---

[6] Wikoff's testimony at Lee's court-martial, p. 198.

posted on the left of Colonel Livingston's regiment; and Varnum's brigade, Lieutenant-Colonel Olney still in command, by General Lee's direct orders, conveyed by Lieutenant-Colonel Brooks, quickly took position behind a fence near by to protect the batteries in case they were compelled to give way under a sudden charge of the British.

Soon after this Varnum's brigade and the detachments under General Lafayette marched off to the right, leaving Scott's own brigade and Colonel Jackson's detachment on the left flank. Captain Thomas Seward's battery of the Third regiment of artillery, by order of General Knox, communicated by his Brigade-Major, Samuel Shaw, then retreated over the middle ravine and took post on the hill on the western slope of the morass. Here Captain Seward opened his guns and fired some fifty shot at the British advance, under cover of which the last half of the retreating Americans got safely over the causeway. Captain David Cook's battery of the Third regiment of artillery also took part in the cannonade. He received the first order to retreat, and the battery with other pieces of artillery, under Lieutenant-Colonel Oswald, took a new position under direction of Captain Edwards, of Lee's staff. While this was being done Captain Seward fired forty more shots and then he too fell back to Oswald's position.

During these trying hours General Lee's self-possession and coolness, under the greatest difficulties, never left him. This is fully established by the opinions of his subordinates. General Maxwell saw no appearance of his being disconcerted; General Knox thought him perfectly master of himself and General Lafayette said he seemed by his voice and features to be as he was in general. Colonel Stewart asserted that Lee "appeared as usual, without being disturbed"; Lieutenant-Colonel Fitzgerald thought he "appeared serious and thoughtful" but Lieutenant-Colonel Smith said he was perfectly calm. Lieutenant-Colonel Olney clearly stated that Lee appeared to possess as much coolness and calmness as any officer he was ever in action with and did not appear to be confused. Lieutenant-Colonel Oswald thought him calm and intrepid and fully possessed of himself; Captain Stith thought he appeared possessed of himself and not in the least disconcerted. Of his three staff officers, who, although they had the best opportunities of judging, were, of course, prejudiced in his favor—Lieutenant-Colonel Brooks said he appeared through the whole course of the day to be cool and deliberate and thoroughly to possess himself; Captain Edwards "did not observe the least embarrassment" in him, but quite the reverse as he delivered every order with the same coolness as when out of the field; Captain Mercer could not but think him exceedingly composed, "as several circumstances happened during the time that evidently evinced it."

The only officers who were disposed to think General Lee was not as self-possessed as was necessary in an officer so high in command were Lieutenant-Colonel Laurens and Lieutenant-Colonel Hamilton. The former thought him a good deal embarrassed and his orders indistinct. This embarrassment he believed was due to want of presence of mind. Although Hamilton had once remarked to Captain Mercer that he thought General Lee self-possessed to a very high degree, he afterward said he heard him give two orders under a hurry of mind. There appeared to be "no want of that degree of self-possession, which proceeds from a want of personal intrepidity," but only a "hurry of spirits which may proceed from a temper not so calm and steady as is necessary to support a man in such critical circumstances."

From all these opinions, expressed by officers whose judgment must have been reliable and who uttered these statements under very solemn surroundings, it is fair to conclude that General Lee was personally brave and intrepid, that he did not hesitate to expose himself in danger, that he was perfectly calm and self-possessed in action, and that he was disturbed only because of the extreme heat and its demoralizing effect upon his men, who were exposed to the scorching rays of the sun.

Up to the time General Lee left Ker's house he had not reported the fact of his retreat to General Washington nor that he was about to throw a body of worn-out men upon the head of the advancing main army. General Lee afterward tried to defend himself from this criminal neglect by saying that although the land in that vicinity had been un-reconnoitered, he hoped every moment to find a suitable position where he could receive the enemy and resist their attack. He declared he never meant to make a general retreat, and said, "The retreat in the first instance was contrary to my intentions, contrary to my orders and contrary to my wishes."[7] But when it did begin he thought first of making the stand on the westerly side of the east ravine with the court house on the right flank, but this position on further examination appeared to be an "execrable" one. The next position was on the hills near William Ker's house and this was abandoned for equally good reasons, and the third position he had just told Captain Mercer that he was about to take when he met Washington in person. General Lee said that when he met General Washington he was about to send a messenger to him, but to have done it before would have been merely to let him know that he was simply looking for a suitable position and that would have conveyed no useful information. He complained bitterly that he had so few attendants but this surely seems without cause. He had such aides as his rank entitled him to, he used some of the light-horse officers as aides, twice he conveyed his messages by the aides of other general officers, many times his orders were taken by members of General Washington's staff who were at hand, he had the volunteer services of two officers of the militia of the County of Monmouth, and he certainly had power to detail any officer from the line at any moment to act as

[7] Lee's defence at his court-martial, p. 219.

an aide. General Lee said he never expected that General Washington would move his main army beyond English-town, and in this opinion he was confirmed by a letter from Lieutenant-Colonel Fitzgerald to Lieutenant-Colonel Laurens, which Laurens showed to him. If General Washington, Lee said, had only posted his force in Englishtown that would have been near enough and it was in such a situation as would have well supported him in the stand he was about to make on the west side of the west ravine. He added that to have sent word to General Washington that he wished him to support him would have been presumptuous.

CHAPTER XVII

GENERAL Washington partook of a late breakfast at the residence of Doctor James English in the village of Englishtown. While he was at this meal the troops of the main army were passing Davis' Tavern and coming up to the village. Before leaving the Doctor's hospitable mansion a remark was made to General Washington in the hearing of Lieutenant William Schanck of the First regiment Monmouth County militia, that it was apparent that a Sunday battle would soon ensue and the General said "he did not like fighting on the Sabbath, but he must yield for the good of his country." General Washington remained in Englishtown some time after his troops had left the little village and wrote a short letter to the President of Congress.[1] In this letter he gave the situation as he knew it just before noon of the day of the battle, and, in reference to the enemy distinctly states that General Lee "had orders to attack their rear if possible." When General Washington left the village his host, Doctor English, accompanied him on horseback and remained with him during all the exciting scenes of the day.

General Washington was giving an order to one of his aides to make some change in the march of his troops when Lieutenant-Colonel Thomas Henderson, the leading physician of that part of the county, noted always in history as a "countryman,"[2] whose residence had been burned the previous day by the British, rode by and told him that the Americans were retreating. Up to this moment General Washington had believed that everything was going well with Lee's division. He had heard of no repulse and had no reason to doubt Lee's success. The General was astounded at the information given by Doctor Henderson

[1] Ford, *Writings of George Washington*, Vol. VII, p. 76.
[2] Tilghman's testimony at Lee's court-martial, p. 91.

and asked him who told him that the advance division was retreating. He said that a fifer who was trudging on just behind had so informed him. The fifer, greatly frightened, had been early in the retreat and was taking good care to place himself as far away from the British as possible. His dress must have been very unsoldierly for Washington asked him if he belonged to the army. The man replied in the affirmative and the General showed his great surprise and indignation. He could not believe it and told the poor fifer that if he spread such a report among his men he would have him whipped. To prevent any alarm of this kind, however, he directed a light horseman of his guard to take charge of the musician and keep his depressing news from going further. To get at the truth of the report General Washington sent out his old Secretary, Lieutenant-Colonel Harrison, on whose judgment he was so accustomed to rely, and his gallant aide, Lieutenant-Colonel Fitzgerald, both of whom had been at times with Lee during the morning, and instructed them to ride ahead rapidly, ascertain the situation and report to him as quickly as possible. General Washington rode on some fifty yards and met several other men, one in uniform, all of whom gave him the same information, that General Lee's division was retreating. General Washington still thought these men the ordinary stragglers of an army and entirely discredited their stories.

The two aides-de-camp of General Washington put spurs to their horses and soon came in sight of the west ravine and rode down to the bridge across that morass. Here they met a small portion of Colonel Grayson's regiment, and Captain Cleon Moore and Captain Strother Jones of that command gave them the first authentic news of the great retreat. They tried to excuse themselves by saying that the men were very much fatigued and had been ordered back to refresh themselves. Next came Colonel John Patton's Second North Carolina regiment in some disorder, the men barely able to walk and greatly distressed by the fatiguing tramp and the excessive heat. Then came Grayson's regiment, also in disorder, and Colonel Henry Jackson's regiment followed. They had left their post on the left of the batteries and of Colonel Livingston's New York regiment, according to orders. The commanding officer, on being asked, said he could give no reason for the retreat as he had lost but one man. Then came Maxwell's New Jersey brigade and Colonel Matthias Ogden of the First regiment, a brave and gallant soldier who, in great anger called out to Harrison, "By God! they are flying from a shadow." Riding with Maxwell's brigade they saw Captain Mercer, General Lee's aide, and Harrison asked him, as an officer who should be well posted, "For God's sake, what is the cause of this retreat?" Mercer replied, "If you will go further you will see the columns of the enemy's foot and horse and that was reason enough for the retreat." As Harrison hurried on he retorted that he presumed they were not greater than when they left Philadelphia and that the Americans all came to that field to meet columns of foot and horse. Then the two aides passed still farther along the line of the New Jersey troops and met Lieutenant-Colonel David Rhea of the Fourth regiment. He appeared greatly agitated, for all this disaster, from which he expected so much glory, was taking place on soil perfectly familiar to him, in the neighborhood of his own homestead and among a people whom he knew and loved. He expressed his disapprobation of this movement in strong terms; at the same time he was greatly concerned for his men. Next they saw bluff old Maxwell in the rear of his brigade and he could give no reason for the retreat, had no orders from anyone and was just moving on with the column uncertain what was expected of him in this crisis. At last they came up to General Lee and he had nothing to say to them which was important enough for them afterward to remember, except that he wished to know where General Washington was.

As General Washington advanced in person toward the bridge he became, as Gordon says, "exceedingly alarmed at what he saw when he came up" and he, as his aides had done, spoke first to Colonel Grayson's and Colonel Patton's men and received the same statement of the great weariness of the troops. He ordered them to go into a wood near by and directed a ration of rum to be issued. He desired that captains of companies should see that their men were kept well together. The plethoric Colonel Israel Shreve, Second New Jersey regiment, then came up, his horse worn out with the weight of the huge soldier he had carried all day, and that officer himself almost exhausted by the intense heat of the day. He told General Washington in a most significant manner that he did not know why they retreated; that he had done so by order, but by whose order he did not say. Major Richard Howell, of the same regiment, expressed himself with great earnestness concerning the retreat of the division and said he had never seen anything like it. Lieutenant-Colonel Rhea told General Washington he knew the farms well, that he thought it good ground to make a stand and that he would be glad to serve him in any way.

It is proper to state, that it appears from what General Lee afterward said of this retreat that he was unaware of a large body of his troops having at this time crossed the bridge at the west ravine. It is true that they followed each other without orders from him, but he should have informed himself of what they were doing if he had any real disposition to make a final stand.

Just at this time, as he clearly saw the condition and position of his advance corps, "suspicion flashed across Washington's mind" as Irving says, "of wrong-headed conduct on the part of Lee, to mar the plan of attack adopted contrary to his counsels."[3]

After riding on a little farther just behind the New Jersey brigade General Washington reined up his horse in

[3] Irving's *Life of George Washington*, Vol. III, p. 454.

front of General Lee who was riding forward to meet him. In a stern voice and with bitter emphasis he said to Lee, "I desire to know, sir, what is the reason, whence arises this disorder and confusion?"[4] Confused by the angry manner and appearance of his chief and in his embarrassment not clearly understanding what he had said to him, General Lee stammered out, "Sir—sir!"[5] In an impatient but decided tone General Washington repeated his question, "What is all this confusion for and what is the cause of this retreat?" Still disconcerted by the manner of General Washington, General Lee replied that he received a variety of contradictory intelligence with regard to the numbers and situation of the enemy, that he knew of no confusion except such as resulted from his orders not being obeyed and that in this way only matters had been thrown into some disorder. He added that it was not to the interest of the army or America to have a general action brought on and that he did not desire to attack the whole British Army with troops in such a situation. He also said the whole plan of any attack was against his expressed opinion. He made this statement with much apparent embarrassment. General Washington, still very angry, replied that "whatever his opinion might have been he expected his orders would have been obeyed."[6] He told Lee that he had certain information that it was but a strong covering party of the enemy. General Lee said it might be so but they were rather stronger than he was and he did not think it was proper to risk so much. General Washington said "he was sorry that General Lee undertook the command unless he meant to fight the enemy."[7] Wash-

---

[4] Lee's defence at his court-martial, p. 219. This was two miles from Freehold, on the Freehold and Englishtown turnpike. "Washington met the first of Lee's retreating troops on the Herbert farm, now [1926] owned by the estate of George Du Bois, and met Lee himself on the Thompson farm, now owned by John M. Laird."—S. C. Cowart.

[5] McHenry's testimony at Lee's court-martial, p. 90.

[6] Tilghman's testimony at Lee's court-martial, p. 93.

[7] Brooks' testimony at Lee's court-martial, p. 169.

ington then rode on toward the rear of the retreating troops.[8]

In addition to this conversation some historians claim that General Washington called General Lee "a damned poltroon." It will be observed by those who carefully examine the proceedings in the trial of General Lee that Lee never asserts that Washington spoke to him in this manner, and that not a single officer puts into the mouth of the commander-in-chief any words of profanity or even of doubtful taste as applied by one officer to another. It seems, however, to be the universal opinion that General Washington used profane language on this occasion, but this is all based on the statement made by General Lafayette, forty-six years after this event, while he was on a visit to America. It does not appear that General Lafayette was present when this interview took place, his memoirs even giving the impression that he was at another part of the field, and it is quite likely that in after years General Lafayette thought Lee deserved such language. It may have been a camp rumor, or, perhaps Lafayette, who in his evidence at the trial did not refer to this interview, supposed that in his great indignation General Washington gave vent to epithets altogether foreign to his life and habits. In after years, in reply to the question, "did Washington swear?" Brigadier-General Scott said, the habit of profanity being strong in his own speech, "Yes, sir, he did once, it was at Monmouth and on a day that would have made any man swear. Yes, sir, he swore that day till the leaves shook on the trees, charming, delightful! Never have I enjoyed such swearing before or since. Sir, on that memorable day he swore like an angel

[8] John Fiske quotes an eye-witness as having heard Washington say, " 'My God! General Lee, what are you about?' General Lee began to make some explanation; but General Washington impatiently interrupted him, and with his hand still raised high above his head, waving it angrily, exclaimed, 'Go to the rear, sir,' spurred his horse and rode rapidly forward. The whole thing occurred as quickly as I can tell it to you." *Essays Historical and Literary*, Vol. I, pp. 91-2 (note).

from heaven!"[9] General Scott does not appear to have been present at Washington's interview with Lee, and, in any case, he should have been with his own command.

Before General Washington reached the rear of the retreating division he met Lieutenant-Colonel Harrison then on his return to report to him, and Harrison told him the British advance was pressing on hard and would be up with them within fifteen minutes. This was the first intelligence Washington had had of the near approach of the enemy. Lieutenant-Colonel Fitzgerald, the aide who had accompanied Harrison, was at this moment a little distance off in a grain-field, on slightly rising ground, with Lieutenant-Colonel De Hart, of the Second New Jersey regiment, trying to reconnoiter the enemy. He joined Harrison and General Washington a few minutes thereafter. General Washington and his aides then retraced their ride, Washington giving orders rapidly and his efficient aides seeing that they were executed. Colonel Shreve and his Second New Jersey regiment, as has been said, took post on a hill, and Colonel Grayson's Virginia regiment and Patton's regiment, Continental infantry, were ordered to form with Colonel Shreve's command. Lieutenant-Colonel David Rhea was ordered to report to General Washington for special duty, as he had volunteered. The regiment of Colonel Livingston, the Fourth New York Continental infantry, was directed to form at the hedge row.

The retreating parties at this time took up such a broad extent of country that a battalion on the extreme left, some distance from the highway, attracted Washington's attention and he feared it was a force of the enemy, but he was undeceived by the report of General Cadwalader and Lieutenant-Colonel Tilghman whom he sent out to ascertain what they were.

[9] This subject is well discussed in Carrington's *Washington the Soldier*, pp. 235-7. See also John Fiske, "Charles Lee, the Soldier of Fortune," in *Essays Historical and Literary*, Vol. I, pp. 53-98, for an able and scholarly discussion of the career of Lee.

CHAPTER XVIII

IT is now necessary to return to the main body of the army, fresh troops, unburdened with knapsacks or blankets, slowly advancing from Englishtown by the same highway which General Lee had taken in the early morning. General Nathanael Greene, the Quartermaster-General, but now in direct command of troops, had first received orders to turn off on a road to the right of the meeting-house and so come in on the south of the Monmouth Court House. Lord Stirling and his division were to keep to the main road and in this way take a position on the left of General Greene's column. But all this was changed during the halt of a few moments near the Tennent church. At that time Lee's retreat, with all its dangerous consequences, began fully to appear to these officers. Then General Greene was ordered to take a very advantageous position, as General Washington thought, on the extreme right of the army, to prevent the enemy from approaching on that flank. Major-General Lord Stirling, with whom General Washington had been riding from Englishtown, was ordered to post his division on a hill on the left of the army, with the west ravine in front, and with orders to prevent any surprise on the upper road. These two bodies of troops were a little over half a mile apart.

At this time all the troops of Lee's division having passed beyond Ker's house, the British cavalry came up, determined to hasten the steps of the retiring Americans across Robert Rhea's farm and the plantation of the late Reverend William Tennent.[1] They charged the few horse which still endeavored to keep guard over the patriots and to warn them of the approach of the foe. These troop-

---

[1] The "parsonage farm" is about two miles west of Freehold, and is now [1926] owned by Joseph Brakely.

ers they dispersed without much difficulty. But just when this was accomplished the British espied Colonel Grayson's detachment, formed as a support to the artillery and the retreating infantry troops, behind a fence which afforded a sure protection against the charge of horsemen. It took but a moment for them to see their danger from the fire of Grayson's men which opened on them and they immediately wheeled off and returned to the British corps to which they were attached.

The position which General Duportail had been anxious for General Lee to occupy and to defend was now virtually abandoned. General Lee was still disposed to continue his retreat and he had his eye, as it was afterward asserted, on the hills pointed out to him by Captain Wikoff, which, unknown to General Lee, were already being occupied by Washington's forces.

General Washington was now giving his orders rapidly and the troops, hailing his clear commands with great enthusiasm and rallying quickly when they felt the influence of his strong, self-reliant personality, were soon placed in position and the retreat checked. The British troops were now in sight, rapidly pressing nearer. The first American officers Washington personally recognized were Colonel Walter Stewart, of the Thirteenth Pennsylvania regiment and Lieutenant-Colonel Nathaniel Ramsay, of the Third Maryland regiment, and, taking Ramsay by the hand and calling him by name he said, "I shall depend on your immediate exertions to check with your two regiments the progress of the enemy till I can form the main army." The reply he received from Colonel Ramsay was characteristic of the man, "We shall check them."[2] His men rallied with the greatest alacrity, within two hundred yards of the approaching enemy—no soldiers ever responded more cheerfully or with better spirit. They clearly understood

[2] Dr. James McHenry's writing on the margin of his own copy of Marshall's *Life of George Washington*, Vol. III, p. 473.

now the reason for the orders given and assumed a position with a determination to hold it until overpowered.

General Washington, as has been said, saw Colonel Walter Stewart, the brave Pennsylvanian, crossing the morass with his men. He had been unable in the course of the retreat to reach General Wayne's detachment, where he belonged, but having gradually inclined his regiment toward the left under cover of a corner of woods, he found himself on the right of General Lee's division. His regiment did not again join Colonel Livingston's and Colonel Wesson's commands, with which it had for some hours been associated. General Lafayette was riding with Colonel Stewart when they met General Washington, and Lafayette gave him a hasty account of the situation and approach of the British.

General Washington also met General Wayne and they agreed on a place on the left, near a wood, where they would make an attempt to stop the British force.

Soon after this decision had been made and General Washington had left for another part of the field, Captain Mercer rode up to General Wayne with an order from General Lee for him to "defend the position to the last." General Wayne having received his orders from a higher authority, brusquely asked him whom he came from. Mercer told him and added that General Lee had again assumed command. Wayne, however, paid no attention to the message nor the explanation but turned away to the conflict now impending.

General Wayne was now smarting under the loss of personal glory which he had hoped to gain that morning. He was indignant at the retreat because of the loss of prestige to the American arms; but he was prompt in placing the regiments of Colonel Stewart and Lieutenant-Colonel Ramsay in a wood on the left of the roadway. He thought the idea of checking the advance of the enemy "exceedingly practicable, provided any effort or exertion was made for the purpose." He was confident that "a very select body of men had been that day drawn off from a body far inferior in number."[3]

The light infantry battalions of the British and their grenadier regiments were at that time hardly four hundred yards distant from the rear of General Lee's retreating column.

The appearance of General Washington as he rallied his broken army was described by General Lafayette in these words: "Never was General Washington greater in war than in this action. His presence stopped the retreat; his dispositions fixed the victory; his fine appearance on horseback, his calm courage roused to animation by the vexations of the morning, gave him the air best calculated to excite enthusiasm."[4] At another time Lafayette said that he "rode along the lines, amid the shouts of the soldiers, cheering them by his voice and example and restoring to our standard the fortunes of the fight. I thought then as now that never had I beheld so superb a man."[5] It is quite certain that his own personal faith and courage aroused a like spirit of confidence in his men and his voice and every act inspired the confidence of victory.

At the beginning of Stewart's and Ramsay's defence of their new position Colonel Walter Stewart, of the Thirteenth Pennsylvania regiment, was sorely wounded and carried off the field of battle.

The British party now in their immediate front was composed of large detachments of Lieutenant-Colonel the Honorable William Harcourt's command, the Sixteenth regiment, light dragoons, and of the Seventeenth regiment, light dragoons, Lieutenant-Colonel Samuel Birch commanding. This latter regiment had been constantly in the saddle since it left the Quaker city and had taken part in all the hard service required of the cavalry, with the American troops constantly hovering on their rear and on

[3] Harrison's testimony at Lee's court-martial, p. 85.
[4] Headley's *Life of General Lafayette*, p. 94.
[5] Custis' *Recollections of Washington*, p. 220.

their flanks. Now it was recalled from the main body to aid the Sixteenth dragoons in pressing on the flight of the retreating patriots.

Lieutenant-Colonel Ramsay, however, held vigorously to his position with his own regiment and Stewart's regiment, of which Lieutenant-Colonel Lewis Farmer was in command after Colonel Stewart had been borne off the battle-field.

The British dragoons pressed stubbornly on Ramsay, but he was able with great efforts to check and engage them for a little time while the main army gained a few needed moments for preparation. At last, by the pressure of superior numbers, Ramsay's force was compelled to fall back, which they did, fighting and in good order. Ramsay was the last man to leave the position. His horse had been killed under him and while dismounted he was attacked by one of the British dragoons who attempted to shoot him with his pistol. It missed fire, however, and the dragoon made a desperate assault with his saber. Then in the very front of the advancing British Army a duel of life and death took place. Ramsay with his short-bladed sword,[6] cut the dragoon down from his horse and was about to mount the animal when a number of the comrades of the disabled trooper came up. Even then the brave Marylander did not hesitate to fight the party. This he did with great courage, inflicting some wounds and being himself wounded. But he was at last overpowered and taken prisoner. Sir Henry Clinton was told the next day of the personal gallantry of Ramsay, and, with a true soldier's love of brave deeds he released him on his parole.[7] In this little episode, brief though it was, Lieutenant-Colonel Ramsay did all in his power to hinder the

[6] This weapon is still preserved in Ramsay's family as a relic of the engagement.

[7] Ramsay soon again entered the American camp, was conveyed to Princeton and remained at the house of Mrs. Jonathan Sergeant.

advance of the foe. The check of a single minute was at this time invaluable.[8]

It is well to add that Lieutenant-Colonel John Laurens, Washington's aide, who was active in aiding Ramsay in this engagement, was himself badly wounded and also had a horse shot under him.

General Washington ordered two more pieces of artillery to take position on the right of the troops of Stewart and Ramsay. They had hardly unlimbered before they found the British artillery sending shot among the men of the Thirteenth Pennsylvania regiment in the woods. Lieutenant-Colonel Oswald now had two field-pieces belonging to General Varnum's brigade with Captain John Compston of the Third regiment artillery in command, two pieces of Captain Thomas Seward's battery of the same regiment and two guns of his own Second regiment, in all six pieces of artillery. The men of these companies were in great distress from heat and fatigue, but still they kept replying to the British cannonade. The desperate condition of these matrosses was very apparent to General Knox.

The musketry and artillery fire between the two lines now became very general and the British advance party, in two distinct columns, pushed forward steadily and evidently gained ground on the little force attempting vainly to check them. Oswald at this moment feared he might lose his guns since the infantry commands just spoken of were out of good supporting distance. He appealed to General Knox to procure him some support. Before this could be obtained, however, Oswald was ordered by General Lee, the order being delivered by Brigade-Major Shaw, to retreat. This he did slowly for about forty yards while the soldiers near him were shouting, "drive on! drive on!" Regardless of this he directed his

---

[8] See very complete and interesting *Sketch of Colonel Nathaniel Ramsay of the Maryland Line,* by Isaac R. Pennypacker, of Philadelphia, Pa., privately printed.

drivers to move steadily. General Knox then appealed to his friend Colonel Henry Jackson to come up and cover the guns, but before he could get his men up as a supporting party on the right of the batteries, the whole artillery line was obliged again to retreat as the enemy had gained the wood on the left and the British dragoons were closing in on the right. Even in this retreat the cannon were frequently unlimbered and shot sent among the enemy. All this time men on horseback on the roadway, seeing the danger to which Oswald's command was exposed, were shouting to him to "retreat! retreat!" His danger was certainly imminent but as he was moving off General Lee directed him to remain there and keep firing until he had direct orders to retreat. Oswald's guns began to fire again when some aides from General Lafayette came up and ordered him to retreat. This order he disregarded for a time because of General Lee's superior orders just given him. He said to Lafayette's aides, "I will remain here and until I have General Lee's orders to retreat I cannot retreat." The aides of Lafayette replied that they had General Lee's orders that he should now retreat and that they should conduct him to a new position in the rear.

During the cannonade at the place they were about to leave, one of the picturesque incidents of this battle took place,—a battle full of dramatic scenes worthy of the painter's brush and the chisel of the sculptor.

The story of Molly Pitcher is related in many different ways.

In Barber and Howe's *Historical Collections of New Jersey* the episode is told somewhat in this manner: During the engagement Molly, the wife of a cannonier, was busy carrying water from a neighboring spring to refresh the weary artillerists. While engaged in this work her husband fell dead at his gun. An officer about this time ordered the gun to the rear. "No," said the woman, "the cannon shall not be removed for the want of someone to serve it; since my brave husband is no more I will use my utmost exertions to avenge his death." She then performed the duties of cannonier and attracted the attention of all in sight. Washington gave her the rank of Lieutenant, and half-pay for life. She wore an epaulette afterward and was called Captain Molly.

Custis, in his *Recollections*, relates very much the same story but gives this as the woman's expression, "Lie there, my darling, while I revenge ye."

The version of the story given by Lossing in his *Field Book* and in his notes to Custis' *Recollections* makes her a young Irishwoman, twenty-two years of age and a sturdy camp-follower. When she heard the order for the removal of the gun, she seized the rammer and with skill and courage tried to avenge her husband's death. The next morning, covered with blood and dirt, she was presented by General Greene to General Washington, who gave her a piece of gold and conferred upon her a commission as sergeant. The fame of "Sergeant Molly" spread throughout the army and the French soldiers, interested in her story, filled her chapeau with silver coin as she passed in front of their ranks.

The Journal of Doctor Albigence Waldo, dated in camp opposite Brunswick on July 3, 1778, gives probably the most accurate account of the incident in these words: "One of the camp women I must give a little praise to. Her gallant, whom she attended in battle, being shot down, she immediately took up his gun and cartridges and like a Spartan heroine fought with astonishing bravery, discharging the piece with as much regularity as any soldier present. This a wounded officer, whom I dressed, told me he did see himself, she being in his platoon, and assured me I might depend on its truth."

Now this statement of Doctor Waldo represents the woman as the sweetheart of an infantry soldier, who fell dead in his platoon, instead of the wife of an artillerist, serving his cannon. A most diligent search of the pension records of the Old War Office at Washington fails to show a pension given, or half-pay for life allowed, to any woman for the death of her lover or husband at the Battle of Monmouth under any of the names by which Molly Pitcher has been known—Molly Maban, Molly Hanna, Molly Hayes or Molly McCauley.

An incident of a similar character occurred at Fort Washington, November 16, 1776. The Supreme Executive Council of Pennsylvania on June 29, 1779, directed that an order be drawn "in favour of Margaret Corbin for Thirty Dollars to relieve her present necessities she having been wounded and utterly disabled by three Grapeshott, while she filled with distinguished Bravery the post of her Husband, who was killed by her side, serving a piece of Artillery at Fort Washington." In the *Pennsylvania Colonial Records*[9] we find that after reciting her services in the language just stated, the Council ordered, "that she be recommended to a further consideration of the Board of War, This Council being of the opinion, that notwithstanding the rations which have been allowed her, she is not Provided for as her helpless situation really requires." In the Second Series of *Pennsylvania Archives*[10] we find her name in Colonel Lewis Nicolas' Invalid Regiment as discharged at the close of the war in April 1783, and thus Margaret Corbin must have been carried on the regimental rolls of the Continental Army for all those years after her heroic exploit in November 1776.[11]

Mention should also be made of the record concerning "Captain Molly" which is found in Boynton's *History of West Point* (page 166). In this work the story is told of her firing the last gun at the British when Fort Clinton was taken October 6, 1777. Then follows the anecdote of her good conduct at Monmouth, nine months afterwards, in the same language as given in Barber and Howe's *Historical Collections of New Jersey*. In addition to this story,

[9] Vol. XII, p. 34.
[10] Vol. XI, p. 277.
[11] *Magazine of American History*, Vol. I, p. 90, and Vol. XVI, pp. 299, 401.

however, extracts are given from manuscript notes made at the Academy by Major George Fleming, Ordnance and Military Storekeeper. These notes are dated October 7, 1786, April 21, June 12 and July 8, 1787, and relate to lodging and food furnished her at the village of Swinstown, now called Buttermilk Falls. This clearly shows that four years after the Revolution the Secretary of War, General Knox, attended to the maintenance of a woman called Molly Pitcher at the government's expense.

The story which is now generally believed, which has same incidental record proof and which is likely to be regarded in the future as the true account, may be related in this wise: Mary Ludwig, daughter of John George Ludwig, who came to this country with the Palatinates, was born October 13, 1744. In the year 1768 she was employed as a domestic in the family of William Irvine, of Carlisle, Pennsylvania, afterward a distinguished general in the Revolutionary War. On July 24, 1769, Mary Ludwig married John Casper Hayes, a barber of Carlisle.[12] On December 1, 1775, her husband, his soldier name being John Hayes, enlisted in Colonel Thomas Procter's First Pennsylvania regiment artillery and served therein one year.[13] He then enlisted in January, 1777, in Captain John Alexander's Company of Colonel William Irvine's Seventh Pennsylvania regiment.[14] It appears that Molly Hayes followed her husband to the war, as we have seen was the custom in the British Army, and to some extent in the American troops. These women nursed the sick and assisted in the cooking and washing. Private Hayes was probably detailed on the battle-field of Monmouth from infantry service to help one of the batteries. His wife was aiding the cause by carrying pitchers of water for the heated and wounded men. When John Hayes was wounded at the gun she took his place and performed

12 *Pennsylvania Archives*, Second Series, Vol. II, p. 181.
13 *ibid.*, Vol. XI, p. 176.
14 *ibid.*, Vol. X, p. 614.

some act of unusual heroism.[15] On the death of John Hayes after the war Molly Hayes married a worthless fellow named John McCauley. Molly McCauley, known familiarly in Carlisle as "Molly Pitcher," lived on the corner of North and Bedford Streets in a house which since has been demolished. On February 27, 1822, the Pennsylvania Legislature granted her the sum of forty dollars and an annuity of the same amount.[16] She died January 22, 1832, and is buried in the old Carlisle cemetery. On the one hundredth anniversary of the Declaration of Independence the citizens of Carlisle erected a neat monument over the heroine's grave,[17] with the following inscription:

> MOLLY MCCAULEY
> RENOWNED IN HISTORY AS
> "MOLLY PITCHER,"
> THE HEROINE OF MONMOUTH.
> DIED JANUARY 22, 1833[18]
> AGED SEVENTY-NINE YEARS.
> ERECTED BY THE CITIZENS OF CUMBERLAND
> COUNTY, JULY THE FOURTH 1876.[19]

[15] "I am satisfied that this spring was in the edge of Gordon's woods near what is known as Gordon's Bridge on the Pennsylvania Railroad, and not where 'Mollie Pitcher's Well' is today pointed out, for the reason that Ramsay's guns were near these woods and the well was not dug until · fifty years after the battle, by Dr. J. C. Thompson, who himself years later told me he dug it." Samuel C. Cowart, in conversation with Ed., August 12, 1926.

[16] *Laws of Pennsylvania* 1821-22, p. 32.

[17] Egle's *Some Pennsylvania Women in the War of the Revolution*, p. 85.

[18] The date should be January 22, 1832. *The Carlisle Republican* in its issue of January 26, 1832, says: "Died on Sunday last in this borough, at an advanced age, Mrs. Molly McCauly," &c.

[19] For a number of years I spent a part of each summer in Carlisle. In 1905 I met there Miss Caroline Ege, a life-long resident, who died in the year 1909 at the advanced age of eighty-seven. As a child she had known Molly McCauley, remembered her well, and told me interesting facts in regard to her. In response to a letter of inquiry to a member of Miss Ege's family I received the following reply (August 1926): "Yes, you are correct in quoting—'Molly was a rough, common woman who swore like a trooper.' She smoked and chewed tobacco, and had no education whatever. She was hired to do the most menial work, such as scrubbing, etc. I think there are some of her descendants still living in Carlisle."—W.S.M.

CHAPTER XIX

BY order of General Lee a march of about a quarter of a mile was made by Oswald's men, during which time four more guns were added to his command. These came from General Maxwell's brigade, which was then emerging from a wood and marching up a hill, and formed the battery attached to his brigade and the battery of Scott's detachment, which General Scott had entrusted two hours previously to the care of Maxwell's troops. Lieutenant-Colonel Oswald, the brave commander, who had gained so much honor on this field had now his own two-gun battery, Captain Compston's two guns, Captain Cook's two guns, Captain Seward's two guns and Captain Well's two guns,—in all ten pieces of artillery.

Colonel Henry B. Livingston and his Fourth New York regiment then received orders from General Lee to support Oswald's artillery as from time to time they fired on the enemy and then retreated. Every moment it was expected that the British would make another fierce cavalry charge for the purpose of capturing these batteries and their gunners. A mistake occurred, however, in reference to the position Livingston's regiment was to take and it was not placed at the post to which it had been assigned. The batteries continued to retreat, and Colonel Livingston's men, still attempting to support them, retreated with them to a hedge fence and there took position on the right side of Varnum's brigade, which Lieutenant-Colonel Alexander Hamilton had assisted Lieutenant-Colonel Olney, the commanding officer, in forming there. General Lee was at this moment in great personal danger from the flying shots of the British, but he appeared brave and self-reliant, although in retreat.

General Washington had ordered General Wayne, who was still enraged at the part he had been obliged to take

during the morning, to make a strong stand along the
hedge fence with Colonel Stewart's regiment, Colonel Livingston's regiment, just referred to, a part of General
Scott's own brigade and two pieces of artillery, and to
dispute every foot of the advance of the foe. It did not
take General Wayne many moments to bring his light
infantry troops in line of battle, and they immediately
began firing on the advancing column of British foot and
dragoons. The fighting soon became quite animated and
considerable execution was done in the ranks of the red-
coats. On the American side Captain Joseph McCracken,
of the Fourth New York regiment, lost his left arm.

General Lee noticed in the distance the active movements of the brilliant and true-hearted Pennsylvania
soldier and he rode up to Wikoff's house, near which
Wayne's command had formed, and inquired of that officer why he formed in a position so exposed to the enemy's
cannon. "By General Washington's orders," Wayne replied, "and he instructed me to defend the post as long
as possible till he could form the troops." General Lee
remarked as he rode away, that he had "nothing more to
say."

Colonel Livingston's regiment was now entirely overcome with heat and fatigue, and although they had tried
as best they could to protect the artillery, they really in-
terfered at times with the proper handling of the pieces.
They seemed not to be able to move quickly right and left
and so give free opening for the discharge of the guns. The
Colonel himself had received a slight wound.

Lieutenant-Colonel William S. Smith, in command of
Lee's Continental regiment, received an order from General Lee that "the blue regiment must form behind the
fence," and one-half of his men turned about to the rear
and went behind the hedge as directed. Colonel Henry
Jackson was angry when he saw the right wing of the
regiment separated from the left, and ordered it back to
its former post. Meeting General Lee soon after, Colonel

Jackson made some remarks about the broken state of the command. Lee was overheard to say angrily to Jackson, with his hand on his sword, that these movements were contrary to his directions, that he meant to effect a retreat, and proposed to station these troops at the fence merely to cover the retreat. Major John S. Tyler, who led the right wing of the detachment, then marched it back and the parts were again united. General Washington, riding near, ordered Lieutenant-Colonel William S. Smith to advance the regiment five hundred yards to a wood, to protect the men from the sun and to give them some advantage if the enemy should advance in that direction. Soon afterward, Colonel Jackson ordered his detachment to file off and retire from the ground.

While the weary soldiers were seeking water at the parsonage well, young Captain Henry Fauntleroy, of the Fifth Virginia regiment, stopped at the well to quench his burning thirst. Seeing the parched and weary enlisted men crowding around and begging for a drink of water he waived his turn again and yet again. As he stood aside unselfishly while others took the cooling draught, a round shot came bounding toward him, shattered his hip and threw him to the ground mangled and dying. He was greatly mourned by his regimental commander, Colonel Josiah Parker, and by the men of his very gallant regiment.

All this time General Maxwell had received no orders to form his New Jersey brigade, and he kept on retreating, expecting every moment that he would be halted by General Lee and posted where he could do some effective service. The officers of his brigade, as has been seen, were still enraged when they passed in column by Washington's aides, and afterward when they saw the General himself. No disposition to turn about and face the enemy was yet apparent in any of the movements, although they had retreated until they were in sight of the meeting-house. Where then, they wondered, was this backward movement to stop! The gallant young Colonel Matthias Ogden begged of General Maxwell that he might be allowed to halt his regiment on the left of a hedge in a small wood near by and in this way to help cover some of the retreating force. His brother, Major Aaron Ogden, General Maxwell's brigade-major, who distinguished himself in the siege of Yorktown, and in after years was made the Governor of New Jersey, rode up and offered to aid Colonel Ogden in forming his men. Maxwell gave Colonel Ogden his consent and the First New Jersey regiment was soon in position near the road which led to the causeway over the west ravine, with a morass on their left. Soon after this General Maxwell sent Major Ogden to General Lee for orders. Major Ogden found him in an orchard not far from Ker's house and told him that Maxwell had posted Colonel Ogden's regiment to cover the retreat. He also expressed the opinion that his brother's troops would give the enemy a warm reception. General Lee impatiently replied, "Don't tell me of what they will do, but tell it to me after they have done it!"[1] At the same time he expressed a wish that they might succeed in checking the foe. Captain Mercer was then sent by General Lee to Colonel Ogden with orders for him to hold his position to the last extremity and cover, if possible, the movement of Lee's division over the narrow bridge.

General Lee told Major Ogden to say to General Maxwell, in response to his request for orders, that he desired him to place his brigade, now consisting of the Second, Third and Fourth New Jersey Continental regiments, in the woods on the right. To do this General Maxwell must needs break through the line of the retreating column and make even more confusion than was now visible. General Maxwell was angry with his brigade-major, for he felt that either General Lee did not know his present position or Major Ogden had brought an incorrect message. Maxwell left his brigade in charge of

[1] Ogden's testimony at Lee's court-martial, p. 109.

Colonel Israel Shreve for a few moments and rode over to where Ogden had informed him that General Lee was riding with his staff. He met General Lee in a large wheat field, and Lee merely repeated the orders as conveyed by Major Ogden. The situation was explained, and General Lee corrected his orders by asking Maxwell to remain on the left side where his brigade then was. He also told him to get water for his men, and, if possible, to shelter them in the underbrush from the intense heat. Brigade-Major Samuel Shaw of the artillery was witness to this interview and afterward had occasion to refer to it under oath.

General Maxwell then returned to his brigade and they crossed a defile, the only causeway over the marsh, and marched into the woods, that they might guard the road on the side which led up from Forman's mill. When they reached their position the retreating column was still moving on both sides of the main roadway and crowding across the ravine in the rear of Maxwell's brigade. The General left his brigade for a moment to reconnoiter the enemy in person, and while he was absent Captain Wikoff rode up and directed Colonel Shreve, by order of General Lafayette, to take his own regiment, the Second New Jersey, over the ravine in the rear of the brigade as then posted. Colonel Shreve instantly marched his men toward the place designated. When General Maxwell returned he halted the regiment, but after the matter was explained to him ordered Lafayette's wishes to be complied with and directed the battery of two guns, which was attached to his brigade and which Lieutenant-Colonel Oswald had just returned, to go with Colonel Shreve and his regiment to the edge of the woods and cover the passage at the west ravine. After some time had elapsed the two other regiments of Maxwell's brigade crossed the defile, followed in the route taken by Colonel Shreve and then joined the Second regiment on the westerly side of the defile, leaving one regiment between the road and the marsh and to cover the road that led from Forman's mill. After all the troops of Lee's division had passed over the bridge General Maxwell's brigade was ordered to form in the rear of General Lord Stirling's command on the hill, which was promptly done.

General Lee had been continuing to give orders to the troops, but was checked by his aide, Captain Mercer, who told him that General Washington was now giving orders direct to the officers of his division and that he should be cautious lest the orders conflict. General Lee thought the suggestion wise, for he had already noticed that General Washington's orders were gradually superseding all that he had issued. When, therefore, he was next asked about the movements of the troops he said that he supposed General Washington meant he should have no further command, and that he scarcely thought he had the right to give any orders. Soon after this he observed General Washington, who had already passed him, crossing the bridge at the west ravine. He rode toward the commander-in-chief, and found him forming the troops for the final conflict of the day. He heard his words of cheer to the men, imparting new faith and confidence to all about him. General Washington noticed General Lee approaching, and in a calmer tone than he had used at their former meeting, asked whether Lee would take the command here, or if he should do it himself. If General Lee would command, Washington said that he would return to the main body and still further arrange them on the next height back. Up to this moment General Washington had not formally deprived Lee of his division, although his own direct orders seemed to supersede Lee's authority. General Lee replied that His Excellency had given him the command before and it was equal with him where he commanded. General Washington then said that he expected him to take proper measures for checking the enemy at that place, and General Lee answered that his orders should be obeyed, that he would do everything in his power and would not be the first to leave the field. General Lee then rode off toward the right wing and was thus expected, with selected troops, to give the enemy a check sufficient to enable the rest of his division to cross the bridge.

During the fighting which followed, and before General Lee was relieved, both of his aides, Captain Mercer and Captain Edwards, had their horses badly wounded, and the horses of Lieutenant-Colonel Brooks and Lieutenant-Colonel de Malmedy were nearly dead with fatigue. Thus these officers of General Lee's staff were dismounted and were carrying his orders on foot. General John Cadwalader had been active in every part of the field, aiding General Washington, and General Joseph Reed had been on the fighting line so often that his horse had been killed under him.

General Washington had just finished his conversation with General Lee and ridden away when his youthful aide-de-camp, Lieutenant-Colonel Alexander Hamilton, full of enthusiasm, came up to General Lee flourishing his sword and exclaiming with great ardor, "I will stay here with you, my dear General, and we will all die here with you on the spot. Let us die here rather than retreat." In a most composed manner and in strong contrast to what he called Hamilton's "frenzy of valour" General Lee asked him if he did not think he looked calm enough to determine what was best to be done in this crisis, and that after he had properly arranged the Continental troops in his command, he would be as ready to die as Hamilton could possibly be. He also said, "When I have taken proper measures to get the main body of them in a good position I will die with you on this spot, if you please."[2] Lieutenant-Colonel Hamilton testified a month later, that he was near General Lee for a short time afterward,[3] but heard no directions given, nor saw any measures taken by him to fulfill his promise to General Washington or

[2] Lee's defence at his court-martial, p. 230.

[3] Not long after his conversation with General Lee, Colonel Hamilton's horse was struck by a bullet and fell, disabling its rider so that he was incapacitated for further service that day.

to carry out the purposes which he had just stated to him. Lieutenant-Colonel Fitzgerald said that he was near General Lee for nearly half an hour, but heard no orders given.

Lieutenant-Colonel Oswald had by this time, returned the battery belonging to Varnum's brigade as well as that belonging to Maxwell's brigade, and Captain Thomas Wells' battery of the Third Continental artillery had been ordered toward Englishtown, the men being entirely disabled by the heat and toil. Oswald then appealed to Lieutenant-Colonel Fitzgerald, who was riding near him, to ask General Washington to send up a fresh artillery force. General Knox, however, coming up just at this moment, promised to see that it was attended to immediately, and ordered Oswald to retire again to a better position a few rods back. The battery of Captain Thomas Seward of the Third regiment of artillery was placed on a little hill back of the hedgerow where the continentals had formed. While the infantry were engaged, the artillery fired grape-shot at the advancing columns of the British through an opening in the fence and over the heads of the line of Americans. Captain Compston's two guns of Varnum's brigade also did excellent service at this time under General Knox's direction. It was a bold and vigorous cannonade at short range and was one of the most effective exploits of the battle. First Lieutenant James McNair, a gallant New York officer, attached to Captain Andrew Porter's company of the Second Continental artillery regiment had his head shot off by a cannon-ball.

We left Lieutenant-Colonel Olney in command of General Varnum's brigade[4] at the hedge fence in front of the bridge over the west ravine. Captain David Cook's battery of the Third Continental artillery regiment was at-

[4] A sketch of Lieutenant-Colonel Olney and of Varnum's brigade, especially the Second Rhode Island regiment and two companies of the First Rhode Island regiment, in this battle, has been prepared by Colonel Asa Bird Gardiner, President of the Society of the Cincinnati in the State of Rhode Island and filed with the archives of said society.

tached to this brigade, and in the position just stated was relied upon to support it. It had but eight matrosses now on duty, yet they stood to their guns ready for the supreme moment. General Knox rode up and down the line and all the guns were loaded with grape under his instructions. On the American right the British dragoons were trotting rapidly up to the charge, and from a copse on the left the enemy could be seen massing their troops for a desperate assault. The contending forces were now within short musket range, and the conflict of the day, the real battle, was impending. Shots were already being exchanged between some eager American marksmen and the British, as the worn-out regiments of Stewart and Ramsay passed the ravine covered by the guns of Olney's men. Large numbers of Colonel Livingston's men would not march by, but crowded in on the right of Varnum's brigade to continue the contest while powder and lead remained.

Just at this time General Wayne learned of a road which led by Taylor's Tavern and he hastily sent to General Washington suggesting that troops should be posted there so as to prevent the British from turning the American right flank. Wayne was thoughtful of the whole army, even though the enemy was about to attack his own position.

The heat was still intense. The mercury registered ninety-six degrees in the shade and the sun beat mercilessly upon the heads of the soldiers exposed to its rays, and upon the wounded and the dying as they fell upon the bloody field. Many, without a wound, crawled along the stream at the west ravine to drink and to die from the heat and fatigue. Doctor Samuel Forman, one of the leading physicians of the county, who was on the battle-field to aid the suffering, said afterward that the tongues of many of the men were so swollen by thirst that it rendered them almost incapable of articulation. The Hessian soldiers, loaded down with heavy clothing, with arms and the weighty and oppressive equipments which they were obliged to carry, swore that they would not fight in such fervid heat. It is not surprising that these men felt the intense heat of the day when we read a description of their stiff and heavy clothing and the great amount of material they had to carry.[5]

While the battle was raging around the parsonage a number of people were gathered on the roof and in the steeple of the church, somewhat more than a mile away, anxiously gazing upon the field. Even as they looked a shot came whirling through the graveyard and struck a man who was seated on a stone, wounding him severely. He was immediately carried into the meeting-house and placed in a pew, but expired there within the same hour. Many years afterward the blood stains on the pew and floor were shown to visitors, and the old grave-stone on which the man sat, and which was broken by the cannon-ball, is still a well-known memento of the incident.

At this stage of the battle an incident of a most ludicrous character occurred.[6] It appears that General Washington's body servant, Billy Lee, who was a fine horseman, with handsome figure, came proudly up on a little hill with a gay party of servants following him. Here he drew forth the General's great spy-glass from its case and proceeded in fine military style to reconnoiter the British column. The enemy discovered the little group, apparently of important officers, spying out their position. General Washington also saw the party collected on the rising ground beyond, and he remarked to his staff: "See those

---

[5] In Dunlap's *History of the American Theatre* we find a description of their appearance on the streets of New York City during the Revolutionary period. "The Hessian with his towering brass-fronted cap, mustachios coloured with the same material that coloured his shoes, his hair plastered with tallow and flour, and tightly drawn into a long appendage reaching from the back of the head to his waist, his blue uniform almost covered by the broad belts sustaining his cartouch-box, his brass-hilted sword and his bayonet; a yellow waistcoat with flaps and yellow breeches were met at the knees by black gaiters and thus heavily equipped he stood an automaton and received the command or cane of the officer who inspected him."

[6] See Custis, *Recollections of Washington.*

fellows collecting on yonder height: the enemy will fire on them to a certainty." A shot from a British six-pounder followed his remark and struck the branches of a sycamore tree near the group, and the proud Billy and his mulatto followers scampered off in undignified haste, causing the General to smile even in this hour of anxiety and danger. It may be added that Billy remained with Washington throughout the war, attended him during his administration as President and was remembered by him in his will.

CHAPTER XX

THE passage of the retreating division over the west ravine, about half a mile southeast of the meeting-house, was practically completed. The troops had fought with great gallantry to cover their brethren, and had sustained some losses. A retreat had been made, as General Lee afterward asserted, for the purpose of gaining a better position, and he boasted that it had been done without the loss of a single piece of artillery or the capture of even part of a battalion. Now, however, contrary to his plans and expectations, his command was about to be absorbed in the main body of the army. He passed the bridge over the deep morass, being the last officer in the column. Colonel Ogden, with his First New Jersey regiment, in an orchard near the bridge, covered the last of the retreat, and then they, too, put the ravine between themselves and the enemy.

Seeing General Washington approaching, General Lee saluted him and said, "Sir, here are my troops! how is it your pleasure that I should dispose of them? Shall I form them in your front, align them with your main body or draw them up in your rear?"[1] General Washington answered that he should march them to the rear of Englishtown Creek and then arrange them. General Lee instantly gave the order to march toward Englishtown, his pet spaniel, which always accompanied him, was called to his side and the balance of the division not already on the march wearily struggled through the tramp of nearly three miles which led them to the little village on the west side of Wemrock Brook.

When his command at the front ended, General Lee said that he thought he merited and had won the praise and congratulation of the army and the country. He did

[1] Lee's defence at his court-martial, p. 217.

not consider himself beaten nor in any way disgraced. He thought he had done nothing worthy of censure, or meriting the reception that Washington had given him, but that he and the troops he commanded deserved and would receive great honor from the people of America. He considered that although the reports he had received were contradictory and often false, and some of his officers had made mistakes or had been disobedient—all of them being ignorant of the country—and despite the weakness of his division in the cavalry arm, the fact that in the face of the very flower of the British Army he had been able to withdraw his men to a better position without material loss, was proof that he deserved the applause of the commander-in-chief and the public.

General Lee was correct in his assertion that the country had not been reconnoitered or mapped out by the American officers, but that no reconnaissance had been made in the night of June 27 and early the following morning was certainly his own neglect. He believed that the ground was well known to the enemy and was quite right in this surmise. Sir Henry Clinton had carefully drawn maps of the county, in constant use.[2]

It was soon after this last interview between the commander-in-chief and General Lee, that the white horse which Governor William Livingston had presented to General Washington while he was at Kingston, June 25, staggered, fell and died, utterly overcome with the intense heat and the severe toil to which he had been subjected by the anxious exertions of his rider. Billy Lee, having now somewhat recovered from his fright, brought up the General's own "chestnut blood mare with long mane and tail," and during the rest of the battle General Washington rode this splendid animal as he dashed about from point to point where the varying fortunes of the day led him.

The detachment commanded by General Scott had

[2] Copies of these maps are now on file in the Library of Congress.

passed on with the retreating column over the west ravine, without receiving orders of any kind from General Lee, but just in front of the meeting-house they were halted by General Washington's order, taken out of Lee's division and sent up on the rising ground to report to General Lord Stirling and form in the line of his command. Lieutenant-Colonel Oswald was also sent up on the hill to report to Lord Stirling.

Major-General Lafayette was now directed to take command of the second line, the troops in reserve in the rear of General Greene and General Lord Stirling. All day Lafayette had been greatly chagrined at the part he had been compelled to play in the contest. Eager to be in the very front, where laurels were to be won, he had sought the advance post, but his visions of conquering the flower of British soldiery had been rudely dispelled by the order to retreat.

Varnum's brigade, with Lieutenant-Colonel Olney still in command, and a portion of Colonel Jackson's detachment, both of which had just borne the brunt of an assault at the hedge fence, were ordered to march to the rear, to refresh themselves, and to prepare, if it became necessary, for renewing the fight later in the day. These men were utterly exhausted with thirst, with fatigue, and with the extreme heat, and slowly and wearily they plodded back by the same road upon which they had advanced in the morning, and at last reached camp at Englishtown.

General Maxwell's brigade, after reaching the hill in the rear of Lord Stirling's position, was also ordered to proceed to Englishtown and form there.

During the fighting of Varnum's brigade and of the regiments of Stewart, of Livingston and of Ramsay, under Wayne, the right and left wings of the main army gradually unfolded, took position and were ranged on good ground in order of battle. The various inequalities of the field and the many attempts to possess and repossess favorable elevations account for the ever-changing features

of this battle. The charges and counter-charges were performed in full view of the main army, and had the effect of gaining the needed time while plans were being matured and formations made in advantageous positions for the final conflict of the day.

While General Wayne was posting his force at the hedge fence, about twelve rods back and northeast of the parsonage, Sir Henry Clinton advanced a strong column of light infantry troops with the Forty-second foot and the Royal Highland regiment on his right flank, with the intention of attacking Major-General Lord Stirling's position on the left wing of the American Army, then being aligned on high ground west of the west ravine. The British battalions, eager and ready for another fight with the brave Continentals, pressed rapidly forward, passing through young John Craig's fields. As they approached that part of the rising ground which lay between Mr. Sutsin's house and that of Mr. Perrine, they were greeted with a heavy discharge of shot and shell from the batteries posted on the right of Stirling's division and commanded by Lieutenant-Colonel Edward Carrington, First regiment Continental artillery. The British also brought up their light guns and soon the fight on this part of the line became general. Never was artillery better served during the war. It was said at the time to have been the "severest artillery fire ever heard in America." The infantry organizations known as Weedon's brigade, Brigadier-General Peter Muhlenberg's brigade and the First and Second Maryland brigades immediately became engaged in the conflict and volley after volley of musketry could be heard between the regular discharges of the artillery. Lord Stirling[3] himself was very active in this part

---

[3] Surgeon Waldo's diary at Valley Forge speaks of Lord Stirling as follows: "Major General Lord Stirling is a man of a very noble presence and the most martial Appearance of any General in the Service; he much resembles the Marquis of Granby—by his bald head—the make of his face, and figure of his Body. He is mild in his private conversation and vociferous in the Field."

of the engagement and was assisted by the presence of General Washington. They moved along the line, accompanied by General von Steuben, and did all they could to encourage the men, to make them forget the burning heat, to keep their energies fixed and their whole souls filled with the clear duty of giving the British a well-merited punishment.

It was a bold and daring manoeuver on the part of the British and it shows to what a state of discipline this "body of troops not equaled if to be surpassed by any in the world" had attained that they dared to attack the fresh troops under Lord Stirling, some of the best drilled of the veterans of the Continental Army and in a position well chosen for defence.

The fighting was terrific for nearly an hour on this part of the line. The artillery hurled the round shot and shell upon the charging ranks of the enemy and the volleys of the foot soldiers carried death into the British columns; but the British replied with great vigor and amid the storm of shell and the rain of lead the form of General Washington could be seen urging his troops to the contest, inspiring them with his own confidence, and by his cheering voice and firm commands bringing order out of what a few hours before had been confusion, and winning a victory where all had been hopeless retreat and defeat.

In the very heat of this conflict on the hill, the Virginia troops lost a splendid young officer, Major Edmund B. Dickinson, of Colonel Richard Parker's First Virginia regiment, who was fearfully shattered by a cannon-ball and instantly killed. He was a soldier of great valor, greatly beloved by his men, distinguished for his courage and daring, an educated gentleman in private life, and a hero in the fight. His sad fate was sincerely mourned by all the Virginians in Muhlenberg's brigade. Lieutenant-Colonel Francis Barber of the Third New Jersey regiment, at this time on Lord Stirling's staff, was badly wounded by a ball passing through his body at the same

time Major Dickinson was killed, and the gallant young Jerseyman had to be carried off the field just as he was winning new laurels. Major James Monroe, one of Lord Stirling's aides, afterward President of the United States, took Lieutenant-Colonel Barber's place and acted as Stirling's adjutant-general during the rest of the battle.

On the British side a popular and brilliant young officer, Lieutenant Harry Gilchrist, of the Forty-second regiment of foot, received a severe wound.

It will never be known exactly how much the veteran Major-General von Steuben contributed to the firm support of Lord Stirling's line. The school of the soldier at Valley Forge now developed its teachings and its value was evident in the thorough discipline which was shown in every movement of the troops. The Continental soldiers who had received von Steuben's instruction now recognized his soldierly presence, his familiar voice, his cool words of command, and responded quickly to the orders of formation. They had full confidence in his ability to post them in the proper position for battle. Although sorely pressed by the enemy they wheeled into line with as much precision as on an ordinary parade and with the coolness and intrepidity of veteran troops. And this discipline was maintained after they had been formed and when the battle was raging. Afterward, in referring to their good conduct, Colonel Hamilton said he had "never known or conceived the value of military discipline till that day."

It may be mentioned here that while General von Steuben was aiding General Lord Stirling in the formation of his line, General Lee passed him without recognition of any kind. A few minutes thereafter, and while the charge on Stirling's line was impending, General Washington ordered von Steuben to ride to Englishtown and form the retreating troops as a reserve. He obeyed promptly, and, accompanied by his aides, Major James Fairlee, Captain

Benjamin Walker and Mr. Jean Baptiste Ternant[4] he galloped rapidly to Englishtown, passing General Lee on horseback in front of a house in that village.

As the enemy pressed sharply on the right of Lord Stirling's division, a party of light infantry, with Colonel Cilley's First New Hampshire regiment, Colonel Parker's First Virginia regiment and Lieutenant-Colonel Dearborn's Third New Hampshire regiment, passed out through the thick woods, over two rail fences, and struck the extreme right flank of the British column with great impetuosity. When they charged they were within sixty yards of the enemy and had just received their severe fire without return. The British gave way as the Americans charged on them and fell back to the low land of the west ravine where they formed again.

In the Reverend Doctor William Gordon's history, the movement of the British infantry and cavalry against the American left wing is graphically described: "The check the British received gave time to make a disposition of the left wing and second line of the main army in the wood, and on the eminence to which Lee had been directed and was retreating. On this were placed some batteries of cannon by Lord Stirling, who commanded the left wing, which played upon the British with great effect, and, seconded by parties of infantry, detached to oppose them, effectually put a stop to their advance. . . . The British finding themselves warmly opposed in front, attempted to turn the American left flank, but were repulsed."[5]

Lieutenant-Colonel Aaron Burr, then but twenty-two years of age, commanded Malcolm's regiment, Continental infantry, attached to a brigade in General Lord Stirling's division. In the midst of the fight of this division Burr observed a party of the enemy issuing from a copse some distance to the south of the other attacking British

[4] On September 25, 1778, Jean Baptiste Ternant was commissioned Lieutenant-Colonel and Inspector, Continental Army.
[5] Gordon's *History of the American Revolution*, Vol. II, p. 377.

force, and he started his command under orders to check their advance. The Third Pennsylvania regiment, Lieutenant-Colonel Rudolph Bunner in command, was the leading regiment in this brigade. The brigade crossed a small bridge over a ravine, and then halted while Lieutenant-Colonel Bunner, Lieutenant-Colonel Henry Miller of the Second Pennsylvania regiment, and Lieutenant-Colonel Caleb North of the Eleventh Pennsylvania regiment ascended a small hill to get a good view of the British. They were gone only a moment, but the enemy opened upon the brigade a most terrific fire. Several men were killed, and many wounded. Burr's valuable horse was severely wounded and Burr was thrown to the ground. Lieutenant-Colonel Bunner arrived from his tour of observation just in time to be pierced by a musket-ball and to fall dead from his horse. The orders to advance were then countermanded and the brigade was withdrawn just when the fire of the enemy slackened and they retreated.

Doctor James McHenry, afterwards Secretary of War, said of Bunner in a letter written soon after the battle, "On our part Lieutenant-Colonel Bunner was killed having very much distinguished himself on the field."

In a letter written by Captain George Gardner, of Malcolm's regiment, to William Ross, member of the New York Assembly, in relation to Aaron Burr's military service we find this reference, "In the battle of Monmouth our regiment suffered very much nearly one-third having been killed or wounded—and Colonel Burr had his horse shot under him."

When the British failed to break the left wing of the American Army, General Cornwallis ordered another column,[6] which by this time had come up, to attack the position of Major-General Greene on the right of the

---

[6] This column consisted of the battalion of grenadiers, the Thirty-seventh and Forty-fourth regiments of foot, the Coldstream guards and the battalion of the guards commanded by those distinguished soldiers Lieutenant-Colonel Sir John Wrottesley and Lieutenant-Colonel Cosmo Gordon.

American line. This force was the very flower of the rear division and of the army and its movements were directed in person by the distinguished Lord Cornwallis. Early in the day, as we have seen, General Greene had been ordered to file off by the church and to move by the old Monmouth road to a position as near as possible to the rear of the court house, so that any attempt to turn the right flank of the main army on the march might be frustrated. Before he could do this, however, the knowledge that Lee had retreated came to him, and caused him instantly to range his division on some high and advantageous ground on the right, just beyond the church and near Mr. Hugin's house. The British had not proceeded far in their effort to attack Greene's position when they were struck by shot straight across their alignment from the six-gun battery in charge of Brevet Lieutenant-Colonel the Chevalier Thomas Antione de Mauduit du Plessis, Brigade Adjutant of General Knox. This is the officer who had greatly distinguished himself in the fight at Red Bank, October 22, 1777, and at Monmouth he did equally good service in directing the severe enfilading fire from Combs Hill, which was somewhat over a quarter of a mile from the British. General Knox took personal charge of the artillery on Combs Hill, and General Woodford's brigade of Virginia Continentals supported the battery. The infantry of General Greene's division also opened on the approaching enemy and between the quick fire of the rifles and the constant discharge of shot and shell the British suffered greatly. So accurate was the gunnery, it is said, that a round shot from one of the pieces struck the muskets from an entire platoon. A number of distinguished officers of the British Army were either killed or wounded on this part of the field. Here Lieutenant Archibald Kennedy of the Forty-fourth foot met his fate and Colonel Henry Trelawney, Commandant of the Coldstream regiment of foot guards and Lieutenant-Colonel Robert Abercromby in command of the Thirty-

seventh regiment of the line received severe wounds. Captain John Powell of the Fifty-second regiment, but now attached to the grenadier battalions, was badly wounded and died a few days after the battle while he was a prisoner of war. Lieutenant Francis Grose of the same regiment also serving with the grenadiers, who had just recovered from wounds received in the Battle of Germantown, October 4, 1777, and had been with his command but a few days, received new injuries. In reference to Captain Powell's death we find in Moorson's history of the Fifty-second British regiment that General Hunter said he was the fourth captain of grenadiers that the Fifty-second regiment had lost during the American war and that the drummer of his company was heard to exclaim, "Well, I wonder who they'll get to accept of our grenadier company now. I'll be damned if I would!" At this time in the war each regiment of the British foot was made up of one grenadier company, one light infantry company and eight companies of the line. The Fifty-second regiment lost Captains Nicholas Addison, William Davison and George Amos Smith at the Battle of Bunker Hill, Captain Andrew Neilson at the Battle of Long Island and Captain Thomas Williamson soon after the Battle of Princeton, although not in the fight itself. This we find from Lieutenant George Inman's manuscript list. The remark of General Hunter refers to one of the captains killed at Bunker Hill, who commanded the grenadier company of that regiment in the battle, and to the deaths of Captains Neilson, Williamson and Powell.

On the American side Hospital Surgeon Samuel Kennedy, formerly Surgeon of the Fourth Pennsylvania Continental battalion, lost his life. Captain Edmund Munro of the Fifteenth Massachusetts regiment was killed, and Captain Paul Ellis of the same regiment had his leg shot off by a cannon-ball and bled to death before assistance arrived.

In describing this attack on Greene's lines, Botta the historian says, "they endeavored to surround"[7] the American troops. This can hardly be said to be correct as the British had not men enough in the immediate neighborhood to effect such a result.

The efficient services of the artillery in breaking the British column in this attack and in creating such demoralization among them drew from General Washington this remark in his General Orders the next day, "It is with peculiar pleasure that the commander-in-chief can inform General Knox and the officers of Artillery that the enemy have done them the justice to acknowledge that no artillery could be better served than ours."

The British column was driven back and no attempt was again made upon General Greene's division. The disposition of his troops and the manner in which he had resisted the assault proved him, as usual, to be one of the most efficient soldiers in the American service.

Simultaneously with the attack on General Greene's division a fierce charge was made by the grenadier battalions, the light infantry battalions and the light dragoons. It was directed at the American soldiers on what might be called the center of the battle-field, on slightly rising ground around the Tennent parsonage.[8] The troops were partly in Mr. Sutsin's orchard, sheltered by the barn, which was about twelve yards back of the parsonage, and at the hedge fence.[9] So confident were the British of success, so certain that if they made but one grand effort, the American force under Wayne would again be turned to

[7] Botta's *History of the War of Independence*, Vol. II, p. 516.

[8] This parsonage, which was taken down in 1861, is described as "a low building, large on the ground, with four lower rooms, two on each side of the hall, with kitchen attached in the rear. Above was the attic room, sloping on one side with rafters, and with a window facing the north, which, as is said, was used as a study by both Mr. Tennent and Mr. Woodhull. During the battle of June 28. 1778, a round shot came through the roof into this room while the conflict raged furiously around the house and in the adjoining orchard." Ellis' *History of Monmouth County, N.J.*, p. 686.

[9] This hedge fence was in 1778, as it is today, the dividing line between the parsonage farm and a farm on the east of it.

flight, that they pressed close to the line of the hedge. But the patriots were now strong in their position and responded to the ringing orders of the brave Pennsylvanian, who felt that now at least he had an independent fighting command, and they poured a terrific volley at close range into the advancing British corps. It was a sudden and staggering rain of lead. The fire-locks of the Continentals did wonderful execution and numbers of the redcoats fell dead and dying on the burning soil that summer afternoon. When the smoke lifted, a young lieutenant of artillery, brave Thomas L. Vaughan, lay dying beside his smoking gun, and Captain Thomas Wills of the Twenty-third foot and Captain Patrick Bellew of the First regiment of foot guards were suffering greatly from deep bullet wounds. Captain Bellew was taken prisoner by the Americans.

The British soldiers instantly formed again, and prepared for a second desperate charge. The gallant Wayne, with keen audacity, let these strong battalions of trained veterans approach near his fence line by the orchard and at the barn, and then the grape-shot from the guns and the leaden balls from the rifles of his own First Pennsylvania brigade and the Rhode Island brigade, wrought havoc in the ranks of the enemy. Numbers of the men from Maxwell's and Scott's brigades, under orders to pass to the rear, had stopped a moment to join their comrades in the impending fight. Again the British line gave way and fell back before the deadly fire. In this second charge the "high sergeant," a British grenadier, seven feet four inches in height, the tallest man in the army, was slain. More than an hour passed while these two attacks were made and before another charge was attempted.

Again, however, for a third time, the line was formed and at the head of the British attacking party appeared the gallant Lieutenant-Colonel Henry Monckton, of the Forty-fifth foot, and now in command of the Second battalion of grenadiers. He was the brother of Earl Galway,

and a man of irreproachable private character, a brave and skilled soldier, admired by all his men. He had been shot through the body by a musket-ball at the Battle of Long Island, August 27, 1776, and lay for many weeks on the verge of death. He recovered, however, rejoined his command, and now by his brave act and untimely death was to make his name immortal in history. Monckton was well on the right of the attacking line and the words of hearty cheer which he spoke to his men could distinctly be heard by the Americans near the parsonage and in the orchard. The two lines were now, it is said, scarcely thirty rods apart. Monckton gave the command to charge the patriot line in solid column. With drawn sword he shouted, "Forward to the charge, my brave Grenadiers." They dashed forward with great fury, led by his presence and inspiring voice. But "Mad Anthony" Wayne, eager for his men to hold their fire, and demoralize the British by wounding their officers, called along the line, "Steady, steady, wait for the word, then pick out the King birds." This was done and the terribly destructive volley flew straight at the breasts of the charging red-coats. The First Pennsylvania regiment, Colonel James Chambers commanding, was the organization which stood the brunt of the assault. In this conflict, by a desperate exertion, they secured the colors of the Royal grenadiers.

This charge was still more important in its fatality on the British side. Captain John Gore, a brave, experienced officer of the Fifth foot, then in command of the First battalion of grenadiers, fell dead at the head of his men. Young Harry Ditmas, a popular officer of the Fifteenth foot, received a severe wound, and Captain Andrew Cathcart, of the same regiment, had his right arm badly shattered. But more conspicuous than all, their gallant leader, Lieutenant-Colonel Henry Monckton, lay dead on the field of honor.[10] His body fell about forty yards

10 "Character of the late Hon. Lieutenant-Colonel Monckton.
"The Hon. Hen. Monckton, late lieutenant-colonel to the forty-fifth regi-

northeast of the parsonage, and so close to the hedge fence that the Continentals, recognizing it, leaped out from their line, coatless and with shirt sleeves rolled up, and made a bold rush for the possession of the body of the dead soldier and for the colors carried near him. His own men, who loved him so well, made every exertion at close quarters, to keep the patriots away. The struggle was desperate but Monckton's body was finally secured and hastily carried off by the Americans. Captain William

ment, of the noble family of the Viscounts Galway, of the kingdom of Ireland, and brother to the present Lieutenant-General Monckton, was a man by nature formed for military greatness, his memory retentive, his judgment deep, his comprehension amazingly quick and clear, his constitutional courage not only uniform and daring perhaps to an extreme, but he possessed that higher species of it, strength, steadiness and activity of mind, which no difficulties could obstruct, nor danger deter; free from pride, with the greatest independence of spirit, generous to a degree, a constant friend to the deserving soldier, whose concerns he always attended to in preference to his own: inferior officers experienced his friendly generosity; he was by temper rather reserved, yet kind and gentle in his manners, and to crown all, sincerity and candor, with a true sense of honor and justice, seemed the inherent principles of his nature, and the uniform tenor of his conduct. He betook himself early in life to the profession of arms, obtaining an ensigncy in the first regiment of guards, in the year 1760 and afterwards a lieutenancy in the same corps. In the year 1769, he purchased the majority of the forty-fifth regiment of foot from Mr. Gates, since so famous for the part he has taken against his country; and in the year 1771, he purchased the lieutenant-colonelcy, remaining with the regiment (then in Ireland) until the breaking out of this unnatural rebellion, in 1775, when he embarked with it for North America. Upon the army's leaving Halifax, the late commander-in-chief, conscious of his courage and abilities, appointed him to the command of the second battalion of grenadiers. In the action on Long Island, the 27th of Aug. 1776, he received a dangerous wound, being shot through the body as he was leading on his battalion to charge a much superior number of the rebels. On this occasion he gave a remarkable proof of that intrepidity that always distinguished him; upon his falling an officer of his battalion came to his assistance, which he nobly refused in these terms: 'Sir, leave me, I am of no consequence at present, go on with the grenadiers.' At Brandywine he received a slight wound in his knee; he continued in the command of his battalion of grenadiers till the 28th of June, 1778, when upon the rear guard of the army's being engaged with the greatest part of the rebel force, in the march through Jersey he gloriously fell in the front of that battalion, nobly exerting himself in the cause of his country, and is now universally regretted by every officer and soldier that knew him, or ever had the honor of serving under his command."—From the *London Chronicle* of September 19-22 and printed in the *Pennsylvania Magazine of History*, Vol. XIV, p. 47.

Wilson[11] and his company of the First Pennsylvania regiment at the same time captured the colors, as has been stated. This flag is now [1899] in possession of one of Captain Wilson's descendants, Captain William Potter Wilson of Bellefonte, Pennsylvania.[12]

Adolphus, the historian, with strange embellishment, says that "relays of grenadiers buried his body, taking turns during the battle and using bayonets for shovels, mingling tears with the earth they cast upon his body."[13] The British bayonet of that day would have made an indifferent tool for grave-digging and the body of their brave commander was wanting as they shed tears to his memory during the excitement of a battle!

A short distance away, on the main roadway, was the old Tennent Church, founded, it is believed, about the year 1692. It is now known as "The First Presbyterian Church of the County of Monmouth." This building with shingled sides and roof, can today be seen from the windows of the fast trains moving pleasure-seekers to the sea-side resorts. The great evangelists Brainerd and Whitefield, and both the Tennents, had uttered their solemn warnings from its sacred desk.

In the yard annexed to this church the body of Lieutenant-Colonel Monckton was carried the day after the battle and was buried there, with those of the other British officers who fell into the hands of the Americans. Full military honors were given to his remains and his grave is within ten feet of the westerly corner of the church.

[11] Captain Wilson resided in Chillisquaque, Northumberland County, Pennsylvania, and after the war he was an Associate Justice of the Court of that county.

[12] In a sketch of this flag given in the *American Historical Record*, June 1874, p. 263, it appears that it is of a light yellow heavy corded silk, five feet four inches by four feet eight inches in size, with the crosses of St. George and St. Andrew on a blue ground twenty inches square. The flag has the appearance of having been wrenched from its staff and bears some traces of blood-stains.

[13] This assertion is repeated in Stedman's *History of the American War*, Vol. II, p. 23.

Present Interior of Tennent Church

Several years after the battle Mr. William R. Wilson,[14] a Scotchman, called familiarly "Dominie Wilson" because he had once been a clergyman, set up a rude monument to mark Monckton's grave. It was a large board painted red with this inscription in black letters—spelling the English soldier's name incorrectly, as is usual—

HIC JACET
COL. MONKTON
KILLED 28 JUNE
1778
W.R.W.

The marble monument standing in the graveyard today has the following inscription:

HIC JACET
LT. COL. HENRY MONCKTON
WHO, ON THE PLAINS OF
MONMOUTH, JUNE 28, 1778, SEALED
WITH HIS LIFE HIS DUTY AND DEVO-
TION TO HIS KING AND COUNTRY.
"COURAGE IS ON ALL HANDS CON-
SIDERED AS AN ESSENTIAL OF HIGH CHARACTER."

———

THIS MEMORIAL ERECTED BY
SAMUEL FRYER WHOSE FATHER, A
SUBJECT OF GREAT BRITAIN,
SLEEPS IN AN UNKNOWN GRAVE.

There were many men who particularly distinguished themselves in the fight at the hedgerow. The old families of Monmouth still relate traditions of the desperate encounters and wonderful escapes of their grandfathers and of their neighbors, who lived in this house or on that farm. It is said of William Lyons, who lived on the battle-field, that he locked bayonets with an English soldier at the brush fence and was about to be overpowered when an

---

[14] William R. Wilson was the schoolmaster at the little schoolhouse near the church. He is often erroneously confounded in histories with the daring soldier Captain Wilson, just spoken of. Mr. Wilson was afterward buried by the side of Monckton.

American officer clove the head of the Britisher with his sword and rescued Lyons.

General Arthur St. Clair, as we find in William Henry Smith's life and public services of this soldier of the Revolutionary War "participated in this engagement and continued with the army without regularly assigned duties." Although we do not find mention in any account of the battle of his active participation therein he wrote an account of the engagement which is given in part in the *Historical Register*, Vol. I, No. 4. In this paragraph it is stated that First Lieutenant David Ziegler, of the First Pennsylvania regiment, so distinguished himself in the charge for Monckton's body and the flag that he received special meritorious mention in the brigade reports for that day.

Soon after the defeat and death of Lieutenant-Colonel Monckton, a large reinforcement came up to the help of the British, and the Americans found themselves completely out-flanked at the hedge fence. It was then necessary for them to retire from the ground which they had defended so bravely and where they had inflicted such severe punishment on the enemy. This movement was made in good order but at that hour it really gave the British no special advantage. The two lines of General Lord Stirling and General Greene were too firmly posted to be at all affected by any of the smaller detachments whose business it had been to hold back the advancing force until the American Army could be properly formed.

CHAPTER XXI

NOTWITHSTANDING all the toil and suffering of the day, General Washington quickly resolved to put some fresh troops in the advance and send them to attack the British before they found an encampment for the night. This was at about fifteen minutes before five o'clock in the afternoon. Brigadier-General Enoch Poor, of New Hampshire, was selected to lead this body of picked troops, and his own brigade, still covered with the glory of Saratoga's battle, went with him; also the North Carolina troops, under command of Colonel Thomas Clark. Brigadier-General William Woodford led a party, composed chiefly of his own brigade, to skirmish on the left of Poor's command. Soon after starting they learned from scouts that the British force had retreated about a mile and a half toward Freehold village and seemed about to take position on the east side of the middle ravine with a narrow causeway in front of the ravine, and thick woods on each side of the troops. The Americans marched over the bridge at the west ravine and then the two general officers separated, though they kept within sight of each other. General Poor took his command over toward the British left and General Woodford's detachment passed off to their right. They intended to attack the British flanks simultaneously. A battery of light artillery, with proper support, continued on the highway, with orders to post themselves on the high ground in front, with the morass between them and the enemy.

Being obliged to leave the main road and march right and left in loose sandy fields, it was just at dusk when the infantry force came within range of the British troops and too late to do any effective work before the night shadows covered them. It was then resolved to lay there with their arms at hand, just west of the middle ravine and close to

the enemy, and await the coming of daylight for an attack. Orders were soon afterward received from General Washington confirming this plan of General Poor and directing that the British be attacked in camp promptly at the first moment of dawn. The Americans were now less than a quarter of a mile from the British encampment and the sentinels of either army could distinguish one another without difficulty.

The countersign on the night of the battle was "Monckton" and the parole "Bunner and Dickinson."

According to orders General von Steuben had been forming all the troops he could collect between the meeting-house and Englishtown. In this way he at last found himself in that village and there met General Lee, who had previously received the same orders. It was important to place that part of the army in some proper position for the close of the day, or, as Lee remarked, "in case of any disaster to the army." By his own exertion and that of his aides, von Steuben was able to get a number of battalions ready for immediate service. General Lee saw him engaged in this work, and asked what his orders were. Finding that they were the same as his own, he expressed himself as glad that von Steuben had taken that labor on himself, as he was tired out. In this way some of Maxwell's brigade which had not tarried with their comrades to fight at the hedge—General Maxwell being with them —and a part of Scott's detachment, were placed in battalion line and posted behind the creek at Englishtown. Late in the afternoon General von Steuben received orders from General Washington to march the force which he had gathered back to the main army, so as to be ready to renew the attack on the British in the morning.

Before dismounting at Englishtown General Lee observed to his aides and the gentlemen standing near him, that it had all happened as he had expected: that it was folly to make such an attempt as had been made that day against an enemy which was so superior in cavalry and

that it was not possible to be successful against such a well-equipped force. From this it is quite evident that he thought the result of the day's battle would be disgraceful to the army and to the cause. He considered the American officers and men brave, patriotic, and devoted, but besides their lack of light-horse, he thought them wanting in discipline. On this very point, however, it had been General von Steuben's duty all the previous winter to instruct the men and the Continental troops had acquired a degree of discipline but little inferior to that of the British line. If, as it certainly appears, Sir Henry Clinton had out-manoeuvered the American advance, the blame was Lee's alone. Lee further said that he had given counsel contrary to a general engagement and thought it very imprudent to bring one on; that the late treaty with France would soon secure independence to the colonies and that it was impolitic to risk so much. He thought the Continental Congress would be displeased to have a battle brought on at this time, when it was sure to result disastrously.

In a letter to Richard Henry Lee dated the night of the battle but probably written the next day, General Lee made these comments on the fight: "What the devil brought us into this level country (the very element of the enemy) or what interest we can have (in our present circumstances) to hazard an action, somebody else must tell you, for I cannot. I was yesterday ordered (for it was against my opinion and inclination) to engage. I did, with my division, which consisted of about four thousand men. The troops, both men and officers, showed the greatest valour! the artillery did wonders! but we were outnumbered! particularly in cavalry, which was, at twenty different times, on the point of turning completely our flanks. This consideration naturally obliged us to retreat! but the retreat did us, I will venture to say, great honour. It was performed with all the order and coolness which can be seen on a common field day. Not a man or officer

hastened his step, but one regiment regularly filed off from the front to the rear of the other. The thanks I received from his excellency were of a singular nature. I can demonstrate that had I not acted as I did, this army, and perhaps America, would have been ruined."[1]

It was six o'clock when Lieutenant-Colonel de Gimat, an aide-de-camp of General Lafayette, galloping rapidly to Englishtown, brought the welcome news that the enemy were falling back, and an order from Washington to bring up reinforcements. It did not take many moments for General von Steuben to wheel his men out into the roadway. He left General Maxwell in immediate command of the troops, which had just been augmented by the arrival of General John Paterson, with three brigades of the second line. These were placed on elevated ground, behind the position of Maxwell's own brigade. A battery was then unlimbered on the right wing, in front of the second brigade, commanded by General Smallwood. Having seen that these dispositions of the troops were being made, General von Steuben with three brigades of fresh troops, which had all day constituted the reserve of the main army, set out, with quick step, for the meeting-house and the battle-field.

Passing through Englishtown, he saw General Lee a second time that day and Lee asked where he was going with the troops. He was informed of General Washington's order and also that the enemy were retreating in confusion. General Lee said they could not be in confusion, that they must be only resting and that there must be some mistake in this order to advance with all these men. One of the brigades under General Muhlenberg was halted and Captain Walker, von Steuben's aide, handed General Lee the original order which Lieutenant-Colonel de Gimat had brought. General Lee was satisfied and said, "then you are

[1] Lieutenant-Colonel Henry Lee's *Memoirs of the War in the Southern Department of the United States*, p. 37.

[224]

to march," and the command instantly continued on the route to the front.

As soon as General von Steuben had started his force, General Lee had fresh horses procured by his aides, and, being somewhat refreshed, he returned to the field of battle. Finding General Washington near the meeting-house he offered his services for any duties which might be required of him. The battle was over, however, for the day, and he was not needed.

Strange indeed must it have been to General Lee, who had asserted at noon that the Americans could not stand before the British grenadiers—and they had not done so while under his immediate command—to find that by night these same invincible soldiers had been beaten and he himself had come up to take part in the pursuit of a retreating foe.

Every act of General Washington in the battle was tactically right. Every move of his, so far as we can now ascertain, was performed in the best possible way. Every disposition of his force after he took immediate control of it has been pronounced correct by skilled military critics who were familiar with the country.

Had the American Army possessed a powerful body of trained cavalry they might have made their success more important and valuable. But such light horsemen as they had, had been for a week in constant active service harassing the enemy, carrying reports of their situation, and in this way had become greatly scattered.

After a whole day of fighting, the longest battle of the war, in the intense heat of the summer sun, in desultory conflicts, in fierce, desperate charges, the American Army was glad to seek such repose as the ground afforded and such a canopy as the stars. Worn out with fatigue the men soon dropped asleep and the night was unbroken by any alarm or by the sound of the challenging picket.

General Washington lay beneath the spreading branches

of an oak.[2] His staff were near him and his young friend
General Lafayette lay by his side, a cloak thrown over
them both. The dead were all around them as they slept.
General Washington must have felt confident of a victory
on the morrow. He had seen his men disorganized, retreating, then forming in embattled ranks, stern and
defiant, punishing the enemy. He knew then that the
discipline acquired at Valley Forge was to be depended
upon and that his weary troops would awake on Monmouth fields in strength and good spirits again to punish
the British line.

[2] "Washington used old Tennent Church and Tennent Parsonage as his
field hospitals and afterwards also the Court House. He slept under a
tree in front of the house on the Herbert (now DuBois) farm the night
after the battle." Samuel Craig Cowart.

CHAPTER XXII

IT was but a short sleep, if any, that the British troops were allowed to take after the battle. At about ten o'clock, according to British accounts, but at least midnight, according to Washington's surmise, General Clinton ordered his army to march toward the Highlands. They moved stealthily, by battalions and brigades, leaving the tired sentries of the Americans none the wiser for their absence, and the standards of the Union proudly floating over the victorious field. By dawn they had put thirteen miles between themselves and the bivouac of the patriots. In the morning the ground they had left presented every evidence of a hasty exit. The dead were lying there unburied, and the whole line of retreat was strewn with arms, knapsacks and accouterments. They also left behind them fifteen prisoners captured from the American Army.

Stedman records the remark that "just as the British were beginning to move, some horses or cattle were straggling through a wood, and a battalion of light infantry, taking them for the enemy, began a fire upon them which continued for five minutes."[1] This certainly must be an error, for a discharge of musketry for that length of time would without doubt have awakened the American advance corps and could hardly have failed to alarm the entire main army, little more than a mile distant.

The moon was four days old on the night of June 28 and set at 10:55 o'clock. It is quite likely that Sir Henry Clinton gave order to his subordinates at about ten o'clock and that he took some advantage of the few minutes of moonlight after that hour, and the partial light which followed it, to withdraw some of the troops farthest removed from the American sentinels; but it is hardly to be supposed that he withdrew his own guards, started his artil-

[1] Stedman's *History of the American War*, Vol. II, p. 23.

[227]

lery, his caissons and his supply wagons at an hour when he could easily have been seen. Yet he succeeded in moving off as noiselessly as General Washington had slipped away from Lord Cornwallis on the banks of the Assunpink Creek in Trenton, eighteen months before, when he performed the great flank movement and effected the surprise at Princeton.

Andrew Bell, Military Secretary to Sir Henry Clinton, who must be considered good authority, says in his Journal that the British Army marched at twelve o'clock at night. Sir Henry Clinton, however, in his report to his King, asserts that, "having reposed the troops until ten at night, to avoid the excessive heat of the day I took advantage of the moonlight to rejoin Lieutenant-General Knyphausen," &c. These moonlight flittings of Sir Henry were the subject of jest as long as he remained in America.[2]

Sir Henry Clinton claimed that he had accomplished all in his power in an offensive demonstration during the day, and that it was right for him to take advantage of the night to push on toward his baggage train and to hasten to New York. But doubtless the punishment he had received

---

[2] A familiar verse written by Colonel Trumbull, in his poem "M'Fingal," became quite current in those days in reference to this march. It runs as follows:

> "He forms his camp with vain parade,
> Till ev'ning spreads the world with shade,
> Then still, like some endanger'd spark,
> Steals off on tiptoe in the dark;
> Yet writes his King in boasting tone
> How grand he march'd by light of moon!"

And again General Clinton is thus apostrophized in the same poem:

> "Go on, great Gen'ral, nor regard
> The scoffs of ev'ry scribbling Bard,
> Who sing how Gods, that fatal night,
> Aided, by miracles, your flight;
> As once they used, in Homer's day,
> To help weak heroes run away;
> Tell how the hours, at awful trial,
> Went back, as erst on Ahaz dial,
> While British Joshua stay'd the moon
> On Monmouth's plain for Ajalon;
> Heed not their sneers or gibes so arch,
> Because she set before your march."

and the loss of many brilliant officers made him reluctant to spend another day in the neighborhood of American rifles and well-sighted guns. Although, as Lieutenant James Moody of the First battalion of New Jersey volunteers (Loyalists), says, Clinton's "intentions seldom lasted longer than the day," in this case his plan of first making his precious baggage secure had been his constant thought day and night for ten days.

The retreat of Clinton does not seem to have been an imperative necessity. His army as an entirety had not been vanquished and it is hardly to be called a brave act to abandon the field with such a force in the manner he did. But the fine carriages of good citizens of Philadelphia had to be placed on the streets of New York, the baggage of the army, the plunder of the Quaker City, had to be safely transferred over the great harbor, and hence his anxiety to reach his destination.

Captain Arthur Ross, of the Queen's rangers, commanded the rear guard of Clinton's retreating column that night. As he passed out of the village of Freehold he liberated fifteen of the citizens of Monmouth County whom they had arrested the previous day. They carried off with them such of the sick and wounded as they could move with safety, but left four officers and forty enlisted men, with their own surgeons, and these were taken to the English church[3] in the village [still standing 1926], which had been turned into a hospital; a few were placed in a barn near by, some in the Court House[4] and others in private houses on the main street of the little hamlet. Both the Tennent Church and parsonage were used as hospitals;

---

[3] The corporate title of this church is St. Peter's Church. In 1778 the Reverend William Ayres was missionary or rector of the church, also of the church at Spotswood, New Jersey, and so continued up to 1799. He lived in Spotswood on property purchased by the two congregations.

[4] The Court House was a wooden building nearly on the present site. It was similar to the English Church with its sides as well as its roof covered with shingles. Of course it was in the very center of the town.

also William Ker's house, all traces of which have disappeared. All the soldiers left behind in the village were badly wounded, so that the British surgeons had not finished binding up their wounds at sunset on Monday.

The dead of the British Army were, of course, left in the possession of the Americans, who held the field of battle. Those who died on the battle-field were buried there or in the Tennent churchyard; those who died near Freehold, or in the hospitals there, were buried by the Americans in a pit on the southeast corner of what is now Main and Throckmorton Streets in Freehold.

General Knyphausen, in command of the strong column protecting the baggage train, and accompanied by General Grant, had been active all day Sunday, as they pushed northward, and "great plunder and devastation had been committed among the friends of liberty in that quarter of the country." Before nine o'clock that night they reached Nut Swamp, about three miles from the little village of Middletown, and there encamped in what they considered a very secure position. To this post Clinton hastened to force Lord Cornwallis' division to march that night. Soon after sunrise on Monday he came up with the rear of Knyphausen's command. At ten o'clock in the morning Clinton marched on three miles to Middletown.

During the afternoon of June 29 Sir Henry Clinton sent back a message under flag of truce to General Washington, commending the wounded which he had left behind to his tender mercies and thanking him for the honors which he had just heard had been paid to the gallant Monckton.

In the morning of June 29 all the fleet except the *Roebuck*, which was at her station off the Delaware Bay, sailed from the Capes off the Delaware, and with wind south, southeast, and then southwest, at about six knots an hour, they made sail all day and night for Sandy Hook. The British fleet commanded by Lord Howe consisted of

six men-of-war of 64 guns each, three of 50 guns each, two of 40 guns each, and some frigates and sloops.[5]

When the British Army had marched from Middletown toward the Highlands of the Navesink on the evening of the thirtieth they found that Sandy Hook had been converted into an island by the force of the ocean wind and tide. Captain John Montresor, the engineer-in-chief of the army, with large details of sailors from the fleet, formed a bridge of boats across the inlet.

Lord Howe's fleet made the Highlands at about ten o'clock on the morning of June 30, and found the *Scorpion* cruising off the Hook. They anchored just outside of Sandy Hook for a short time but soon after sailed inside of the bay and anchored near the frigate *Amazon*, which for a long time had been the guard-ship to the defences of New York.

In leaving Philadelphia, this fleet had barely escaped an encounter with the French naval vessels, twelve ships of the line[6] and six large frigates, with about 4,000 troops on board, under command of the Count Charles Hector D'Estaing, which left Toulon April 30 and arrived off the Capes of the Delaware July 8. The British fleet arrived in safety, however, on Tuesday morning, and were distinctly seen by the British force as they marched that evening to Sandy Hook. They encamped that night at the Highlands under protection of the guns of the fleet.

On July 5 the British Army passed over the bridge of boats which had been constructed, as before mentioned, and were taken on transports and conveyed to New York.

The morning of June 29 dawned with the same sultry

---

[5] The *Roebuck* joined the fleet at a later day, so that when the British Army reached New York City the squadron at Sandy Hook consisted of the following vessels: *Eagle*, the flag-ship of Lord Howe, *Somerset*, *Roebuck*, *St. Albans*, *Nonesuch*, *Pearl*, *Venus*, *Preston*, *Isis*, *Richmond*, *Experiment*, *Trident*, *Ardent*, *Phoenix*, *Vigilant* and the *Vesuvius* and *Aetna*, fire-ships.

[6] These vessels were as follows: *Languedoc*, 90 guns; *Tonnant*, 80; *Caesar*, 74; *Guerriere*, 74; *Protecteur*, 74; *Provence*, 64; *Valliant*, 64; *Saggitaire*, 54; *Chiniere*, 30; *L'Engeante*, 26; *L'Alemcnce*, 26; *L'Arimable*, 26.

heat that had characterized the Sabbath, and the soldiers of the American Army awoke only to find that the enemy had stolen away. General Washington and his officers thought that, after such an interval of time, to pursue them would be "impracticable and fruitless." It would have cost them the lives of many of their best men and have been barren of results, as they knew that the British Army would soon be under the protection of the guns of Lord Howe's fleet.

General Washington found that many of his men had died during the night from prostration, even those who had not been wounded. During the early morning General David Forman, Colonel Thomas Henderson and Colonel Nathaniel Scudder, the two latter being physicians as well as officers, of the State troops, and other prominent citizen soldiers of Monmouth County, called on General Washington and expressed the opinion that the American Army could now do the British no injury, no matter in what force they attempted it, on the barren sand reef of Sandy Hook. This opinion is expressed more fully in the letter written by General Washington from Englishtown, July 1, to the President of Congress: "Being fully convinced by the gentlemen of this country that the enemy cannot be hurt or injured in their embarkation at Sandy Hook, the place to which they are going, and unwilling to get too far removed from the North River, I put the troops in motion early this morning."

The New Jersey brigade under General Maxwell and the rifle corps under Colonel Morgan were sent out to keep near the British rear, to prevent them from sending out forage parties or detachments to annoy the patriot farmers and, if possible, to encourage desertions from the British Army, which were daily on the increase.

In reference to this action of General Washington, in not pursuing the British with all his force, Colonel Henry Lee remarked, "The enemy having united his columns on the heights of Middletown, an attempt to dislodge him

would have been blind temerity. Had sir Henry Clinton not possessed this vast advantage, the victory would have been improved; and in any other period of the retreat might have been made decisive in all probability."[7]

The fatigue parties of the American Army were busy all day June 29 gathering up the dead of both armies. Two brigades of Continental troops were posted near the court house to cover the burial parties. In this work the whole day passed and just before five o'clock the men on fatigue duty and their guard, joining the rest of the army near the old meeting-house, marched to Englishtown and to the fields where they had left their camp equipage and dropped their blankets and knapsacks in the early morning of the previous day.

General Washington made this preliminary official report to the Honorable Henry Laurens, President of the Continental Congress:

Fields, near Monmouth Ct. House
29 June, 1778.

SIR:

I have the honour to inform you, that, about seven o'clock yesterday morning, both armies advanced on each other. About 12 o'clock they met on the grounds near Monmouth Court House, when an action commenced. We forced the enemy from the field and encamped on their ground. They took a strong post in our front, secured on both flank by morasses and thick woods where they remained till about 12 at night, and then retreated. I cannot at this time go into a detail of matters; when opportunity will permit, I shall take the liberty of transmitting to Congress a more particular account of the proceedings of the Day. I have the honour to be, with gt. resp't

Sir, your most obt. servt.

Go. WASHINGTON.

To Hon. Henry Laurens, Esq., &c., &c.

---

[7] Lieutenant-Colonel Henry Lee's *Memoirs of the War in the Southern Department of the United States*, p. 37.

General Washington also issued this order to his troops on Monday:

Headquarters, Freehold
29th June 1778.

The Commander-in-Chief congratulates the Army on the Victory obtained over the Arms of his Britannic Majesty yesterday, and thanks, most sincerely, the gallant officers and men who distinguished themselves upon the occasion and such others as, by their good order and coolness, gave the happiest presages of what might have been expected had they come to action.

General Dickinson and the Militia of this State are also thanked for the noble spirit which they have shown in opposing the enemy on their march from Philadelphia, and for the aid which they have given by harrassing and impeding their motions so as to allow the Continental troops time to come up with them.

A Party consisting of two hundred men to parade immediately to bury the slain of both Armies; Gen'l Woodford's Brigade to cover this party.

The officers of the American Army are to be buried with military honours, due to men who have nobly fought and died in the cause of Liberty and their Country.

Doctor Cochran will direct what is to be done with the wounded and the sick. He is to apply to the Quarter Master General and Adjutant General for necessary assistance. The several detachments (except those under Col. Morgan) are to join their respective Brigades immediately, and the lines to be formed agreeable to the order of the 22d instant. The Army is to march from the left, the second line in front, the Cavalry in the rear. The march to begin at five o'clock this afternoon.

A Sergeant, Corporal and twelve men from General Maxwell's Brigade to parade immediately to guard the sick to Princetown Hospitals. Doctor Craig will give directions to the guard.

Colonel Martin is appointed to superintend collecting the sick and wounded on the Army's route through Jersey, between Coryell's and Monmouth and send them to Princetown Hospitals—he will call immediately at the orderly office for further orders.

It is with peculiar pleasure, in addition to the above, that the Commander-in-Chief can inform General Knox and the officers of Artillery that the enemy have done them the justice to acknowledge that no artillery could be better served than ours.[8]

The army remained perfectly quiet all day June 30 in and around Englishtown, resting from the severe labors

[8] General Edward Hand's *Orderly Book, Continental Army*, p. 288.

of the two previous days and preparing for the long march about to be made in the summer heat.

General Washington then issued the following order:

Headquarters, Englishtown
30th June 1778.

The men are to wash themselves this afternoon and appear as clean and decent as possible. Seven o'clock this evening is appointed that we may publickly unite in thanksgiving to the Supreme Disposer of human events for the victory which was obtained on Sunday over the Flower of the British Troops. Accurate returns of the killed, wounded and missing in the Battle of Monmouth are immediately to be made to the Adjutant General's Office. The troops are to be completed with provisions for tomorrow and have it cooked to-day. The whole Army, except Maxwell's Brigade, is to move at two o'clock to-morrow morning— and every thing is to be in the most perfect readiness tonight. General Maxwell will apply at Headquarters for particular orders. Complaint having been made to the Commander-in-Chief that certain persons belonging to the army have seized the property of inhabitants which had been concealed in order to escape the ravages of the enemy, he calls upon the commanding officers of corps to order a strict search of the soldiers' packs at parade time, that the offender may be discovered and brought to condign punishment. Such articles as may be found agreeable to a list left at the Adjutant General's are to be sent to his office that they may be returned to their owners.

The General further gives notice that the detestable crime of marauding will henceforth be punished with instant death.[9]

General Washington deemed it best to move around New York harbor and up the Hudson River and on the first day of July the entire army left Englishtown, and passing through thick pine woods they reached the village of Spotswood. Men dropped by the roadway continually, overcome by the heat, and were placed in the army wagons and carried on the march. Upon their arrival the following brief order was promulgated:

[9] *ibid.*, p. 290.

THE BATTLE OF MONMOUTH

Head Quarters Spottswood,
Wednesday July 1st 1778.

The General will beat at twelve o'clock, troop at half-past twelve and the march begins at one. The troops are in the mean time to take as much sleep and refreshment as possible that they may be the better prepared.

On July 2 the army marched to Brunswick and encamped on the north and south banks of the Raritan River, and remained there until after the Fourth.

General Maxwell and his New Jersey brigade, Colonel Morgan and his rifle corps, Colonel Moylan's dragoons and Captain Allan McLane's Delaware partisan company of foot were detached, as we have seen, to do what damage they could to the retreating enemy.

On July 6 this force just started on their return to the main army which, having marched by the way of Paramus, Bergen County, New Jersey, and Haverstraw, New York, was at that time approaching King's Ferry. They took with them a number of prisoners, some horses and cattle, and much stores and baggage which they had captured. Upon reaching Elizabethtown General Maxwell's brigade was halted and remained there and at Woodbridge and Newark for some time, while Morgan's corps and the rest of the command marched on to the main army.

Immediately after the battle the militia of New Jersey were discharged from the tour of duty on which they had been called out, and they returned to their homes. This body of militia was the second contingent of the summer campaign and their "thirty days" expired June 30.

It may be noted here that General Greene, who in time of battle was commander of a division, was also Quartermaster-General of the Continental Army in the field and had to busy himself for several weeks after the fight at Monmouth in procuring a large number of horses to replace those killed and disabled at the time of the battle.

The ability of the Continental line to fight the best troops of Great Britain, was fully established on Mon-

mouth battle-field. When they came under the leaders
with whom they had practised the school of the soldier at
Valley Forge they were fit to cope with the best of European soldiery. The fight at the hedge fence, with the flash-
ing of bright bayonets in the fierce sunlight, in the hands
of those who in all the world knew best how to use them,
was enough to try the stoutest patriot heart. But they
stood the onset well and no unfavorable criticism can ever
be made on their conduct as fighting men. The American
patriot proved himself the right material from which to
make a good soldier, the American artillerist proved himself a match for the batteries of Britain, the American
general officer proved himself able to manoeuver his men
in a crisis, and to hold his troops against a fierce assaulting
column. The American Chieftain appeared reliable in
every contingency, and with a fertility of resource and
strategic skill equal to any emergency which might arise.
General Washington himself, as has been said, was the
hero of Monmouth.

In a letter published in the *Gazette* at Trenton, July 3,
1778, General Lee says, "the behaviour of the whole
army, both men and officers, was so equally good, that it
would be unjust to make distinctions; tho' I confess it is
difficult to refrain from paying compliments to the artillery, from General Knox and Colonel Oswald, down to
the very driver."

General Knox wrote to Colonel Lamb, July 19, "Our
corps, as usual did themselves the justice to behave like
men, contending in the great cause of liberty and their
country."

The fighting of that portion of Sir Henry Clinton's
Army which left Freehold in pursuit of the retreating
forces of General Lee was all that could be expected of
such superb troops.[10] The commanding officers of the Brit-

[10] Referring to the Royal regiment which he commanded, General James
Pattison said, in orders, "The very handsome and obliging terms in which
the General officers and others have repeatedly spoken of the appearance,
discipline and good conduct of the Corps of Artillery, and particularly of

ish foot, of the Guards and of the Dragoons handled their men with the skill and ability which years of study and experience had given them. No better drilled and disciplined force had ever been placed in line of battle, and they fought with all possible courage. They were clearly superior to any fighting men in the world at that time. To defeat such soldiers at any time, and under any circumstances, to cause such men to abandon the battle-field was glory enough for any army.

Opinions varied as to Clinton's course in the march from Philadelphia to New York. Mr. Coke, in the House of Commons, said, that the whole march from Philadelphia to New York "was universally allowed to be the finest thing performed during the present war."

The Earl of Shelburne called it "the shameful retreat from Philadelphia when the General escaped with his whole army rather by chance and the misconduct of the enemy than by the natural ability of the force under his command."

Baron von Ochs, the Hessian general officer, in "Reflections on the Art of War," said, that "Clinton's march across New Jersey was more remarkable than the march of Moreau across the Black Forest in October 1796."

Clinton himself afterward said, in reference to having so long a baggage train, "I was certainly to blame for permitting it. I lost not a cart however." In reference to the battle, he said to Major Thomas Clarke, of the Coldstream regiment of foot guards, "Tell General Phillips that on that day I fought upon velvet; he will fully understand me."

Referring to Washington, Stedman, the English his-

the conduct, care and attention of all the officers who have been detached with the several Brigades and Battalion guns, cannot fail to be pleasing and satisfactory to the Brigadier-General. He therefore takes this occasion to give them his best thanks and to express further his entire approbation of the regularity and observance of duties that have been shown by all ranks during the late march and of the cheerfulness and alacrity with which they have undergone the great fatigue of it." Duncan's *History of the Royal Regiment of Artillery*, Vol. I, p. 322.

torian, says: "Having come up with the main body of his army, fresh and untired troops, he should have endeavored to turn one of General Clinton's flanks. Had he succeeded, that part of the British army must have been destroyed."[11] But Clinton made light of this remark about turning his flanks by saying, "When the author knows the country a little better, and possibly military movements in it a little better this question may be answered."

Horace Walpole wrote to Sir —— Mawn, "The Royal army has gained an escape."[12] Clinton himself writes thus, as we find in his manuscript notes: "Sir Henry Clinton had been ordered to embark the army at Philadelphia and proceed to New York. For various reasons he ventured to disobey the King's commands, and by that disobedience saved both army and navy. The principle of the British army was retreat at this period. Washington's avant guarde passes to marshy boggy branches at single bridges and attacks the British rear-guard; probably with no other intent than to amuse while another corps attempted the baggage. The British rear-guard forces Lee back over all these branches beyond the Lake. Lee is met by Washington arriving in column from Englishtown. Here of course the business would have finished: but the ungovernable impetuosity of the light troops had drawn them over the morass, and till they returned it became necessary to mask the 4th (west) ravine to prevent the enemy from passing it and cutting the above corps; and the 1st Guards and 33rd regiment under Col. Medows and Webster, maintained the ground exposed to a cross-fire, and with severe loss, till the light troops had retired over the bog in safety."[13]

In the same manuscript Sir Henry Clinton gives the

[11] Stedman's *History of the American War*, Vol. II, p. 24.

[12] Walpole *Correspondence*, Vol. III, p. 96.

[13] "It took Clinton and his red coats from June 18th to June 27th to travel sixty miles from Philadelphia to Freehold, nine days—less than seven miles a day—but after the battle of Monmouth was fought on the 28th of June it only took him one day to reach Sandy Hook, which was twenty-four miles away." S. C. Cowart.

opinion of Frederick the Great, as if in confirmation of his conduct in the battle. After Frederick had read of Lee's trial and Clinton's report to his King, he said, "When two opposite gentlemen agree in describing the ground and the events of the day, they must both be right."

CHAPTER XXIII

WHATEVER General Lee's real motives may have been on the field of battle he could not but feel during the evening of June 28 that his conduct was displeasing to many of the officers of the army, and his proud, arrogant nature could not brook the thought that he should be criticised by provincial troops who had never drawn sword in any of the Continental wars. His education as a soldier, his experience in bloody engagements forbade the idea that he had done anything wrong. He said to his staff around him that night that he was thoroughly persuaded that he had more than done his duty, and that he had obeyed the instructions he had received to the utmost of his power. He felt also, and so expressed himself, that he had extricated his command by a retrograde movement, from a most dangerous situation, with the loss of but few men and no material and that he had baffled and checked the enemy. Then why not congratulation and applause from his comrades, and why these slights and reproaches which he could not but feel in the conduct of his subordinates? As the officers gathered together at the evening meal, and as the soldiers lay down in groups in the early moonlight, they talked over the events of the day and few were found to say a word in favor of General Lee. This gossip of the camp did not fail to reach Lee's ear and, withal, the stern words of the chief, whom he envied, kept his mind in active thought that Sabbath night. He said that all day on Monday, he expected General Washington would have made him some apology when he had become better informed of the facts, but no such words came from His Excellency. Before Lee retired for the night, his mind harassed by the current topic of conversation in all the army outside his own quarters, and when all his boasted self-control had certainly left him,

he wrote a disrespectful letter to General Washington, which, in his agitation, he dated July 1 when it should have been June 29. It is generally believed that this letter did not come into Washington's hands until the next morning.

On June 30 General Washington replied to General Lee's discourteous letter and charged him with misbehavior before the enemy in not attacking them, and in making an unnecessary retreat.

On receipt of this letter from General Washington, by the hands of Lieutenant-Colonel John Fitzgerald, of his staff, General Lee requested him to remain while he wrote a reply. This second offensive letter, while apologizing for a former error, he also misdated, making it the very day of the battle instead of two days afterward, June 30, when it was actually written. In his letter he expresses a desire to retire from the active service in the army until his vindication can be secured.

During the afternoon of the same day General Lee wrote a third letter to the commander-in-chief on the same subject. At last he had ascertained the correct date.[1] In this letter he asked for a court of inquiry, but states that he would prefer a court-martial. His preference was complied with.

General Washington was prompt in dealing with General Lee. The court-martial was ordered on the first halt in the march of the army, and the charges exhibited. On the afternoon of June 30, General Washington's gallant adjutant-general, who afterward gave his life for freedom's cause in the trenches before Yorktown, Virginia, served a copy of the charges upon General Lee, with the following letter:

---

[1] The mistake in dates is admitted by Lee, in a letter addressed to the President of Congress, under date of October 16, 1778. See *Lee Papers*, Vol. III, p. 242.

Head Quarters, Englishtown, 30 June 1778.

SIR:

Your letter by Colonel Fitzgerald and also one of this date have been duly received. I have sent Colonel Scammell, the Adjutant General, to put you in arrest, who will deliver you a copy of the charges on which you will be tried.

I am, Sir, your most obedient servant

GO. WASHINGTON

MAJOR GENERAL LEE.

The charges against General Lee were, *First*: For disobedience of orders, in not attacking the enemy on June 28, agreeable to repeated instructions.

Secondly: For misbehavior before the enemy on the same day, by making an unnecessary, disorderly and shameful retreat.

Thirdly: For disrespect to the Commander-in-Chief in two letters dated July 1 and June 28.

On the same day, June 30, Brigadier-Generals Anthony Wayne and Charles Scott addressed an important letter to General Washington, giving their version of General Lee's conduct in the retreat. This letter was not referred to in the trial, but was no doubt carefully considered by General Washington when he framed the charges.[2]

On the following day the general orders convening the court were promulgated.

Head Quarters, Spotswood, 1 July 1778.

A General Court Martial, whereof Lord Stirling is appointed President will set in Brunswick tomorrow (the hour and place to be appointed by the President) for the trial of Major-General Lee. Brigadier-Generals Smallwood, Poor, Woodford and Huntington and Colonels Grayson, Johnston, Wigglesworth, Febiger, Swift, Angel, Clarke and Williams are to attend as Members.

By order of the Commander-in-Chief

ALEXANDER SCAMMELL
Adjutant General.

[2] This letter, with those exchanged between Lee and Washington, may be found in Appendix IV to this volume.

It was not until Saturday, July 4, however, that the court first convened, at the inn of Hyndert Voorhees, in the town of Brunswick, New Jersey, in the same room in which the Provincial Congress of New Jersey held its meetings from January 31 to March 2, 1777. In the meantime, the members of the court had been somewhat changed by orders, but on that day they were all present and sworn.[3]

The court-martial held twenty-six sessions, three at Brunswick, and six at Paramus church, in New Jersey; three at Peekskill, and fourteen at North Castle in New York.

General Lee pleaded not guilty.

Twenty-six persons testified against him in the trial.[4]

On behalf of the defence thirteen witnesses were called and gave their testimony.[5]

[3] The members of the court were: Major-General Lord Stirling, President; Brigadier-Generals William Smallwood, Enoch Poor, William Woodford, and Jedediah Huntington; Colonels William Irvine, Seventh Pennsylvania regiment, William Shepard, Fourth Massachusetts regiment, Herman Swift, Seventh Connecticut regiment, Edward Wigglesworth, Thirteenth Massachusetts regiment, Israel Angell, Second Rhode Island regiment, Thomas Clark, First North Carolina regiment, Otho H. Williams, Sixth Maryland regiment, Christian Febiger, Second Virginia regiment, and Colonel John Lawrence, Judge Advocate.

[4] Witnesses against General Lee: Major-Generals the Marquis de Lafayette and the Baron von Steuben; Brigadier-Generals Charles Scott, Anthony Wayne, David Forman, and William Maxwell; Colonels Joseph Cilley, First New Hampshire regiment, William Grayson, Grayson's Continental regiment, Walter Stewart, Thirteenth Pennsylvania regiment, Richard Butler, Ninth Pennsylvania regiment, and Matthias Ogden, First New Jersey regiment; Lieutenant-Colonels John Fitzgerald, Richard K. Meade, Alexander Hamilton, John Laurens, Robert H. Harrison, Tench Tilghman, all on Washington's staff, Samuel Smith, Fourth Maryland regiment, David Rhea, Fourth New Jersey regiment, and William S. Smith, Jackson's Continental regiment; Captains David Lennox and Benjamin Fishbourne, of Wayne's staff; Brigade-Major Aaron Ogden, of Maxwell's staff; Doctors James McHenry, of Washington's staff, and David Griffith, of Woodford's staff, and Monsieur Langfrang (probably Captain Pierre Charles L'Enfant, of the Continental Engineers).

[5] Witnesses for General Lee: Brigadier-Generals Louis Lebeque Duportail and Henry Knox; Colonel Henry Jackson, Jackson's Continental regiment; Lieutenant-Colonel Jeremiah Olney, Second Rhode Island regiment, Jeremiah Gilman, First New Hampshire regiment, Eleazer Oswald, Second Continental artillery regiment, and John Brooks, of Lee's staff; Captains John F. Mercer of Lee's staff, John Compston and Thomas Seward, Third Conti-

General Lee read to the court, on August 9, a carefully prepared paper in defence of his conduct.

On August 12, Major-General Lord Stirling announced the decision of the court-martial, as follows:

The Court having considered the first charge against Major-General Lee, the evidence and his defence, are of opinion, that he is guilty of disobedience of orders, in not attacking the enemy on the 28th of June, agreeable to repeated instructions: being a breach of the latter part of Article 5th Section 2d of the Articles of War.[6]

The Court having considered the second charge against Major-General Lee the evidence and his defence, are of opinion he is guilty, of misbehaviour before the enemy on the 28th of June, by making an unnecessary, and in some instances, a disorderly retreat;[7] being a breach of the 13th Article of the 13th Section of the Articles of War.

The Court having considered the third charge against Major-General Lee, are of opinion that he is guilty of disrespect to the Commander-in-Chief in two letters dated the 1st of July and the 28th of June: being a breach of the 2d Article, Section 2d of the Articles of War.

The Court do sentence Major General Lee to be suspended from any command in the Armies of the United States of North America, for the term of twelve months.

nental artillery regiment, Evan Edwards, of Lee's staff, and John Stith, serving with the Third Continental light dragoons; Brigade-Major Samuel Shaw, of Knox's staff.

The affidavit of Captain Peter Wikoff, Second regiment Monmouth County militia, was also received.

[6] The paragraphs in the Articles of War, adopted by the Continental Congress, September 20, 1776, and referred to in above finding, are:

Section II, Article 5. Any officer or soldier who . . . shall disobey any lawful command of his superior officer shall suffer death or such other punishment as shall according to the nature of his offence, be inflicted upon him by the sentence of a court-martial.

Section XIII, Article 13. Whatsoever officer or soldier shall misbehave himself before the enemy and run away or shamefully abandon any fort or guard which he or they shall be demanded to defend or speak words inducing others to do the like . . . every such offender being duly convicted thereof . . . shall suffer death or such other punishment, as by a general court-martial shall be inflicted on him.

Section II, Article 2. Any officer or soldier who shall behave himself with contempt or disrespect towards the general or other commander-in-chief of the forces of the United States or shall speak words tending to his hurt or dishonor shall be punished according to the nature of his offense by the judgment of a court-martial.

[7] The word "shameful" in the charge was omitted.

After much delay by the Continental Congress, in session at Philadelphia, the sentence of the court-martial of General Lee was approved December 5, 1778, by a vote of thirteen to seven, or rather, five states voting aye, two states voting nay, and the rest divided or not voting. The order of Congress was in these words: "Resolved, That the sentence of the General Court Martial upon Major General Lee be carried into execution."[8]

General Lee received this sentence with bitter abuse and severe reproaches. Doctor James Thacher says that, pointing to his dog, he said, "Oh that I was that animal, that I might not call man my brother."[9] During the rest of his life he was bitter and abusive in conversation and his letters were devoted to detraction of the army and of General Washington.

General Lee had no sympathy with the Commander-in-Chief. He did not appreciate his greatness of character, he was thoroughly jealous of his power and position and was not disposed to do anything that would reflect honor on the head of the army.

Charles Botta the historian very justly remarks, "Nevertheless the court martial found him guilty of all the charges, bating the epithet of shameful, which was expunged, and sentenced him to be suspended for one year; a judgment certainly too mild if Lee was guilty, or too severe, if innocent."[10]

General Carrington says, "If he had been in sympathy with Washington he would have received no censure. If he had exercised reasonable self-control at the close of the action he would have saved his commission."[11]

It is apparent that on the evening of the battle Washington had determined to give Lee no further reproof. General Lee's conduct after their first interview in doing what he could to check the retreat which his incompetency

[8] *Journals of Congress*, Vol. IV, pp. 488 *et seq.*
[9] Thacher's *Military Journal*, Appendix, p. 462.
[10] Botta's *History of the War of Independence*, Vol. II, p. 520.
[11] Carrington's *Battles of the American Revolution*, p. 445.

or indifference had caused, was quite evident even to General Washington, whose deep sense of gratitude for the heroic endurance and fortitude of his soldiers had dispelled all feeling of anger. Had it not been for Lee's arrogant and disrespectful letters after the fight, Washington would certainly have passed over his strange conduct on the battle-field. Even as late as the morning of June 30 General Washington named Lee in general orders as the Major-General for July 1. But the reproof Lee had publicly received, which had now become the gossip of the camp, annoyed and fretted him and he felt that he had been badly used. He worked himself into a bitter state of mind which prompted him to write discourteous letters, assuming the authority of a superior, and requiring reparation for injury sustained. If General Lee had waited until the next day and in a calm and respectful manner made a full explanation of his conduct on the battle-field, instead of writing petulant and unbecoming letters to the commander-in-chief, the outcome of his affairs would undoubtedly have been very different. Lee's downfall commenced from that hour and his military career was at an end.

In this connection we quote from the memoirs of Henry Lee:

The records of the court martial manifest on their face the error of the sentence; and it is wonderful how men of honour and of sense could thus commit themselves to the censures of the independent and impartial. If General Lee had been guilty of all the charges as affirmed by their decision, his life was forfeited; and its sacrifice only could have atoned for his criminality. He ought to have been cashiered and shot; instead of which the mild sentence of suspension, for a short time, was the punishment inflicted. The truth is, the unfortunate general was only guilty of neglect in not making timely communication of his departure from orders, subject to his discretion, to the commander-in-chief, which constituted no part of the charges against him. This was certainly a very culpable omission: to which was afterwards added personal disrespect, where the utmost respect was not only due, but enjoined by martial law, and enforced by the state of things;

two armies upon the very brink of battle, himself intrusted with the direction of an important portion of one of them, for the very purpose of leading into action, to withhold the necessary explanations from his chief, and to set the example of insubordination by his mode of reply to an interrogatory, indispensably though warmly, put to him, merited punishment. But this offence was different, far different from "disobedience to orders," or a "shameful retreat," neither of which charges were supported by testimony; and both of which were contradicted by fact.[12]

In Belsham's memoirs the following passage occurs: "It was suspected that the commander-in-chief was not displeased at the dismissal of a man so haughty and impracticable; nor did the army in whose estimation he had been visibly lessened since the disaster which had befallen him, appear much to regret his loss. For though the capture of general Lee was merely fortuitous, misfortune is in the minds of men nearly allied to disgrace, disgrace produces contempt, and contempt verges towards alienation and hatred."[13]

In the edition of Leudrum's history, published in Boston in 1795, we find this statement: "Many were displeased with this sentence because it had been submitted to his discretion whether to attack or not, and likewise when and in what manner; and they thought that suspension from command was not a sufficient punishment for his crimes, if guilty. They therefore inferred his innocence from the lenient sentence of his judges."[14]

Chief Justice Marshall remarks, "Whatever judgment may be formed on the propriety of retreating before the enemy, it seems difficult to justify either the omission to keep the commander-in-chief continually informed of his situation and intentions or the rude letters written after the action was over."[15]

In his comments on the trial, General de Peyster says,

[12] Lieutenant-Colonel Henry Lee's *Memoirs of the War in the Southern Department of the United States*, p. 38.
[13] Belsham's *Memoirs of the Reign of George III*, Vol. II, p. 352.
[14] Leudrum's *History of the American Revolution*, Vol. II, p. 71.
[15] Marshall's *Life of George Washington*, Vol. III, p. 418.

"The decision of this Court is very unsatisfactory. If guilty Lee's punishment was altogether too mild for the offences charged; and if innocent it was totally unjustified."[16]

It may also be remarked that General Lee's defence was a masterly one. He endeavored to prove that any other course than that which he pursued would have given the enemy great advantage and have hazarded the destruction of the entire army. He stated distinctly that at "the several councils of war, held both in Pennsylvania and on this side of the Delaware, on the subject of the operations to be pursued in the Jerseys, he reprobated the idea of risking a general engagement, as a measure highly absurd in the present or rather then circumstances of America (for since the time these councils were held, circumstances are much altered). . . . The most sanguine of these councils only recommended to seek and seize some favourable opportunity of striking some important but partial blow."[17]

The Honorable Elias Boudinot made this criticism on Lee's conduct:

Gen'l Lee had considerable Military Knowledge & did very well on a small scale,—but I have no doubt that whenever anything on a very large scale struck him, that a partial Lunacy took place. His behaviour this morning discovered this state of mind, which might have been increased from the peculiarity of his situation, and his exalted idea of the prowess of British Troops. In the midst of the Engagement, he rode up to a Lt. Coll. of my acquaintance who had a single field piece firing and called to him Coll. have you seen anything improper in my Conduct this morning? the Coll. (who had been convinced of something wrong in the Gen'l all the morning, yet not choosing to acknowledge it) answered no, by no means —well then said the General do you remember that.—Such an Extraordinary Question form a Commander in Chief of a division, under such Extraordinary Circumstances, is full proof that he must have felt something unusual in himself. The issue was that he was beat, and had not Gen'l Washington have come up in a

16 De Peyster's "Consideration of the Case of Lee" in *Old Times in Old Monmouth*, p. 43.
17 Lee's defence at his court-martial, p. 199.

lucky moment & turned the fortune of the Day, It might have been fatal to America.[18]

After a careful study of the conduct of General Lee from the time he marched his division from Washington's camp at Valley Forge until he reached Englishtown after the close of the battle, it is difficult to prove that he exhibited one traitorous act. General Lee was a professional soldier, personally a brave man, and his life had been spent in studying in the schools and in practising on the field the art of war. His experience in Continental wars warranted the American Congress in bestowing upon him his high rank. Experienced soldiers were needed in the patriot army and the people looked to General Lee to furnish that peculiar skill which they were ready to believe was not found in any of our general officers, not even in Washington. That he was not true to the cause of American independence is conclusively proved by his conduct in the previous year while a prisoner of war in New York. His suggestive plans, an eight-page manuscript endorsed "Mr. Lee's plan," dated March 29, 1777, and addressed to the British commanding general show that he was at that time full of treason to the sacred cause, although it does not appear that any of his compatriots at this time had the slightest idea of the extent of his turpitude. That his heart was not perfectly true to General Washington in the high office which he held needs no particular proof, but that any of his acts during that period exhibited the disposition of a traitor is questionable. He promptly obeyed the order to march to the banks of the Delaware River, he crossed the river with his division without delay, the halt at Hopewell was not by his order, and the opinion expressed by him at the council of war in that village was concurred in by other well-known patriot officers. It was at least a worthy ambition, if there was to be a fight with the British Army, to desire to lead at the very front, his orders from Washington were to some extent discretion-

18 Boudinot's *Journal of Events in the Revolution*, p. 81.

ary, and his plan of carefully attacking the rear of the covering party, or rather inviting them to attack him while he could take a force from his left flank, divide the British column, and so, if possible, surround them, had been successfully tried in other battles, and was certainly feasible at that time. That General Lee was not equal to the management of 5000 men in such a country, so full of thickets, woods, and marshes was his misfortune and not due to treachery. He certainly failed to use his force as he might have done, because he had not the sharp cooperation of Dickinson's New Jersey militia nor of Morgan's rifle corps. They had no orders when the fighting began and so were inactive at the very moment Lee needed them. He had given his general officers no idea of his plans before the battle, and evidently had matured no plans in his own mind. When General Lee saw his right column retreating he gave his left no orders of any kind. When he found Scott had fallen back he did not attempt to change his movements. In this he was grievously wrong. His whole force was not handled with skill and seems virtually to have taken care of itself. He failed to concentrate and control his forces, and by distinct, definite orders to keep his troops well in hand. At last, when he found his division giving way, he said he had it in mind to secure a new line of defence, where he might check the foe for the time, and although his troops seemingly got out of his control in their retrograde movement, he said (probably an after-thought in his defence) that he hoped to re-form them on the very ground where Washington was at that moment bringing up his supporting column. Before he was able to make his statement good, the control of the division had passed out of his hands by the presence of superior rank. Lee's reply to Washington, his indignant exclamation, was not traitorous, his indirect supervision of the first fighting at the hedge fence was certainly all that could be expected of him, for he obeyed General Washington's orders and the fighting of his weary troops

was superb. His head and heart might not have been thoroughly in accord with what Washington expected of him in the hour of battle, but he apparently executed to the best of his ability the reasonable plans which an experienced general should form at such a time. General Lee may have supposed that Clinton was in too great force for him to attack him with any hope of success. Perhaps he thought that his division was likely to be overwhelmed before Washington could come to his support, and, therefore, judged that a short retreat was best. Although he differed from Washington in his plans for the day, his orders were discretionary, and, of course, his judgment was not infallible. Certain it is that the active work of a more skillful leader was imperatively needed at the front that day. It will be noticed that Washington, although amazed at Lee's unexpected retreat, did not promptly relieve him of command. It was over two hours later that Lee was sent to the rear with a body of weary troops.

It is not generally thought by students of this battle that the brigade commanders did their full duty in supporting General Lee. It is difficult at this time to explain why they lacked confidence in him, for it does not appear that he had publicly done anything to specially detract from his great military reputation. It is certain, however, that General Lee thought it advisable to make only a partial demonstration against the foe. According to his discretionary orders, which he interpreted to be almost unlimited, he did not think it best to attack the main army. It is also possible that he did not at that time care to have such a measure of success as would turn the whole British column upon him, or in any way disprove his predictions given at the council of war a week previous.

It may be well to note that the life of General Lee was full of complaints, of disagreements with his comrades, and of quarrels with his superior officers. His temper was rough and vindictive, his morals bad, his manner snarling and cynical and his conversation full of impiety and pro-

fanity. His correspondence, which seems to have been large for that time, was always in a critical, complaining, or vindictive style.

But with all these personal characteristics, with full knowledge of his nationality and early training, keeping in mind also the "Plan," which he had beforehand given to General Howe for the subjugation of America, it is scarcely just to assert that in his conduct on the battle-field Lee exhibited one disloyal act, that he did anything that his military judgment might not have approved, or that any other general officer perfectly true to the cause might not have done.

In addition to the court-martial of Major-General Lee, a Court of Enquiry was ordered, to "enquire into and state Facts relative to the conduct of Col. Henry Jackson at the battle of Monmouth he thinking his character much injured and his Reputation highly reproached." The complaint was signed by sixteen officers, ten of his own regiment, four of Colonel David Henley's regiment Continental infantry, and two of Colonel Lee's regiment Continental infantry. His complaint is dated July 26, 1778. The court was held at the court house in Providence, at as late a date as April 17, 1779, by order of Major-General Horatio Gates. After the testimony had been taken, the court did not resume its sessions in Providence until July 5, 1779, when Colonel Jackson made an address to the court in his defence, and the following decision was rendered:

> The Court upon fully and maturely considering the Evidence & Col. Jackson's Defence and also the Confusion of the advanced Corps of Gen'l Lee's Division on that Day are of opinion that there appears not anything against Col. Jackson sufficiently reprehensible to call him before a Court Martial.[19]

After General Lee's trial and conviction Major-General the Baron von Steuben took exception to the

[19] Complete proceedings of this Court in the *Lee Papers.* Vol. III, pp. 209 *et seq.*

statements of General Lee at the trial, and toward the close of the year some bitter correspondence took place between them. Von Steuben's letter was written in French and was dated in Philadelphia, December 2, 1778.[20]

The grievance of General von Steuben was in consequence of words used by General Lee in the written document he read in his defence, and for this expression von Steuben desired satisfaction on the field of honor. "Of all the very distant spectators of the manoeuvers on this day and those a very trifling part of them, the Baron Steuben is, I think, the only gentleman who has stepped forth to prove their demerits. He has certainly shown a very laudable zeal for bringing a criminal officer to condign punishment; but the next time he takes the field of prosecution in the cause of an injured community I hope his prudence will dictate to him the necessity of being furnished with a better apparatus."[21]

General Lee replied to von Steuben's challenge and his explanation seems to have been satisfactory for we find that the subject was dropped.

On December 3, 1778, General Lee published, in the *Pennsylvania Packet* of Philadelphia, a lengthy and carefully written "vindication to the public" of his character and conduct "especially on the field of Monmouth."[22]

General Lee also received a challenge from Lieutenant-Colonel John Laurens, of Washington's military family, on account of Lee's constant personal abuse of the character and conduct of General Washington. The challenge was accepted and the duellists met on the Point-no-Point Road in a woods near the four-mile stone just below Philadelphia, at half-past three in the afternoon of December 23, 1778. Lieutenant-Colonel Alexander Hamilton was Lauren's second and Captain Evan Edwards, of

---

[20] *Lee Papers*, Vol. III, p. 253.

[21] Lee's defence at his court-martial, p. 232.

[22] Washington, in a letter of December 12, 1778, to Joseph Reed, President of Pennsylvania, charges Lee with downright falsehood. This letter may be found in Ford, *Writings of Washington*, Vol. VII, p. 280.

Lee's staff, was his second. They fired at six paces distance and General Lee was slightly wounded in his right side.[23]

Soon after General Lee left his command in the army, he retired to a farm near Shepherdstown, Berkeley County, [now West] Virginia, and spent his time in seclusion in a miserable, dilapidated house, a servant and a large number of dogs his only companions.[24] He continued, however, even from this forlorn retreat, which he called Prato Rio, to send out to the public venomous attacks on General Washington which were powerless to injure him, and scarcely even annoyed him.

During the year 1779 General Lee still continued his severe and contemptible criticisms of Washington in conversation with his friends and with those who were willing to listen to his scathing aspersions. When Congress had made some movement toward striking his name from the army lists, he wrote to the President of Congress a weak and undignified letter, undated, from his farm in Berkeley County, Virginia.[25]

When Congress received this letter from General Lee the following resolution was passed:

Monday January 10, 1780.—"Resolved That Major General Lee be informed, that Congress has no further occasion for his services in the army of the United States."

General Lee replied to this action of Congress in a letter addressed to its President, dated January 30, 1780.[26] He apologized for his former communication and attempted to justify himself by the peculiar circumstances under which he had written the letter, the fact that he was not

---

[23] The narrative of this duel is found in the *Lee Papers*, Vol. III, pp. 283 *et seq.*

[24] "He had led a kind of hermit life on his estate; dogs and horses were his favorite companions. His house is described as being a mere shell, destitute of comforts and convenience. For want of partitions the different parts were designated by lines chalked on the floor. In one corner was his bed; in another was his books; his saddles and harness in a third; a fourth served as a kitchen." Irving's *Life of George Washington*, Vol. III, p. 471.

[25] *Lee Papers*, Vol. III, p. 405.

[26] *ibid.*, p. 407.

well, that he dictated and did not write himself and that
he was just at the moment about to leave his home. His
object in writing this last letter is not very clear,—but
it apparently had no effect upon Congress.

During the year 1779 Lee had written many articles
for the journals of the day, attacking General Sullivan
and General Wayne, abusing his former friend General
Reed, and making gross insinuations against the military
skill of General Washington. One of the most widely
circulated of these attacks was published in the *Maryland
Journal and Baltimore Advertiser*, July 6, 1779, "containing twenty-five queries political and military humbly
offered to the consideration of the public." This document he dated from Philadelphia. It created much excitement at the time.[27]

In the latter part of the year 1782, this soldier of fortune, tired of his poor life on the old Virginia plantation,
convinced, too, that at that time the cause he had despised,
if not tried to betray, had become triumphant, came to
Philadelphia and took lodgings in a small inn. Here he
was taken with lung disease, which after five days' illness
proved fatal and he died at ten o'clock on the evening of
Wednesday, October 2, 1782, aged fifty-one years. His
thoughts to the very last were of the soldier life he had
led and he expired shouting, as he supposed to his troops,
"Stand by me, my brave grenadiers!" His funeral on
October 4, from the City Tavern, was attended by a large
gathering of the people of Philadelphia and officers of the
army, and apparently more respect was shown him at his
death than he had received in the last four years of his
life. In his will he desired not to be buried in any churchyard or within a mile of any Presbyterian or Anabaptist
meeting-house giving the following reason: "I have kept
so much bad company while living, that I do not choose
to continue it when dead." His body, however, was buried
in Christ Churchyard, Philadelphia.

[27] The *Lee Papers*, Vol. III, pp. 341 *et seq.*

Thus, in a little room in the "Canastoga Wagon" tavern, in the capital of the country he had so poorly served, ended a life which, as has been said, "was little less than the history of disputes, quarrels and duels in every part of the world."

CHAPTER XXIV

THE desertions from the British Army on their passage through New Jersey were very many. On July 4 General Arnold made a return of the number which had come back to Philadelphia and he makes the list include, 136 British and 440 Hessians, in all 576 men. This was afterward increased to over 600 men, as Washington says in one of his letters. He also added the statement that many of the Germans came over to the American Army, others wandered into the country from the line of march so that he "believed the whole number of deserters may be estimated as about 800."

Judge Jones, in his Tory history, says of the British Army that "from the intense heat, different skirmishes, and desertion, it consisted upon its arrival at the Hook, of at least 1,500 men less, than it contained when it left Philadelphia."[1]

Captain Montresor, in his Journal, says that "350 Germans deserted from us on the march," and General Knyphausen wrote Frederick II, Landgrave of Hesse Cassel July 6, 1778, that 236 of his men had deserted in New Jersey.

General Washington wrote to General Arnold from Brunswick, July 6, that he believed that from desertion and the action "Clinton's Army had experienced a diminution of 2000 men at least since it left Philadelphia." Of course, this number included the 300 killed, 800 wounded and 100 prisoners.

It is quite evident that these desertions were principally from the ranks of the German mercenaries, and that they preferred to go back to their sweethearts and wives

---

[1] Jones' *History of New York during the Revolutionary War*, Vol. I, p. 263.

in Philadelphia rather than continue in the ranks of an army employed to crush out freedom in America.

Surgeon James Thacher, of the American Army, gives this strange, and we must conclude very inaccurate, account of the British losses: "If reports are accurate, the loss of the royalists consists of four officers and two hundred and forty-five rank and file killed, and left in the field, buried by our people; one thousand two hundred and fifty-five wounded; one hundred and seventeen prisoners; and one thousand five hundred and seventy-two deserted during the march; total of their loss, after they left Philadelphia, according to accounts circulated, three thousand one hundred and eighty-nine. Of the Continentals, according to returns, sixty-nine were killed, one hundred and forty-two wounded and about one hundred missing. The intense heat of the weather, great fatigue, and drinking cold water, proved fatal to about sixty or eighty men of each party."[2]

Stedman says, "three sergeants and fifty-six men died without a wound." This refers to the British Army and was a result of the intense heat.[3]

In Lamb's *Journal* we find the following remark: "The total disagreement between the British and American accounts of this action, is not a little perplexing to the impartial narrator; both parties claim the advantage; but the Americans, particularly at that time, had their reasons for their misrepresentations—reasons which did not at all influence the reports of the British commanders."[4] Are we then to conclude that General Washington designedly misstated to Congress in an official letter the real loss of the British column? This is manifestly improbable.

In Mackinnon's *History of the Coldstream Regiment of Foot Guards*, it is mentioned that while Sir Henry Clinton made a full report of the names and casualties

[2] Thacher's *Military Journal*, p. 165.
[3] Stedman's *History of the American War*, Vol. II, p. 12.
[4] Lamb's *Journal of Occurrences during the Late American War*, p. 242.

among his officers, "no separate return was made of the loss in men." This statement seems to be correct. The British records do not appear to show the names of the enlisted men killed and wounded in this fight. We are, therefore, left to conclude that Clinton either did not estimate correctly, or did not wish to know, and made no effort to get the exact number of his loss before the next muster of his command; and that he then neglected to send it to Lord Germaine. Consequently, we must accept the report of General Washington as more nearly correct, for he had ample opportunity to get the exact numbers from his own burial parties.

Lieutenant-Colonel Henry Lee remarks concerning the British dead, "Judging from the official statements which were published, the loss was trifling and not very unequal; but the stubborn fact of burying the dead, manifests a great error in the report made by Sir Henry Clinton to his government. He rated his dead and missing at one hundred and eighty-eight: whereas we buried on the field of battle two hundred and forty-nine."[5]

The following is the official return of the killed, wounded and missing of the American Army:

KILLED. *Infantry*—1 lieutenant-colonel, 1 major, 3 captains, 2 lieutenants, 1 sergeant, 52 rank and file. *Artillery*—1 lieutenant, 7 mattrosses, 1 bombadier.

WOUNDED. *Infantry*—2 colonels, 8 captains, 4 first lieutenants, 2 second lieutenants, 1 ensign, 1 adjutant, 8 sergeants, 1 drummer, 120 rank and file. *Artillery*—1 captain, 1 sergeant, 1 corporal, 1 gunner, 10 mattrosses.

MISSING. *Infantry*—3 sergeants, 126 rank and file. *Artillery*—1 mattross.

Some of the missing dropped through fatigue and hardship, since come in. Six horses killed and two wounded.

This return was made by General Washington July 1, and it was not complete, especially in reference to the wounded officers. It shows 8 officers and 61 enlisted men

[5] Lee's *Memoirs of the War in the Southern Department of the United States*, p. 37.

killed, 19 officers and 142 enlisted men wounded, and 130 enlisted men missing, a total of 360 casualties. Fiske the historian says, 362 loss. Bancroft gives the number of killed and wounded as 229. A carefully prepared roster of the casualties of the American Army in the battle, will be found in the appendix to this work. This roster is not taken from any report, but has been compiled from pages of history, biography, genealogy, and especially from pension records. All the commissioned officers killed and wounded, except one ensign wounded, are now identified. Many of those numbered and named as missing and those recorded as sent to hospital on account of the heat and fatigue afterward rejoined their regiments.[6] In addition to the horses reported as above, killed and wounded, it may be noticed that a large number became utterly prostrated by the heat and died or had to be abandoned. For weeks afterward their dead bodies made the air of the battle-field intolerable.

The following is the official return of the killed, wounded, missing, &c., of the British Army:

Total British—1 lieutenant-colonel, 1 captain, 2 lieutenants, 4 sergeants, 56 rank and file killed; 3 sergeants, 45 rank and file died with fatigue; 1 colonel, 1 lieutenant-colonel, 1 major, 7 captains, 5 lieutenants, 7 sergeants, 137 rank and file wounded; 3 sergeants, 61 rank and file missing.

Total German—1 rank and file killed, 11 rank and file died with fatigue, 11 rank and file wounded.

General Total—1 lieutenant-colonel, 1 captain, 2 lieutenants, 4 sergeants, 57 rank and file killed; 3 sergeants, 56 rank and file died with fatigue; 1 colonel, 1 lieutenant-colonel, 1 major, 7 captains, 5 lieutenants, 7 sergeants, 148 rank and file wounded; 3 sergeants, 61 rank and file missing.

This return of 4 officers and 61 enlisted men killed, 15 officers and 155 enlisted men wounded, 64 enlisted men missing and 59 enlisted men died of fatigue, a total of 358 casualties, was made by Sir Henry Clinton July 5 and accompanied his official report of the battle. A report was made to General Washington the day after the battle as

[6] Appendix V.

to the number of British and American soldiers who had been interred by the American burial parties that day, under charge of Lieutenant-Colonel Cornelius Van Dyck, of the First regiment, New York Continental infantry. This report gives the number as 217 British and 29 Americans and this does not include those of the enemy buried by the British themselves. A roster of such casualties among the officers as have been found among the records of Great Britain has been compiled from the "Army lists of British officers Serving in America," and while it is by no means complete, every effort has been made to make it accurate as far as the records give us information. After the return was forwarded one Lieutenant-Colonel and one Captain were found to have been wounded.[7]

The historian Fiske says 416 loss, and according to Mr. Bancroft the number of killed and wounded was more than 400.

The third day after the battle General Washington sent his official report to Honorable Henry Laurens, President of the Continental Congress.

Englishtown, 1 July 1778.

Sir,

I embrace this first moment of leisure to give Congress a more full and particular account of the movements of the army under my command since its passing the Delaware, than the situation of our affairs would heretofore permit. I had the honour to advise them that on the appearance of the enemy's intention to march through Jersey becoming serious, I had detached General Maxwell's brigade, in conjunction with the militia of that State to interrupt and impede their progress by every obstruction in their power, so as to give time to the army under my command to come up with them and take advantage of any favorable circumstances that might present themselves. The army having proceeded to Coryell's Ferry and crossed the Delaware at that place, I immediately detached Colonel Morgan with a select corps of six hundred men to reinforce General Maxwell and marched with the main body towards Prince Town. The slow advance of the enemy had greatly the air of design and led me, with others to suspect that General Clinton, desirous of a general action was endeavouring to draw us down

[7] Appendix VI.

into the lower country in order, by a rapid movement, to gain our right, and take possession of the strong grounds above us. This consideration and to give the troops time to repose and refresh themselves from the fatigues they had experienced from rainy and excessively hot weather, determined me to halt at Hopewell township about five [eight] miles from Princeton where we remained till the morning of the 25th. On the preceding day I made a second detachment of fifteen hundred chosen troops under Brigadier General Scott to reinforce those already in the vicinity of the enemy, the more effectually to annoy and delay their march. The next day the army moved to Kingston; and having received intelligence that the enemy were prosecuting their route towards Monmouth Court House, I despatched a thousand select men under Brigadier-General Wayne and sent the Marquis de Lafayette to take the command of the whole advanced corps, including Maxwell's brigade and Morgan's light infantry, with orders to take the first opportunity of attacking the enemy's rear. In the evening of the same day the whole army marched from Kingston where our baggage was left with intention to preserve a proper distance for supporting the advanced corps, and arrived at Cranberry [Cranbury] early the next morning. The intense heat of the weather and a heavy storm unluckily coming on, made it impossible to resume our march that day without great inconvenience and injury to the troops. Our advanced corps, being differently circumstanced, moved from the position it had held the night before and took post in the evening on the Monmouth road about five miles from the enemy's rear, in expectation of attacking them next morning on their march. The main body having remained at Cranberry, the advanced corps was found to be too remote, and too far upon the right to be supported in case of an attack either upon or from the enemy; which induced me to send orders to the Marquis to file off by his left towards English Town which he accordingly executed early in the morning of the 27th. The enemy in marching from Allentown, had changed their disposition, and placed their best troops in the rear, consisting of all the grenadiers, light infantry, and chasseurs of the line. This alteration made it necessary to increase the number of our advanced troops; in consequence of which I detached Major General Lee with two brigades to join the Marquis at English Town, on whom of course the demand of the whole devolved, amounting to about five thousand men. The main body marched the same day and encamped within three miles of that place. Morgan's corps was left hovering on the enemy's right flank; and the Jersey militia, amounting at this time to about seven or eight hundred men, under General Dickinson, on their left. The enemy were now encamped in a strong position with their right extending

about a mile and a half beyond the Court-House to the parting of the roads leading to Shrewsbury and Middletown, and their left along the road from Allentown to Monmouth, about three miles on this side of the Court-House. Their right flank lay on the skirt of a small wood, while their left was secured by a very thick one, a morass running towards their rear, and their whole front covered by a wood, and for a considerable extent towards the left, with a morass. In this situation they halted till the morning of the 28th. Matters being this situated and having had the best information, that, if the enemy were once arrived at the Heights of Middletown, ten or twelve miles from where they were, it would be impossible to attempt any thing against them with a prospect of success, I determined to attack their rear, the moment they should get in motion from their present ground. I communicated my intention to General Lee and ordered him to make his disposition for the attack, and to keep his troops constantly lying upon their arms to be in readiness at the shortest notice. This was done with respect to the troops under my immediate command. About five in the morning General Dickinson sent an express informing that the front of the enemy had begun their march. I instantly put the army in motion and sent orders by one of my aids to General Lee to move on and attack them unless there should be very powerful reasons to the contrary, acquainting him at the same time, that I was marching to support him and for doing it with the greater expedition and convenience, should make the men disencumber themselves of their packs and blankets. After marching about five miles, to my surprise and mortification, I met the whole advanced corps retreating, and as I was told, by General Lee's orders, without having made any opposition, except one fire, given by a party under the command of Colonel Butler, on their being charged by the enemy's cavalry, who were repulsed. I proceeded immediately to the rear of the corps, which I found closely pressed by the enemy, and gave directions for forming part of the retreating troops, who by the brave and spirited conduct of the officers aided by some pieces of well-served artillery, checked the enemy's advance, and gave time to make a disposition of the left wing and second line of the army upon an eminence, in a wood a little in the rear, covered by a morass in front. On this were placed some batteries of cannon by Lord Stirling, who commanded the left wing which played upon the enemy with great effect, and seconded by parties of infantry detached to oppose them effectually put a stop to their advance. General Lee being detached with the advanced corps the command of the right wing for the occasion was given to General Greene. For the expedition of the march, and to counteract any attempt to turn our right I had ordered him to file off by the

new church, two miles from Englishtown and fall into the Monmouth road, a small distance in the rear of the Court-House, while the rest of the column moved directly on towards the Court-House. On intelligence of the retreat he marched up and took a very advantageous position on the right. The enemy by this time, finding themselves warmly opposed in front, made an attempt to turn our left flank; but they were bravely repulsed and driven back by detached parties of infantry. They also made a movement to our right with as little success, General Greene having advanced a body of troops with artillery to a commanding piece of ground; which not only disappointed their design of turning our right, but severely enfiladed those in front of the left wing. In addition to this, General Wayne advanced with a body of troops, and kept up so severe and well-directed a fire that the enemy were soon compelled to retire behind the defile where the first stand in the beginning of the action had been made. In this situation the enemy had both their flanks secured by thick woods and morasses, while their front could only be approached through a narrow pass. I resolved nevertheless to attack them; and for that purpose ordered General Poor, with his own and the Carolina brigade to move round upon their right and General Woodford upon their left and the artillery to gall them in front. But the impediments in their way prevented their getting within reach before it was dark. They remained upon the ground they had been directed to occupy during the night with the intention to begin the attack early the next morning; and the army continued lying upon their arms in the field of action, to be in readiness to support them. In the mean time the enemy were employed in removing their wounded, and about twelve o'clock at night marched away in such silence that though General Poor lay extremely near them, they effected their retreat without his knowledge. They carried off all their wounded, except four officers and about forty privates, whose wounds were too dangerous to permit their removal. The extreme heat of the weather, the fatigue of the men from their march through a deep sandy country almost entirely destitute of water, and the distance the enemy had gained by marching in the night, made a pursuit impracticable and fruitless. It would have answered no valuable purpose, and would have been fatal to numbers of our men, several of whom died the preceding day with heat. Were I to conclude my account of this day's transactions, without expressing my obligations to the officers of the army in general I should do injustice to their merit and violence to my own feelings. They seemed to vie with each other in manifesting their zeal and bravery. The catalogue of those who distinguished themselves is too long to admit of particularizing individuals. I cannot, however, forbear

mentioning Brigadier General Wayne, whose good conduct and bravery through the whole action deserves particular commendadation. The behaviour of the troops in general, after they recovered from the first surprise occasioned by the retreat of the advanced corps, was such as could not be surpassed. All the artillery, both officers and men that were engaged distinguished themselves in a remarkable manner. Enclosed Congress will be pleased to receive a return of our killed, wounded and missing. Among the first were Lieutenant-Colonel Bunner of Pennsylvania and Major Dickinson of Virginia both officers of distinguished merit and much to be regretted. The enemy's slain, left on the field and buried by us, according to the return of the persons assigned to that duty were four officers and two hundred and forty-five privates. In the former number was the honourable Colonel Monckton. Exclusive of these, they buried some themselves, as there were several new graves near the field of battle. How many men they may have had wounded cannot be determined; but, from the usual proportion the number must have been considerable. There were a few prisoners taken. The peculiar situation of General Lee at this time requires that I should say nothing of his conduct. He is now in arrest. The charges against him, with such sentence as the court-martial may decree in his case shall be transmitted for the approbation or disapprobation of Congress as soon as it shall be passed. Being fully convinced by the gentlemen of this country, that the enemy cannot be hurt or injured in their embarkation at Sandy Hook, the place to which they are going, and unwilling to get too far removed from the North River, I put the troops in motion early this morning and shall proceed that way, leaving the Jersey brigade, Morgan's corps and other light parties (the militia being all dismissed) to hover about them, to countenance desertion, and to prevent depredations as far as possible. After they embark, the former will take post in the neighborhood of Elizabeth Town, the latter rejoin the corps from which they were detached. I have the honor to be,

Go. Washington.

On July 7, 1778 "Congress took into consideration the letter of June 29th and that of July 1st from General Washington, giving an account of his movements from Valley Forge to Monmouth Court-House, in the state of New Jersey, in pursuit of the enemy, and of a victory obtained over the British army commanded by general sir H. Clinton, in a battle near Monmouth Court-House, on the 28th of June; whereupon

"*Resolved*, unanimously, That the thanks of Congress be given to General Washington for the activity with which he marched from the Camp at Valley Forge, in pursuit of the enemy; for his distinguished exertions in forming the line of battle; and for his great good conduct in leading on the attack and gaining the important victory of Monmouth over the British grand army, under the command of general sir H. Clinton, in their march from Philadelphia to New York.

"*Resolved*, That General Washington be directed to signify the thanks of Congress to the gallant officers and men under his command, who distinguished themselves by their conduct and valour at the battle of Monmouth."

In acknowledgment of this action of the Continental Congress General Washington wrote to the President of Congress:

Camp, at Paramus, 12 July 1778.

Sir,

The vote of approbation and thanks which Congress have been pleased to honour me with gives me the highest satisfaction and at the same time demands a return of my sincerest acknowledgments. The other resolution I communicated with great pleasure to the army at large in yesterday's orders.

. . .   .

I have the honor to be.——

Go. Washington.

Sir Henry Clinton also sent his report of the engagement to Lord George Germaine, Colonial Secretary of George III.

New York, 5 July, 1778.

My Lord:

I have the honour to inform your lordship that pursuant to his majesty's instructions I evacuated Philadelphia on the 18th of June at three o'clock in the morning and proceeded to Gloucester Point without being followed by the enemy. Every thing from thence being passed in safety across the Delaware, through the excellent disposition made by our admiral to secure our passage the army marched at ten o'clock and reached Haddonfield the

[267]

same day. A strong corps of the enemy having upon our approach abandoned the difficult pass of Mount Holly, the army proceeded without any interruption from them, except by what was occasioned by their having destroyed every bridge on our road. As the country is much intersected with marshy rivulets, the obstructions we met with were frequent; and the excessive heat of the weather rendered the labour of repairing the bridges severely felt. The advanced parties of our light troops arriving unexpectedly at Crosswicks, on the 23rd, after a trifling skirmish, prevented the enemy from destroying a bridge over a large creek at that village: and the army passed it the next morning. One column under the command of his excellency Lieutenant General Knyphausen, halted near Imlay's town; and as the division train and heavy artillery were stationed in that division, the other column, under Lieutenant General Earl Cornwallis, took a position at Allen's town, which covered the other encampment. Thus far, my lord, my march pointed equally toward Hudson River and Staten Island, by the Raritan. I was now at the juncture when it was necessary to decide ultimately what course to pursue. Encumbered as I was by an enormous provision train, &c., to which impediment the probability of obstructions and length of march obliged me to submit, I was led to wish for a route less liable to obstacles than those above mentioned. I had received intelligence that Generals Washington and Lee had passed the Delaware with their army, had assembled a numerous militia, from all the neighboring provinces; and that Gates with an army from the northward, was advancing to join them on the Raritan. As I could not hope that, after having always hitherto so studiously avoided a general action, they would now give in to it, against every dictate of policy, I could only suppose his views were directed against my baggage &c. in which part I was indeed vulnerable. This circumstance alone would have tempted me to avoid the difficult passage of the Raritan; but when I reflected that from Sandy Hook I should be able, with more expedition to carry his majesty's further orders into execution, I did not hesitate to order the army into the road which leads through Freehold to the Navisunk. The approach of the enemy's army being denoted by the frequent appearance of their light troops on our rear, I requested his excellency Lieutenant General Knyphausen to take the baggage of the whole army under the charge of his division, consisting of the troops mentioned in the margin.[8] Under the head of baggage was comprised not only all the wheel-carriages, of every department, but also the bat-horses; a train

[8] Seventeenth light dragoons, 2nd battalion of light infantry, Hessian Yagers, 1st and 2nd brigades British, Stirn's and Loo's brigades of Hessians, Pennsylvania Loyalists, New Jersey Volunteers, Maryland Loyalists.

which, as the country admitted but of one route for carriages, extended near twelve miles. The indispensable necessity I was under of securing these is obvious, and the difficulty of doing it, in a most woody country, against an army far superior in numbers, will I trust be no less so. I desired Lieutenant General Knyphausen to move at daybreak on the 28th; and that I might not press upon him, in the first part of the march, in which we had but one route, I did not follow him with the other division[9] until near eight o'clock. Soon after I had marched reconnoitering parties of the enemy appeared on our left flank. The Queen's Rangers fell in with and dispersed some detachments among the woods in the same quarter. Our rear-guard having descended from the heights above Freehold into a plain near three miles in length, and about one mile in breadth, several columns of the enemy appeared likewise descending into the plain; and about ten o'clock they began to cannonade our rear. Intelligence was this moment brought me that the enemy were discovered marching in force on both our flanks. I was convinced that our baggage was their object; but it being in this juncture engaged in the defiles, which continued for some miles, no means occurred of parrying the blow, but attacking the corps which harassed our rear and pressing it so hard as to oblige the detachments to return from our flanks to its assistance. I had good information that General Washington was up with his whole army, estimated at about 20,000; but as I knew there were two defiles between him and the corps at which I meant to strike, I judged that he could not have passed them with a greater force than what Lord Cornwallis's division was well able to engage; and had I even met his whole army in the passage of these defiles, I had but little to apprehend but his situation might have been critical. The enemy's cavalry commanded it is said by M. Lafayette, having approached our reach, were charged with great spirit by the Queen's Light Dragoons. They did not wait the shock, but fell back, in confusion, upon their own infantry. Thinking it possible that the event might draw to a general action, 1 sent for a brigade of British and the 17th Light Dragoons, from Lieutenant General Knyphausen's division; and having directed them on their arrival, to take a position effectually covering our right flank of which I was most jealous, I made a disposition of attack on the plain. But before I could advance, the enemy fell back and took a strong position on the heights above Freehold court-house. The heat of the weather was intense and our men already suffered severely from fatigue. But our circumstances obliged us to make a vigourous

[9] Sixteenth light dragoons, 1st battalion of British grenadiers, 2nd ditto, 1st battalion of light infantry, Hessian grenadiers, guards, 3rd, 4th, 5th brigades British.

THE BATTLE OF MONMOUTH

exertion. The British Grenadiers, with their left to the village of
Freehold, and the Guards on the right of the Grenadiers, began the
attack with such spirit, that the enemy gave way immediately.
The second line of the enemy stood the attack with great obstinacy,
but was likewise completely routed. They then took a third position, with a marshy hollow in front, over which it would have
been scarcely possible to have attacked them. However, part of the
second line made a movement to the front, occupied some ground
on the enemy's left flank and the Light Infantry and Queen's
Rangers turned their left. By this time our men were so overpowered
with fatigue that I could press the affair no further; especially as
I was confident the end was gained for which the attack had been
made. I ordered the Light Infantry to rejoin me, but a strong detachment of the enemy having possessed themselves of a post
which would have annoyed them in their retreat, the 33rd regiment
made a movement toward the enemy; which, with a similar one
made by the first Grenadiers, immediately dispersed them. I took
the position from which the enemy had been first driven, after they
had quitted the plain; and having reposed the troops until ten at
night, to avoid the excessive heat of the day, I took advantage of
the moonlight to rejoin Lieutenant General Knyphausen, who had
advanced to Nut Swamp, near Middeltown. Our baggage had
been attempted by some of the enemy's light troops, who were
repulsed by the good dispositions made by Lieutenant General
Knyphausen and Major General Grant, and the good countenance
of the 40th regiment, whose piquets alone were attacked and one
troop of the 17th Light Dragoons. The two corps which had
marched against it, (being, as I since learn, a brigade on each flank)
were recalled, as I had suspected, at the beginning of the action. It
would be sufficient honour to the troops to barely say that they
had forced a corps, as I am informed of near 12,000 men, from
two strong positions: but it will, I doubt not, be considered doubly
creditable when I mention they did it under such disadvantages of
heat and fatigue, that a great part of those we lost fell dead as they
advanced. Fearing that my order had miscarried, before I quitted
the ground I sent a second, for a brigade of infantry, the 17th
Light Dragoons and the 2nd battalion of Light Infantry to meet
on the march, to which additional force had General Washington
shown himself the next day, I was determined to attack him; but
there being not the least appearance of an enemy I suspected he
might have passed a considerable corps to a strong position, near
Middeltown; I therefore left the rear-guard on its march and detached Major General Grant to take post there, which was effected
on the 29th. The whole army marched to this position the next day,
and then fell back to another near Navisunk; where I waited two

days in the hope that Mr. Washington might have been tempted to advance to the position near Middeltown, which we had quitted; in which case I might have attacked him to advantage. During this time the sick and wounded were embarked and preparations made for passing to Sandy Hook island, by a bridge, which by the extraordinary labours of the men was soon completed, and over which the whole army passed, in about two hours time; the horses and cattle having been previously transported. Your lordship will receive herewith a return of the killed, wounded, missing &c. of his majesty's troops, on the 28th of last month. That of the enemy is supposed to have been more considerable especially in killed. The loss of Lieutenant Colonel Monckton, who commanded the 2d battalion of Grenadiers, is much to be lamented. I am much indebted to Lord Cornwallis for his zealous services on every occasion; and I found great support from the activity of Major General Grey, Brigadier Generals Matthew, Leslie and Sir William Erskine. I beg leave to refer your lordship, for any other particulars which you may wish to be informed of, to Colonel Patterson, who will have the honour to deliver these despatches, and whose services in this country entitle him to every mark of your lordship's favour.

I have the honour to be, &c.

H. CLINTON.

Lord George Germaine made this reply to the official report of Sir Henry Clinton:

Whitehall, 2nd September 1778.

Sir Henry Clinton

SIR,

On the 22d of last Month I had the pleasure to receive your Dispatches No. 5 and 6, by Colonel Patterson and immediately laid them before The King. His Majesty's reliance on the Valour and Affection of His Troops, and His Confidence in the Zeal & Ability of His General, had not suffered a Doubt to arise in His Royal Breast that your march through the Jersies would be other than successful from the time your former Letter was received; but it was with the greatest satisfaction His Majesty dwelt upon every Circumstance of your very difficult Passage, so fully and clearly detailed in your Dispatch; and was graciously pleased to express the highest Approbation of your whole Conduct in the Dispositions you made, and the Spirit and Address with which you effected your purpose. The Wisdom of your Choice of the Route by Freehold to Sandy Hook was particularly remarked by His Majesty, to

which and the highly Military and spirited Resolution you took of attacking the Enemy in their Main Body, and your forming so true a Judgement of the Effect of that Operation in obliging the Enemy to recall the Detachments which were ordered to attack the Corps under the command of Lieut. General Knyphausen, His Majesty imputes the unexampled Event of conducting an Army, encumbered with so long a Train of Baggage thro' a very difficult Country, in the Face of a numerous Enemy, without the loss of a single Carriage. The Commendations you so properly give to the Officers and Soldiers under your Command appear to His Majesty to have been fully merited and it is His Majesty's Command that you acquaint them that their Intrepidity & Perseverance in so arduous a Service, is highly approved by The King. It would however, be injustice to Lieut. Generals Knyphausen & Earl Cornwallis, as well as to Major General Grey and Brigadier Generals Mathew, Leslie and Sir William Erskine, whose services you distinguish, were I not to acquaint you that His Majesty desires you will convey to each of them in particular, His fullest Approbation. The Arrival of Mor. d'Estaing's Squadron on the Coast was undoubtedly a sufficient Reason for Lord Howe to defer making the Embarkations directed in His Majesty's Secret Instructions of the 21st March and as you will soon have heard that Admiral Byron's Squadron which followed the French Fleet, had the Misfortune of being separated in a Gale of Wind off Newfoundland, the propriety of that step will be still more evident. But I trust so many of Admiral Byron's Fleet will have kept together, as, when joined to the Ships with Lord Howe will have enabled his Lordship to act with Success against Mor. d'Estaing, and that an opportunity will then have offered of carrying those Instructions into Execution.

I am &c.

GEO. GERMAINE.

On July 4, the anniversary of the Declaration of Independence, the army being still on the south bank of the Raritan River at Brunswick, celebrated the day by firing thirteen pieces of artillery and a *feu de joie* of firearms along the whole line drawn up on the bank of the river at five o'clock in the afternoon.

On July 7 the whole army was in motion and marched to Scotch Plains, Springfield, Aquackanonk, Paramus, Haverstraw, and then across the Hudson River at King's Ferry on July 17, 18, and 19. On Friday, July 24, the army joined the division of General Gates at White Plains.

General Washington sums up his opinion of the whole campaign, nearly two months after the battle, in a letter to General Nelson of Virginia, August 20, 1778: "After two years' manoeuvreing and undergoing the strangest vicissitudes, that perhaps ever attended any one contest since the creation, both armies are brought back to the very point they set out from, and that which was the offending party in the beginning is now reduced to the use of the spade and pick-axe for defence."[10]

In commenting on this battle it will suffice to make a few clear statements the truth of which will be apparent to any one who enters carefully into the study of the affair in all its changing phases.

The Battle of Monmouth was the very first fruits of the good cheer which the new alliance with the French nation had brought to the hearts of every patriot soldier. It destroyed the cabal which had hounded the Commander-in-Chief, it cheered the patriots at home, it gave new courage to the patriots in the field, it gave new confidence to Congress.

It was the strong, unequivocal reply which the American Army made to the offer of the British Government for peace and the proposals for conciliation tendered by the Commissioners.

It was the hour of creation, of the establishment of the regular military service of America. It demonstrated the fact to the men themselves, to the Congress and to the world (although Edmund Burke had said "it is evident they cannot look standing armies in the face") that the soldiers of the regular Continental Line did not hesitate for a moment to make a stand in front of or to attack a body of British regulars and that they possessed an equal amount of courage and endurance, of drill and discipline. This fact is to the honor and glory of the first American soldiers.

It was, as General de Peyster has truly asserted, the last

[10] Ford's *Writings of George Washington*, Vol. XII, p. 761.

battle in which 10,000 men in the British Army and at least 10,000 men in the American Army fought or were present. It was the only battle of the Revolutionary War in the open field wherein the main forces of both armies, with a majority of their most brilliant officers, participated.

It is quite clear that the early part of the fight was lost because of Lee's failure to grasp the situation in the manner in which an officer who enjoyed such a reputation as he seems to have had in America should have done. He certainly did not even execute the plan of the day which he professed to have in his own mind.

It is apparent that the second part of the battle was turned to victory by the personal magnetism of General Washington. The soldiers certainly made a prompt response to every order he gave. They had full faith in his ability to bring them out of confusion and to vanquish the approaching enemy.

It was a simple escape which Sir Henry Clinton accomplished and this in no sense can be called a victory for him. It is true that he secured a safe retreat, the end he asserts he most desired, but this was not a victory. It is also quite true that the British soldier displayed on this field all the courage and all the discipline for which he has ever been celebrated. No better troops in that day marched to the field of battle than the light infantry, the guards and the grenadiers of the British Army. To cope with such men on the open field was glory indeed for Washington, and for Greene, Stirling, Lafayette, Wayne and Knox.

The American Army made their camp on the battlefield and the nation had a right to call such an act a victory. The next day the patriot army buried the dead of both armies—the unpleasant duty of victors.

By this battle the soil of New Jersey became indeed, as has been said, the great battle-ground of the Revolution. Trenton and Princeton and Red Bank had brought mili-

tary fame to the State. Monmouth added new luster to those victories and secured to the Commonwealth immortal honor.

APPENDIX I

A *Weekly Return* of the Continental Army under the Command of His Excellency GEORGE WASHINGTON ESQ'R, General and Commander in Chief of the Armies of the Independent States of America. (An extract very carefully prepared.)

Camp June 13, 1778.

BRIGADE	COLONELS	LT.-COLS.	MAJORS	CAPTAINS	SUB'S.	STAFF	SERGEANTS	DRUM AND FIFE	RANK AND FILE FIT FOR DUTY
Woodford		1	1	13	33	16	66	30	494
Scott	2	2	1	21	26	19	89	33	478
1st Pennsyla.	2	1	3	14	27	12	64	46	442
2nd Pennsyla.		3	2	7	11	12	40	28	260
Poor	3	4		16	37	15	94	49	941
Glover	2	4	1	24	51	14	90	46	703
Larned	1	2	2	12	30	13	56	33	450
Patison	3	2	2	18	44	14	92	35	548
Weedon	3	3	4	22	49	19	83	40	667
Muhlenberg	3	5	5	21	49	21	91	49	783
Maxwell									
1st Maryl'd	2	2		10	52	21	97	35	913
2nd Maryl'd	2	2	2	12	19	13	47	20	779
Conway	2	3	4	12	34	25	92	55	509
Huntington	2	3	2	21	36	17	110	50	903
Varnum		1	3	15	26	8	80	43	688
N. Carolina	2	2	1	11	29	11	49	29	683
Jackson's Detach't	1	1		9	17	3	22	27	236
Vanchaicks Reg't	1	1	1	6	16	5	31	12	327
Silen's Comp'y				2	3		8	2	21
At Fish Kills.	2	6	4	6	143	24	237	115	1.830
Hartleys Reg't	1	1		4	7	3	27	15	121
Total,	34	49	38	276	744	285	1,565	792	12,776

Return of part of the Corps of Artillery in the service of the United
States.

BRIGADE	COLONELS	LT.-COLS.	MAJORS	CAPTAINS	SUB'S.	STAFF	SERGEANTS	CORPORALS, BOMBARDIERS, GUNNERS, &C.	MATTROSSES
9 Companies Col. Crane's				6	26	3	37	98	154
5 Companies Col. Lamb's		1		4	14		16	39	70
Col. Proctors Reg't	1	1	1	2	15	4	14	57	68
Col. Harrison's Reg't	1	1	1	12	29	6	24	107	207
Capt. Kingsbury's Co.				1	4		5	14	9
Total,	2	3	2	25	88	13	96	315	508

Return from Fisk Kill dated May 16th, Hartleys May 31st. No return of Gen'l Maxwell's brigade.

ALEX. SCAMMELL, *Adj't. Gen*.

[Endorsed by General Washington on the back of the original.]
Weekly & Gen¹ Return 13th June 1778.

APPENDIX II

Field Return of the Troops under the Command of His Excellency
GENERAL WASHINGTON at Corya[e]ll's Ferry, June 22, '78.

OFFICERS PRESENT, FIT FOR DUTY

BRIGADES	FIELD			COMMIS-SIONED		NON COM-MISSIONED		
	COLONELS	LT.-COLS.	MAJORS	CAPTAINS	SUB'S.	SERGEANTS	DRUM AND FIFE	RANK AND FILE FIT FOR ACTION
Woodford's		3	2	11	33	61	25	562
Scott's	1	2	1	19	37	81	42	518
1st Pennsylvania			1	15	29	58	51	514
2nd Pennsylvania	3	4	3	17	26	66	45	664
Poor's	2	4	1	18	46	76	46	871
Glover's	2	4	1	26	51	83	50	781
Larnd's	2	2	2	13	32	55	36	561
Paterson's	3	2	2	21	45	85	41	570
Weedon's	4	3	5	20	46	81	42	664
Muhlenberg's	3	5	4	19	49	80	55	752
Late Conway's	1	3	4	12	28	88	54	541
Huntington's	2	2	2	18	40	94	56	755
Varnum's		1	3	16	24	73	48	674
No. Carolina	2	2	1	11	27	47	34	728
1st Maryland	1		2	11	49	93	40	1,000
2nd Maryland	2	2	1	11	21	52	26	542
Total,	28	39	35	258	583	1,173	691	10,697

ALEXD[R]. SCAMMELL,
Adj't Genl.

APPENDIX III

A SKETCH OF MAJOR-GENERAL LEE

GENERAL Charles Lee had been a soldier almost from his birth. His father was colonel of the Forty-fourth regiment British foot, and it is said that the son held a commission in the British service when he was but eleven years of age. In 1751, at the age of twenty, we find him on the army list as a lieutenant in the regiment which his father, who died the previous year, had commanded, and he came with that organization to America in 1754. He was present at the disastrous defeat of Braddock on the Monongahela River, and became a captain in his regiment in June, 1756. At the assault on Ticonderoga, July 8, 1758, he was badly wounded by a musket-ball, breaking his ribs and passing through his body. During the following year, however, he took part in the attack on the French Army in garrison at Niagara, and in 1760 he was with General Amherst at the fall of Montreal.

Returning to England immediately thereafter, he was made major of the One hundred and third regiment of foot, then successively major and lieutenant-colonel on half-pay. In 1762 he was in the service of the King of Portugal under General Burgoyne, and in "a very gallant action" surprised the Spaniards in camp on the south bank of the Tagas, near the castle of Villa Velha, and gathered up many prisoners and much valuable booty. In 1769 he was a major-general by the King of Poland, and in 1773 he appears again in America as a private citizen, although still borne on the half-pay list of Britain.

His appearance was described by Dr. Thomas Girdlestone, in a work published in London in 1813, to prove that Lee was the author of the Junius letters, as "a remarkably thin man." The book is illustrated with a most singular caricature of General Lee. Another description of him was, "as plain in his person, even to ugliness, and careless in his manners, even to a degree of rudeness: his nose was so remarkably acquiline that it appeared as a real deformity. His voice was rough, his garb ordinary, his deportment morose. He was ambitious of fame, without the dignity to support it. In private life he sank into the vulgarity of the clown."

His character was that of a self-sufficient, overbearing, abusive officer. He delighted to ridicule his superiors in rank, and to write words of keen satire against those who stood in the way of his rapid advancement. He was rude in his actions, very

profane in his language, yet withal, was able to impress everyone with the idea of his great military genius, skill, and experience, and this faculty never failed him. As Alexander Hamilton said of him in after years, he had "a certain preconceived and preposterous notion of his being a very great man," and Tom Paine remarked, "that he was above all monarchs and below all scum."

This, then, is the idea we have of the officer who solicited a high command in the provincial army, and received it June 17, 1775. Congress soon after took great pains to compensate him for his pecuniary loss in dropping his British commission and taking up his sword on behalf of America.

In the fall of 1776, although ordered by General Washington, who had retreated through New Jersey and over the Delaware River, to join his feeble force on the west bank of that river, he tardily left the Hudson River with his division, and leisurely passed on toward Morristown and New Jersey. A few hours' rapid march would have enabled him to reinforce his commander-in-chief, but he cared not to sink his separate command in the main army. He was captured unceremoniously by a detachment of British dragoons, December thirteenth, and without hat, coat or boots, the British troopers hurried away with their odd-looking captive, and carried him off to Pennington and then to Brunswick. Great rejoicing was made at the British posts when they heard that he who was considered the "American Paladium" had been taken prisoner, and consequent dejection followed in the army of the republic, where he was the "idol of the officers and possessed still more the confidence of the soldiers." At the British headquarters in New York General Lee was considered, and at first treated, as a deserter from their army, and thrice under orders was he placed on shipboard to be sent to England for trial. This, however, was never done.

[For a sound and able study of Charles Lee, see John Fiske, *Essays, Historical and Literary*, Vol. I, pp. 53-98. Also see Stryker's *The Battles of Trenton and Princeton*, pp. 53-9.]

APPENDIX IV

Camp, English Town, 1 July, 1778

SIR:

From the knowledge I have of your Excellency's character I must conclude that nothing but the misinformation of some very stupid or misrepresentation of some very wicked person could have occasioned you making use of so very singular expressions as you did on my coming up to the ground where you had taken post: they implied that I was guilty either of disobedience of orders, of want of conduct or want of courage; your Excellency will therefore infinitely oblige me by letting me know on which of these articles you ground your charge, that I may prepare for my justification, which I have the happiness to be confident I can do to the army, to the Congress, to America and to the world in general. Your Excellency must give me leave to observe that neither yourself nor those about your person could from your situation be in the least judges of the merits or demerits of our manoeuvres; and, to speak with a becoming pride, I can assert, that to these manoeuvres the success of the day was entirely owing. I can boldly say that had we remained on the first ground or had we advanced or had the retreat been conducted in a manner different from what it was, this whole army and the interests of America would have been risked being sacrificed. I ever had and hope ever shall have the greatest respect and veneration for General Washington: I think him endowed with many great and good qualities: but in this instance I must pronounce that he has been guilty of an act of cruel injustice towards a man who certainly has some pretensions to the regard of every servant of this country; and I think, Sir, I have a right to demand some reparation for the injury committed, and, unless I can obtain it, I must, in justice to myself, when this campaign is closed (which I believe will close the war) retire from a service at the head of which is placed a man capable of offering such injuries: but, at the same time, in justice to you, I must repeat, that I from my soul believe, that it was not a motion of your own breast, but instigated by some of those dirty ear-wigs who will forever insinuate themselves near persons in high office; for I really am convinced, that when General Washington acts for himself no

man in his army will have reason to complain of injustice or indecorum.

> I am, sir, and hope ever shall have
> > Reason to continue your most sincerely
> > > Devoted, humble servant

CHARLES LEE

HIS EXCELLENCY GENERAL WASHINGTON.

GENERAL WASHINGTON TO GENERAL LEE

Head Quarters, English-Town 30 June 1778.

SIR:

I received your letter (dated through mistake the 1st of July) expressed, as I conceive, in terms highly improper. I am not conscious of having made use of any very singular expressions at the time of my meeting you, as you intimate. What I recollect to have said was dictated by duty and warranted by the occasion. As soon as circumstances will permit, you shall have an opportunity either of justifying yourself to the army, to Congress, to America and to the world in general or of convincing them that you were guilty of a breach of orders and of misbehaviour before the enemy on the 28th inst., in not attacking them as you had been directed and in making an unnecessary, disorderly and shameful retreat.

I am, sir, your most obedient servant

GO. WASHINGTON.

MAJOR GENERAL LEE.—

GENERAL LEE TO GENERAL WASHINGTON

Camp, 28 June 1778

SIR:

I beg your Excellency's pardon for the inaccuracy in mis-dating my letter. You cannot afford me greater pleasure than in giving me the opportunity of showing to America the sufficiency of her respective servants. I trust that the temporary power of office, and the tinsel dignity attending it, will not be able by all the mists they can raise, to offiscate the bright rays of truth: in the mean time your Excellency can have no objection to my retiring from the army.—

> I am, sir, your most obedient
> > Humble servant

CHARLES LEE.—

GENERAL WASHINGTON.—

THE BATTLE OF MONMOUTH

GENERAL LEE TO GENERAL WASHINGTON

Camp, 30 June, 1778

SIR:

Since I had the honour of addressing my letter by Colonel Fitz-gerald to your Excellency I have reflected on both your situation and mine and beg leave to observe, that it will be for our mutual convenience that a court of inquiry should be immediately ordered: but I could wish it might be a court-martial, for if the affair is drawn into length, it may be difficult to collect the necessary evidences and perhaps might bring on a paper war betwixt the adherents to both parties, which may occasion some disagreeable fends on the continent, for all are not my friends, nor all your admirers. I must entreat, therefore, from your love of justice, that you will immediately exhibit your charge, and that on the first halt, I may be brought to a trial, and am, sir, your most obedient, humble servant,

CHARLES LEE.—

HIS EXCELLENCY GENERAL WASHINGTON.—

GENERALS WAYNE AND SCOTT TO GENERAL WASHINGTON

Englishtown, 30th June, 1778

SIR:

We esteem it a duty, which we owe to our country, ourselves and the officers and soldiers under our command, to state the following facts to your Excellency:

On the 28th instant, at five o'clock in the morning we received orders to march with the following detachments, namely, Scott's and Varnum's brigades, Colonels Butler and Jackson in front, amounting to seventeen hundred men; Colonels Wesson, Livingston, and Stewart, with one thousand men, commanded by General Wayne; a select detachment of fourteen hundred men, rank and file, under General Scott, with ten pieces of Artillery properly distributed among the whole.

About eight o'clock, the van under Col Butler arrived on the left of Monmouth Court House, on the rear of the left flank of the enemy, who were in full march, moving in great haste and confusion. At this time our main body under General Lee, were formed at the edge of a wood about half a mile distant from the Court House. General Wayne, who was in front reconnoitring the enemy, perceiving that they had made a halt and were preparing to push Colonel Butler with their horse and a few foot, gave direction for

him to form and receive them and at the same time sent Major Byles to General Lee, requesting that those troops might be advanced to support those in front, and for the whole to form on the edge of a deep morass, which extends from the east of the Court House on the right a very considerable distance to the left. The troops did arrive in about an hour after the requisition, and were generally formed in this position.

About the same time General Scott's detachment had passed the morass on the left, and the enemy's horse and foot that had charged Colonel Butler, were repulsed. The number of the enemy now in view might be near two thousand, though at first not more than five hundred exclusive of their horse. The ground we now occupied was the best formed by nature for defence of any, perhaps in the country. The enemy advanced with caution, keeping at a considerable distance in front. General Scott, having viewed the position of the enemy, as well as the ground where about twenty-five hundred of our troops were formed, repassed the morass and took post on the left, in a fine open wood, covered by said morass in front.

Whilst this was doing, General Wayne perceiving that the troops on the right from the wood to the Court House, were retreating, sent Major Fishbourne to General Lee, requesting that the troops might return to support him. In the interim General Wayne repassed the morass, leaving Colonel Butler's regiment to keep post on the right flank of the enemy. Generals Scott and Wayne then went together along the morass to the Court House, when Major Fishbourne returned, and said that General Lee gave no other answer, than that he would see General Wayne himself, which he never did. The enemy having now an opening on the right of General Scott began to move on, when General Wayne and General Scott sent to General Lee to request him at least to form, to favor General Scott's retreat, but this requisition met with the same fate as the last. The troops kept still retreating, when General Scott perceiving that he would not be supported, filed off to the left. General Wayne ordered Colonel Butler to fall back also. Thus were these several select detachments unaccountably drawn off without being suffered to come to action, although we had the most pleasing prospect from our number and position, of obtaining the most glorious and decisive victory. After this we fortunately fell in with your Excellency. You ordered us to form part of those troops, whose conduct and bravery kept the enemy in play until you had restored order.

We have taken the liberty of stating these facts, in order to convince the world that our retreat from the Court House was not occasioned by the want of numbers, position, or wishes of both

officers and men to maintain that post. We also beg leave to mention that no plan of attack was ever communicated to us, or notice of a retreat, until it had taken place in our rear, as we supposed by General Lee's order. We are &c.

ANTHONY WAYNE.
CHARLES SCOTT.

MAJOR-GENERAL LEE TO ROBERT MORRIS

Brunswick, July ye 3rd 1778.—

MY DR. SIR,

To use the words of my Lord Chatham, have we not a gracious Prince on the Throne? is he not still the same?—I trust he is: but there is something rotten betwixt him and his People—not content with robbing me and the brave men under my command of the honour due to us—a most hellish plan has been formed (and I may say at least not discourag'd by Head Quarters) to destroy for ever my honour and reputation—I have demanded a Court Martial which has fortunately been granted—if I had been let alone, I should with patience has suffered 'em to pick up the laurels which I had shaken down and lay'd at their feet; but the outrageous attacks made are enough to drive patience itself to madness—I shall not trouble you at present with a detail of the action, but by all that's sacred Gen'l Washington had scarcely any more to do in it than to strip the dead—by want of proper intelligence we were ordered to attack the covering party supposed to consist only of fifteen hundred men—Our intelligence as usual was false—it proved to be the whole flower of the British Army, Grenadiers, L Infantry Cavalry and Artillery amounting in the whole to Seven thousand men—by the temerity, folly, and contempt of orders of General Wain we found ourselves engaged in the most extensive plain in America—separated from our main body the distance of eight miles—The force we cou'd bring to action not more than three thousand men—in danger every moment of having our flanks turn'd by their Cavalry—it required the utmost presence of mind and courage to extricate ourselves out of this dangerous situation, and on this occasion it is no crime to do justice to myself. Upon my Soul I feel I know the whole Army saw and must acknowledge that I did exhibit great presence of mind and not less address—altho' my order's were perpetually counteracted I manoeuvred my antagonists from their advantageous ground into as disadvantageous a one—no confusion was seen, the Battalions and artillery supported and were supported by each other through a plain of four miles, without losing a single gun, a single color, or sacrificing a single Battalion until I led 'em totally exhausted into the

ground where the general was posted, who had as I observ'd before nothing to do but strip the dead—it is true they cannonaded each other for some time but the Enemy were so completely worn down that they cou'd never attempt the least impression—The General has the madness to charge me with making a shameful retreat—I never retreated in fact (for 'till I join'd him it was not a retreat but a necessary and I may say in my own defence masterly manoeuvre) I say I never retreated but by his positive order who invidiously sent me out of the field when the victory was assur'd—Such is my recompense for having sacrificed my Friends, my connexions, and perhaps my fortune for having twice extricated this man and his whole army out of perdition, and now having given him the only victory he ever tasted. Do not my Dr. Friend, imagine I talk in this heated manner to every man—to you I venture to pour out my indignation—but I give you my word I am so sensible of my ticklish situation that I am with others perfectly moderate and guarded—the cool parts of this letter I wish you wou'd read to Richard Henry Lee and Duar, to what others you think prudent.—

I am most sincerely and affectionately Yours

C. LEE.[1]

[1] The *Lee Papers*, Vol. II, p. 457.

APPENDIX V

A LIST, compiled, of the *killed, wounded, missing* and *died of fatigue* of the American Army.

KILLED

LIEUTENANT-COLONEL RUDOLPH BUNNER, Third Pennsylvania regiment.

MAJOR EDMUND B. DICKINSON, First Virginia regiment.

CAPTAIN PAUL ELLIS, Fifteenth Massachusetts regiment.

CAPTAIN HENRY FAUNTLEROY, Fifth Virginia regiment.

CAPTAIN EDMUND MUNRO, Fifteenth Massachusetts regiment.

FIRST LIEUTENANT JAMES MCNAIR, of Captain Andrew Porter's company, Second Artillery regiment, head shot off by cannon-ball.

SECOND LIEUTENANT NATHAN WEEKS, of Lieutenant-Colonel Jeremiah Olney's company, Second Rhode Island regiment.

SURGEON EBENEZER HAVILAND, Second New York regiment.

HOSPITAL SURGEON SAMUEL KENNEDY, formerly surgeon of the Fourth Pennsylvania battalion.

SERGEANT JOSEPH KENYON, of Captain William Allen's company, Second Rhode Island regiment.

CORPORAL THOMAS TRUMBULL, of Captain Seth Drew's company, Second Massachusetts regiment.

FIFER DAVID MCCLAREN, of Captain John Davis's company, Fourth New York regiment.

MATTROSS REUBEN ELLIS, of Captain Andrew Porter's company, Second artillery regiment.

PRIVATE THOMAS ATKERSON, of Captain Reuben Lipscomb's company, Seventh Virginia regiment.

PRIVATE JOHN BATES, of Captain Samuel Mattock's company, Eighth Connecticut regiment.

PRIVATE MCINTIRE BENJAMIN, of Captain Nathaniel Tomm's company, Malcolm's regiment.

PRIVATE AZELL BENNETT, of Lieutenant-Colonel Jeremiah Olney's company, Second Rhode Island regiment.

PRIVATE JOHN BUYS, of Lieutenant-Colonel Peter R. Fell's battalion, New Jersey State troops.

PRIVATE GEORGE BROWN, of Captain Christopher Darrow's company, First Connecticut regiment.

[288]

PRIVATE MATTHEW BURVE, of Captain Joseph McCracken's company, First New York regiment.

PRIVATE PATRICK CATON, of late Captain Sylvenus Shaw's company, Second Rhode Island regiment.

PRIVATE MICHAEL FIELD, First regiment Middlesex county New Jersey militia, wounded, prisoner of war, and died the day after the battle.

PRIVATE JOHN FINNEY, of Captain Seth Drew's company, Second Massachusetts regiment.

PRIVATE JAMES P. FITCH, of Captain Abner Bacon's company, Fourth Connecticut regiment.

PRIVATE ANSEL FOX, of an artillery regiment.

PRIVATE CHRISTIAN GUTHRIE, of Captain John Copp's company, First New York regiment.

PRIVATE SAMUEL HALL, of Major Theodore Woodbridge's company, Seventh Connecticut regiment.

PRIVATE JOHN HAMILTON, of Captain Jonathan Forman's company, Fourth New Jersey regiment.

PRIVATE NATHANIEL JESUP, of Captain Sylvanus Brown's company, Eighth Connecticut regiment.

PRIVATE AARON MONSON, of Major David Smith's company, Eighth Connecticut regiment.

PRIVATE GEORGE MUNRO, of Captain Edmund Munro's company, Fifteenth Massachusetts regiment.

PRIVATE JOHN PARKERSON, of Captain Reuben Lipscomb's company, Seventh Virginia regiment.

PRIVATE EBENEZER ROGERS, of late Captain Elisha Lee's company, Fourth Connecticut regiment.

PRIVATE WILLIAM P. STEWART, of Captain Peter Dolliver's company, Jackson's regiment.

PRIVATE JOHN WALKER, of Captain John Sandford's company, Malcolm's regiment.

WOUNDED

COLONEL JOHN DURKEE, Fourth Connecticut regiment, wounded in right hand, permanently disabled.

COLONEL HENRY B. LIVINGSTON, Fourth New York regiment.

COLONEL WALTER STEWART, Thirteenth Pennsylvania regiment.

COLONEL JAMES WESSON, Ninth Massachusetts regiment, cannon-ball grazed his shoulder and back.

LIEUTENANT-COLONEL FRANCIS BARBER, adjutant-general to Major-General Lord Stirling, musket-ball passed through his body.

LIEUTENANT-COLONEL JOHN LAURENS, aide-de-camp to General Washington.

LIEUTENANT-COLONEL NATHANIEL RAMSAY, Third Maryland regiment.

—————— TOUSSARD, lost an arm.

MAJOR SIMEON THAYER, Second Rhode Island regiment, lost the sight of an eye, by the windage of a cannon-ball.

MAJOR BENJAMIN TITCOMB, First New Hampshire regiment.

CAPTAIN THOMAS BUTLER, Third Pennsylvania regiment.

CAPTAIN DAVID COOK, Third artillery regiment.

CAPTAIN MOSES ESTEY, Fourth regiment Hunterdon county New Jersey militia, in thigh.

CAPTAIN JOSEPH McCRACKEN, First New York regiment, left arm shot off by a cannon-ball.

CAPTAIN JEREMIAH MILLER, First Massachusetts regiment.

CAPTAIN WILLIAM SATTERLEE, Second Canadian regiment.

CAPTAIN ROBERT SMITH, Malcolm's regiment.

CAPTAIN PHILIP SNOOK, First regiment Hunterdon county New Jersey militia.[1]

CAPTAIN ANDREW WAGGONER, Twelfth Virginia regiment.

ADJUTANT PETER TAULMAN, Malcolm's regiment, shot in the throat.[2]

FIRST LIEUTENANT ANDREW JOHNSON, quartermaster First Pennsylvania regiment, right leg.

FIRST LIEUTENANT JAMES MONELL, Malcolm's regiment, lost an eye.

FIRST LIEUTENANT ABRAHAM NEELY, Malcolm's regiment, right thigh.[3]

FIRST LIEUTENANT CHARLES PARSONS, First New York regiment.

FIRST LIEUTENANT JONATHAN PUGH, Fifth Pennsylvania regiment.

SECOND LIEUTENANT EZEKIEL HOWELL, of Captain Andrew Porter's company, Second artillery regiment.

SECOND LIEUTENANT DANIEL McLANE, Second artillery regiment.

GEORGE WALKER, a volunteer, acting as an officer, "with reputation, without pay," Second New Jersey regiment (commissioned as an ensign in same organization September 12, 1778), wounded in the side.

SERGEANT HENRY BECKER, of Captain Jonathan Pearcy's company, Fourth New York regiment, died of his wounds July 27, 1778.

---

[1] Colonel Joseph Phillips, First regiment Hunterdon County New Jersey militia, certified to the War Department that Captain Snook had the "honor of receiving a shot through the thigh" in this battle.

[2] See Barber and Howe's *Historical Collections of New Jersey*, p. 342.

[3] *ibid.*, p. 343.

SERGEANT BALTUS COLLINS, of Captain Gibbs Jones' Pennsylvania artillery company, left arm and leg.

SERGEANT BURR GILBERT, First Connecticut regiment.

SERGEANT ATCHISON MELLEN, of Captain Michael Simpson's company, First Pennsylvania regiment.

SERGEANT THOMAS SNOWDEN, of Captain Thomas B. Bowen's company, Ninth Pennsylvania regiment, ball shattered his ankle.

SERGEANT DAVID WELCH, First artillery regiment, right foot.

CORPORAL JOHN WILLIAMS, of Captain John Anderson's company, Fourth New Jersey regiment, wounded four times.

CORPORAL WILLIAM WOODRUFF, Fifth Connecticut regiment.

MATTROSS JOHN KELLY, of Captain Andrew Moodie's company, Second artillery regiment. He died of his wounds July 19, 1778.

DRUMMER ROBERT LETFORD, First Pennsylvania regiment.

GUNNER HENRY SMITH, of Captain Andrew Moodie's company, Second artillery regiment.

PRIVATE RICHARD ALLISON, of Captain John Smith's company, Fourth New York regiment, prisoner of war, severely wounded on head and neck with a sword.

PRIVATE NICHOLAS BEARZS, of Captain Thomas Butler's company, Third Pennsylvania regiment.

PRIVATE JOSHUA BENNETT, of late Captain Benjamin Pelton's Company, Second New York regiment, died of his wounds October 1778.

PRIVATE JOHN BLAIN, Fourth Pennsylvania regiment.

PRIVATE JAMES BODEN, of Captain William Tucker's company, First regiment Hunterdon county New Jersey militia.

PRIVATE JOSEPH COX, Fifteenth Massachusetts regiment, lost right leg.

PRIVATE JOHN DAVIS, Second Pennsylvania regiment.

PRIVATE WILLIAM ELBERTSON, of Captain David Van Ness's company, First New York regiment.

PRIVATE JOHN FLEMING, of Captain William Helm's company, Second New Jersey regiment, wounded on head and right shoulder by saber cut, and right arm became useless.

PRIVATE BENJAMIN GRAY, of Captain Benjamin Walker's company, Fourth New York regiment. He died of his wounds July 5, 1778.

PRIVATE WILLIAM HOWELL, Fourth New Jersey regiment.

PRIVATE ELIJAH HOYT, Thirteenth Massachusetts regiment, right side by a bayonet.

PRIVATE CAESAR JOWLER, of Captain Sylvanus Brown's company, Eighth Connecticut regiment. He died of his wounds August 8, 1778.

PRIVATE JAMES KIRKPATRICK, of Captain John Mott's company, Third New Jersey regiment.

PRIVATE JOHN LORAINE, of Captain Francis Nichols' company, Ninth Pennsylvania regiment.

PRIVATE EPHRAIM MARSH, (probably First) regiment Essex county New Jersey militia, wounded in the stomach by saber, died from the effects of the wound.

PRIVATE ALEXANDER McQUILLEN, of Captain Jacob Weaver's company, Tenth Pennsylvania regiment.

PRIVATE NICHOLAS MOONEY, of Captain Andrew Waggoner's company, Twelfth Virginia regiment.

PRIVATE BARNEY MURPHY, Ninth Pennsylvania regiment, elbow of right arm.

PRIVATE WILLIAM ORMOND, Second Maryland regiment, right hand.

PRIVATE ROBERT SAUNDERS, of Captain John Graham's company, First New York regiment.

PRIVATE JAMES SEARCH, of Captain Ephraim Anderson's company, Second New Jersey regiment.

PRIVATE JOHN LEONARD SPANG, of Captain John Doyle's company, Eleventh Pennsylvania regiment.

PRIVATE CAESAR SPRAGUE, Fourth Massachusetts regiment, left foot shot off by cannon-ball.

PRIVATE ROBERT VERNON, Second Pennsylvania regiment, right arm.

PRIVATE AARON FORMAN WALKER, First regiment Monmouth county New Jersey militia, in the side.

MISSING

CAPTAIN THOMAS THEODORE BLISS, Second artillery regiment, prisoner of war.

SECOND LIEUTENANT THOMAS LITTLE, Third regiment Monmouth county New Jersey militia, taken prisoner June 27, 1778.

SERGEANT ROBERT GORE, of Captain Joseph McClellan's company, Ninth Pennsylvania regiment.

SERGEANT ANDREW HALLIDAY, of Captain John Stith's company, Fourth Virginia regiment.

PRIVATE JOHN BRITTON, of Captain Daniel Nevin's company, Malcolm's regiment.

PRIVATE PETER CHAPMAN, of Captain George Wall's company, Fourth Virginia regiment.

PRIVATE JOHN DEMPSEY, of Captain Daniel Nevin's company, Malcolm's regiment.

APPENDIX V

PRIVATE THOMAS KIDDER, of Captain Joshua Brown's company, Fifteenth Massachusetts regiment.

PRIVATE SAMUEL POST, of late Captain Jonathan Pearcy's company, Fourth New York regiment.

PRIVATE ANDREW SKILLING, of Captain George Wall's company, Fourth Virginia regiment.

DIED OF FATIGUE

SERGEANT HENRY BAKER, Lieutenant-Colonel's company, died July 27, 1778.

SERGEANT STEPHEN WHITE, First North Carolina regiment, on June 28, 1778.

CORPORAL SAMUEL ANDREWS, of Captain Daniel Barnes' company, Fifteenth Massachusetts regiment, on July 1, 1778.

CORPORAL JAMES BUTLER, of Captain Samuel Darby's company, Second Massachusetts regiment, on July 1, 1778.

PRIVATE JAMES BEAL, of Captain Caleb Robinson's company, Second New Hampshire regiment, on June 29, 1778.

PRIVATE DAVID BLACK, of Captain Davis's company, Fourth New York regiment, on July 9, 1778.

PRIVATE ELIAKIM BROOKS, of Captain James Keith's company, Eighth Massachusetts regiment, on July 1, 1778.

PRIVATE SAMUEL BURCH, of Captain McKean's company, First New York regiment, on July 20, 1778.

PRIVATE JOHN P. CLARK, of Captain Joshua Eddy's company, Fourteenth Massachusetts regiment, on July 1, 1778.

PRIVATE JOHN COOPER, of Captain George Dunham's company, Second Massachusetts regiment, on June 30, 1778.

PRIVATE JAMES CRATON, of Captain William Rowell's company, Second New Hampshire regiment, on June 30, 1778.

PRIVATE WILLIAM DAVIS, of Captain George Wall's company, Fourth Virginia regiment, on July 2, 1778.

PRIVATE JOEL DENSLOW, of Captain Abner Prior's company, Fifth Connecticut regiment, on July 1, 1778.

PRIVATE JOHN DEPEW, of Captain Wright's company, Second New York regiment, in August, 1778.

PRIVATE JOSEPH DESILVE, of Captain Moses Knapp's company, Fourth Massachusetts regiment, on June 28, 1778.

PRIVATE JOHN P. DRESSAR, of Captain Joseph Hodgkins' company, Fifteenth Massachusetts regiment, on June 29, 1778.

PRIVATE ANDREW GAGE, of late Captain James Gray's company, Third New Hampshire regiment, on July 1, 1778.

PRIVATE JOHN GROVEHAM, of Captain Reuben Lipscomb's company, Seventh Virginia regiment, on June 30, 1778.

PRIVATE WILLIAM HADOCK, of Captain Samuel Sackett's company, Fourth New York regiment, on June 29, 1778.

PRIVATE PETER HARDISON, of Captain Daniel Pilsbury's company, Thirteenth Massachusetts regiment, on July 1, 1778.

PRIVATE WILLIAM HARRICK, of Captain Samuel Sackett's company, Fourth New York regiment, on June 29, 1778.

PRIVATE BENJAMIN LAND, of Captain Hallett's company, Second New York regiment, in July 1778.

PRIVATE KENDRICK LENT, of Captain Hallett's company, Second New York Regiment, on July 10, 1778.

PRIVATE WILLIAM MAHANE, of Major William Scott's company, First New Hampshire regiment, on July 1, 1778.

PRIVATE JOHN MAIN, of Captain Phineas Beardeley's company, Seventh Connecticut regiment, on June 30, 1778.

PRIVATE LAURENCE NEAL, of Captain George Wall's company, Fourth Virginia regiment, on July 5, 1778.

PRIVATE JOHN P. ORBOLTON, of Captain Joseph Stetson's company, Fourteenth Massachusetts regiment, on June 28, 1778.

PRIVATE MOSES RANDALL, of Captain Smith's company, Fourth New York regiment, on July 22, 1778.

PRIVATE MATTHEW RHOADES, of Captain John Van Anglen's company, First New Jersey regiment, on June 29, 1778.

PRIVATE JOHN SHEELY, of Captain Finn's company, First New York regiment, on July 9, 1778.

PRIVATE SAMUEL SPICER, of Major Benjamin Throop's company, First Connecticut regiment, on July 1, 1778.

PRIVATE NATHAN TERRELL, of Captain Abner Prior's company, Fifth Connecticut regiment, on June 30, 1778.

PRIVATE PETER P. TOBEY, of Captain Joseph Wadsworth's company, Fourteenth Massachusetts regiment, on June 30, 1778.

PRIVATE JOSEPH TUCKER, of Captain Joseph Pettingill's company, Ninth Massachusetts regiment, on July 1, 1778.

PRIVATE WILLIS UPTON, Second North Carolina regiment, on July 1, 1778.

PRIVATE SAMUEL WATERMAN, of Captain Ten Eyck's company, Second New York regiment, in July 1778.

PRIVATE TIMOTHY WILCOTT, of Captain Thomas Willington's company, Thirteenth Massachusetts regiment, on July 1, 1778.

SICK IN HOSPITAL

CAPTAIN DANIEL BARNES, Eighth Connecticut regiment, exhaustion from the heat.

FIRST LIEUTENANT JOHN GRACE, First Massachusetts regiment, suffering from his great exertions in the excessive heat.

QUARTERMASTER-SERGEANT WILLIAM LOVE, Third New Jersey regiment, ruptured.

CORPORAL WILLIAM ANDERSON, Fifth Connecticut regiment, incapacitated by the heat.

CORPORAL ASA BUNCE, Third Connecticut regiment, exhausted.

FIFER JACOB LOOMES, Second Massachusetts regiment, incapacitated by the heat.

FIFER GIDEON NOBLE, Second Connecticut regiment, ruptured.

PRIVATE BENJAMIN PRESSEY, Ninth Massachusetts regiment, convulsions caused by the intense heat.

APPENDIX VI

A LIST, compiled, of the *killed* and *wounded* officers of the British Army.

KILLED

LIEUTENANT-COLONEL THE HONORABLE HENRY MONCKTON, Forty-fifth regiment of foot, in command of the Second battalion of grenadiers.

CAPTAIN JOHN GORE, Fifth regiment of foot, in command of the First battalion of grenadiers.

LIEUTENANT ARCHIBALD KENNEDY, Grenadier company of the Forty-fourth regiment of foot.

LIEUTENANT THOMAS L. VAUGHAN, Royal regiment of artillery.

WOUNDED

COLONEL HENRY TRELAWNEY, Coldstream regiment of foot guards.

LIEUTENANT-COLONEL ROBERT ABERCROMBY, Thirty-seventh regiment of foot.

LIEUTENANT-COLONEL JOHN GRAVES SIMCOE, Captain Fortieth regiment of foot, lieutenant-colonel commanding Queen's rangers, wounded in the arm.

MAJOR WILLIAM GARDINER, Tenth regiment of foot.

CAPTAIN PATRICK BELLEW, First regiment of foot guards, prisoner of war.

CAPTAIN WILLIAM BRERETON, Seventeenth regiment of foot.

CAPTAIN ANDREW CATHCART, Fifteenth regiment of foot, right arm.

CAPTAIN HARRY DITMAS, Fifteenth regiment of foot, on duty with the Second battalion of grenadiers.

CAPTAIN BALDWIN LEIGHTON, Forty-sixth regiment of foot.

CAPTAIN JOHN LLOYD, Forty-sixth regiment of foot.

CAPTAIN JOHN POWELL, Fifty-second regiment of foot, prisoner of war, and died soon afterward on account of his wounds.

CAPTAIN THOMAS WILLS, Twenty-third regiment of foot, or Royal Welsh Fuzileers.

LIEUTENANT PATRICK BELLEY, of the Guards.

LIEUTENANT ——— DESBOROUGH, of the Marines, on duty with the Second battalion of grenadiers.

LIEUTENANT HARRY GILCHRIST, Forty-second regiment of foot, or Royal Highland regiment.

LIEUTENANT FRANCIS GROSE, Fifty-second regiment of foot. He had also been wounded in the fight at Forts Clinton and Montgomery, October 6, 1777.

LIEUTENANT GEORGE KELLY, Grenadier company of the Forty-fourth regiment of foot.

LIEUTENANT MUNGO PAUMIER, Forty-sixth regiment of foot.

INDEX

ARNOLD, Benedict, 64-5, 72-3.

BAYLOR, Col. George, 152.
Beesley, Capt. Jonathan, 52.
Boudinot, Elias, 45, 249-50.
Brooks, Lieut.-Col., 171.
Burr, Lieut.-Col. Aaron, 210-11.
Butler, Col. Richard, 78, 127-8, 135-6, 138, 143-4, 154-5.
Byles, Capt. Thomas L., 144-5.

CADWALLADER, Gen. John, 10, 58, 73, 74, 91, 199.
Carlisle, Abraham, 65-6.
Cilley, Col. Joseph, 78, 142, 157, 164, 210.
Clarke, Lieut.-Col. Alured, 54.
Clinton, Sir Henry, assumes command, 27-8, 29-32; character,
    33-4; evacuates Philadelphia, 41, 47-9; march through New
    Jersey, 49-56, 82-97; at Battle of Monmouth, 129-31, 147-8,
    151-2, 186, 238; retreat, 227-32; official report, 267-71.
Continental Congress, treaty with France, 16-17; British peace
    commission, 34-7; orders council of war, 40; approves Lee
    sentence, 245, 255; congratulates Washington, 266-7.
"Conway Cabal," 8-9.
Conway, Gen. Thomas, 9.
Cornwallis, Lord, 33-41, 53, 82, 88, 89, 131, 166, 211.

DE PEYSTER, Gen., quoted, 92.
Dickinson, Maj. Edmund B., 208-9.
Dickinson, Gen. Philemon, 19, 41, 54, 67, 79, 88, 104, 110,
    118-19, 122-6.
Duportail, Gen., 24, 57, 77, 168, 183.
Durkee, Col. John, 131, 134.

EDWARDS, Capt. Evan, 141, 153, 158, 169, 171, 172, 254-5.
English, Dr. James, 175.

FISHBOURNE, Capt. Benjamin, 144-5.